THE FRENCH DRAMA
OF
THE UNSPOKEN

BY

MAY DANIELS

GREENWOOD PRESS, PUBLISHERS
WESTPORT, CONNECTICUT

Library of Congress Cataloging in Publication Data

Daniels, May.
    The French drama of the unspoken.

    Reprint of the 1953 ed. published by the University
Press, Edinburgh, which was issued as no. 3 of Edinburgh
University publications, language and literature.
    Originally presented as the author's thesis, Edinburgh,
1948, under title: Experiments with the unexpressed in
the modern French drama.
    Bibliography: p.
    Includes index.
    1. French drama—20th century—History and criticism.
I. Title. II. Series: Edinburgh. University.
Edinburgh University publications : language and lit-
erature ; no. 3.
[PQ558.D3 1977]   842'.9'109   77-2374
ISBN 0-8371-9464-4

Originally published in 1953 at the University Press,
Edinburgh

Reprinted with the permission of Edinburgh University Press
Reprinted from a copy in the collections of the Brooklyn
Public Library.

Reprinted in 1977 by Greenwood Press, Inc.

Library of Congress catalog card number 77-2374

ISBN 0-8371-9464-4

Printed in the United States of America

FOREWORD

THIS book is the text, with minor alterations, of a thesis pre-
sented to the University of Edinburgh, 1948, for the Degree of
Doctor of Philosophy in the Faculty of Arts, under the title
Experiments with the Unexpressed in the Modern French Drama.
I wish to acknowledge with gratitude and respect the sympathetic
guidance and invaluable advice given by Professor John Orr and
Dr. Georges Poulet of the University of Edinburgh during the
course of my studies.

MAY DANIELS

CONTENTS

PAGE

FOREWORD   V

CHAPTER

I. THE PROBLEM   1

II. THE FRENCH THEATRE AFTER 1870   17

III. MAURICE MAETERLINCK : I   46

IV. MAURICE MAETERLINCK : II   73

V. THE FRENCH THEATRE AFTER 1918   100

VI. CHARLES VILDRAC   121

VII. DENYS AMIEL   144

VIII. JEAN-JACQUES BERNARD : I   172

IX. JEAN-JACQUES BERNARD : II   211

X. CONCLUSION   238

BIBLIOGRAPHY   247

INDEX   259

CHAPTER I

THE PROBLEM

ONE of the hardest tasks of the literary critic is to attempt to define the nature of drama. Aristotle's dictum on tragedy was a description of the art as it already existed, and efforts to enclose the drama in rules have continually been defeated by the triumphant self-justification of some new theatrical form. In France, *Hernani* broke the shackles of the unities. The Théâtre Libre freed the theatre from the ingenious mechanics of the " well-made play ". Maeterlinck produced the " static drama ", a contradiction in terms according to the hitherto recognized " laws " of the theatre, and in more recent times the drama was given a new twist by the experiments of the Expressionists. The critic can indeed do little more than indicate the bare essentials which condition a work of dramatic art, and which distinguish it from other literary forms.

A play is obviously intended to be performed in a theatre before a public—even Alfred de Musset must have had an ideal theatre in mind when writing his *Spectacle dans un fauteuil.* So far, throughout the changeful history of the drama, four factors have remained constant : an audience, a stage of a kind upon which the attention of that audience is focused, peopled with living actors using as a medium of communication the spoken word. Without these essentials a play in the proper sense cannot exist. The art form apparently nearest it, the cinema, while offering the illusion of a stage and speech, dispenses with living actors, and hence with the restrictions on the form inherent in the necessity for their physical presence, and this, in conjunction

with the power of the camera to conquer space visually and concentrate on detail by means of the " close-up ", imposes different
laws.

Obviously, more than these essentials is required to constitute
drama, as distinct from, let us say, a recital of verse, or for that
matter the efforts of a pair of cross-talk comedians. But they
provide, as it were, the climate and habitat of a play. The rest,
its anatomical and physiological structure, dependent to a great
extent upon them, is not at this stage the subject of our interest.
We are at present concerned with the fourth-mentioned factor,
the spoken word, which constitutes the drama as a special and
unique form of the Spectacle that uses the physical presence of
the actor, differentiating it, for example, from the mime or the
dance. Drama exists and survives by virtue of its text, the tran-
scription of the spoken word intended for the use of living actors
on a stage in the presence of an audience.

The purpose of the drama throughout the ages has been in
the main to represent through the above-mentioned media human
experience in one or many of its significant aspects. In high
tragedy and in serious drama the author is at pains to communicate to us the fundamental truths of humanity; as well as external
speech and action, it is necessary to convey or suggest what lies
behind, the complex psychological laws within man, and the
mysterious hidden forces governing the universe of which he is
a part. The restrictive medium of the spoken word creates great
difficulties in this respect, for while flat documentary realism is
not the purpose of any art, the credulity of the audience must not
be overtaxed. At least, the conventions employed by the dramatist must impose themselves on the spectator and make him willing
to adjust himself to a changed vision of the world. To express
the deeper aspects of human experience the ancient Greeks made
use of the Chorus, the English Elizabethans and the French
seventeenth-century Classics of the soliloquy, unrealistic devices,
but accepted by contemporary audiences because of the high
degree of emotional tensity imposed upon them by the compelling

truth of the work, and the heightened language of its utterance.[1] But such a state of affairs was possible mainly because of the moral and social climate of the ages which produced those flowerings of dramatic art. The theatre appeals to massed humanity, broadly and directly, and before communication can be established, there must be, shared in common by public and dramatist, a background of recognized human laws. The religious nature of the ancient Greek drama, with its idea of fate, found a deep spiritual response in the people ; heroism, honour, duty, the compelling force of an external moral law, were accepted by seventeenth-century French audiences ; hence for them the tragic conflict had a deep poignancy, and moved them to such a degree that they were ready to dispense with rigid realism in dialogue, and willingly allowed on the stage the use of the spoken word in forms which would never occur in everyday life.

From the eighteenth century onwards the collective emotions and beliefs of the people with regard to the laws governing human life and conduct gradually fell away, and with them poetry on the stage. Tragedy was to be replaced by—at its best—serious drama, which, with all its qualities, could never quicken the emotions to such a degree as to make possible the acceptance of grossly unrealistic conventions. A calmer and more critical public required greater verisimilitude in dialogue. The problem of combining this with the representation of humanity in depth became more acute. The dramatist might tackle it, as Ibsen did, by presenting the hero at a time of crisis and arranging events in such a way that at a certain stage he would be forced to speak out and put into words deep feelings which, but for the stress of circumstances, might have normally remained unspoken. The tragic moment is the moment when the hero speaks out; the construction of the play, the expectation of the audience, are directed to that point where the secret thoughts and emotions become explicit.

[1] Cf. Una Ellis-Fermor, *The Frontiers of Drama* (1945), ch. 6, where some of the points raised in this chapter are discussed.

But again, with dramatic realism in mind, writers have sensed that tragedy in contemporary everyday life is rarely explicit. W. B. Yeats, speaking of the problem of dealing in dramatic form with the deeper feelings of modern men and women, points out that these feelings generally remain hidden. " When they are deeply moved, they look silently into the fireplace." [1]

In his *Lectures on Dramatic Literature*,[2] Schlegel had already given some indication of the problems which were to pre-occupy the writers in whom we are interested. Complaining of the absence of the contemplative element in the French drama, he says :

> It is like a music from which the *piano* should be altogether excluded, and in which even the difference between *forte* and *fortissimo* should not be distinguishable from the mistaken emulation of the performers. I find too few resting-places in their tragedies, such as we have everywhere in the ancient tragedies where the lyric enters. There are moments in human life which are dedicated by every religious mind to self-meditation, and when the view is turned towards the past and the future. This sacredness of the moment I do not find to be held in sufficient reverence ; the actors as well as the spectators are always equally hurried on to what follows ; and we shall find very few scenes indeed where the development of a mere condition is tranquilly represented independently of the causal connexion. The question with them is always *what* happens, and not sufficiently *how* it happens. And yet this is the main thing when an impression is to be made on the witnesses of human events. Hence everything like silent effect is almost entirely excluded from the province of their dramatic art. The only leisure which remains to the actor for silent pantomime is during the delivery of the long discourses addressed to him, when it more frequently serves to embarrass

---

[1] " Discoveries " (1906), in *Essays* (1924), p. 339, quoted by Una Ellis-Fermor, *op. cit.* p. 118.

[2] A. W. von Schlegel, *A Course of Lectures on Dramatic Art and Literature*, translated by John Black, 1815, Lecture x, pp. 377-8. Lectures delivered in Vienna in 1808, printed in 1809 and 1811 under the title *Vorlesungen über dramatische Kunst und Literatur*, translated into French by Madame Necker de Saussure under the title *Cours de littérature dramatique* (1814).

him than to assist him in the development of his part. They are satisfied if the weaving of the intrigue proceeds in its rapid measure without interruption, and if in the speeches and answers the ball is diligently kept up to the conclusion.

He goes on to say that when the contemplative side of dramatic poetry is neglected, " the representation then engenders, from its very rapidity and animation, only a deafening noise in our mind, instead of the inward music which ought to accompany it ".

The writers with whom our study is concerned endeavour to deal with the problem by the systematic exploitation of the dramatic possibilities of the Unexpressed. We are made to realize that the spoken word has its complement in silence, which can be used as effectively as the distribution of space in architecture or shadow in painting. This group of dramatists is generally known as the *Théâtre du Silence*, but an examination of their theory and practice will show that they are interested not only in the dramatic use of silence, but also in the evocative and suggestive power of dialogue. Theirs is a special manipulation of the essential medium of the spoken word. The group aims at a realistic reticence of emotion and speech, and the dramatists produce their most telling effects either by a skilful use of eloquent silences or by a sober unpretentious dialogue, rich in undertones and suggesting more than it superficially communicates. For this reason we prefer to employ the less used term *Théâtre de l'Inexprimé* ; it is, moreover, the term preferred by the *chef d'école*, Jean-Jacques Bernard.

The earlier dramatists were not liberal in their use of stage directions ; yet there is no doubt that the imaginative *metteur en scène* must have made use of the simplest form of silence, the pause or suspension of dialogue. Diderot advocates the use of pantomime for purposes of realism, ". . . il y a des scènes entières où il est infiniment plus naturel aux personnages de se mouvoir que de parler . . ." and he illustrates : " Deux hommes, incertains s'ils ont à être mécontents ou satisfaits l'un de l'autre en attendant un troisième qui les instruise, que diront-ils jusqu'à ce que ce troisième soit arrivé ? Rien. Ils iront, ils viendront, ils montreront de l'impatience ; mais ils se tairont." [1] But he often uses the term " pantomime " in the sense of " production ". " La pantomime est le tableau qui existait dans l'imagination du poète lorsqu'il écrivait ; et qu'il voudrait que la scène montrât à chaque instant lorsqu'on le joue." He is, however, sensitive to the intrinsic value of silence as a powerful instrument for moving an audience. In a letter to Voltaire,[2] written after a performance of *Tancrède*, he says : " Ah ! mon cher maître, si vous voyiez la Clairon traversant la scène, à demi renversée sur les bourreaux qui l'environnent, ses genoux se dérobant sous elle, les yeux fermés, les bras tombants comme morte ; si vous entendiez le cri qu'elle pousse en apercevant Tancrède, vous resteriez plus convaincu que jamais que le silence et la pantomime ont quelque-fois un pathétique que toutes les ressources de l'art oratoire n'at-teignent pas. J'ai dans la tête un moment de théâtre où tout est muet, et où le spectateur reste suspendu dans les plus terribles alarmes." And we are told " how he used to go to the highest seats in the house, thrust his fingers into his ears and then, to the astonishment of his neighbours, watch the performance with the sharpest interest. ' They could not refrain from hazarding questions to which I answered coldly that everybody had his own way of listening and that my way was to stop my ears, so as to understand better . . . ! ' " [3] Although the last few words seem a fore - shadowing of Maeterlinck, the passage does little more than indicate Diderot's extreme sensitivity to good miming. Certainly in his plays he did not put his theories into practice. As Émile Faguet puts it : " La presque suppression du dialogue par le geste l'attitude et l'action ; c'est ce qu'il prêchait. Il est vrai que quand il écrivait il faisait tout le contraire. Mais ce qu'il a écrit

---

[1] *De la poésie dramatique* (1758), xxi, " De la pantomime ".
[2] 28th Nov. 1760.
[3] A. B. Walkley, *Still More Prejudice* (1925), " Pantomime and Drama ", p. 221.

montre à quel point il aurait eu raison de se conformer à ses
théories. . . ." [1]

That the importance of mime was recognized and perhaps
exaggerated in the eighteenth century is clear from Sheridan's
famous passage in *The Critic* on Lord Burleigh's shake of the
head :

> PUFF. Why, by that shake of the head, he gave you to
> understand that even though they had more justice in their
> cause, and wisdom in their measures—yet, if there was not a
> greater spirit shown on the part of the people, the country
> would at last fall a sacrifice to the hostile ambition of the Spanish
> Monarchy.
>
> SNEER. The Devil ! did he mean all that by shaking his
> head ?
>
> PUFF. Every word of it—if he shook his head as I taught
> him.

Diderot does indicate an interrelationship of pantomime and
text. " C'est elle qui fixera la longueur des scènes, et qui
colorera tout le drame." But actually mere suspension of dialogue at certain points in the play had in the past only a limited
dramatic value. The text remained sufficient in itself. The pause,
in addition to producing effects of realism, could enhance the
value of that text by creating suspense and focusing the attention
of the audience on an approaching crisis. But the crisis itself was
led up to and expressed in words. It was for Bernard to express
the crisis in the pause itself. We shall see when we come to
examine his plays how the pause is a logical outcome of the text,
how it is inextricably bound up with it, and how the spoken word
is dramatically subordinated to the silence.

A different type of pause is sometimes observed in the
Hugoesque Romantic drama, that which results from the rhythm
and pace of the dialogue. Since a constant high pitch of lyricism cannot be indefinitely maintained, a natural diminuendo
and rest, as in music, may effectively relax the tension and offer a

---

[1] Lugné-Poe, *Le Sot du tremplin* (1930), p. 224 ; letter from Faguet to Lugné-Poe.

breathing-space. An example of this comes in *Ruy Blas* [1] where Don César and Ruy Blas stand for a moment with clasped hands, gazing at each other with an expression of sadness and confident friendship. Similarly there is the sinister, fateful pause before the hero launches into a new tirade, as, for example, when Ruy Blas discovers the ministers discussing the illicit profits they plan to make from the taxes.[2] Such silences have a degree of realism, but they are chiefly, as it were, a by-product of an intensely lyrical and unrealistic style, and though effective enough on the stage, they are comparatively superficial in nature. Silence is also used to emphasize a dramatic climax, as, for example, in *Lucrèce Borgia*, when, after the orgy, the great door at the back opens to reveal the sinister monks singing the " De Profundis ". This tense pause prepares for the entrance of Dona Lucrezia and her long speech to the men she has poisoned. It produces the thrill of authentic melodrama, but need not claim our serious attention.

A more fruitful kind of silence is that of the mute character placed beside the speaking actors, most effectively used by Aeschylus. We think of Atossa in the *Persae*, of Prometheus, who proudly awaits the departure of Might, Violence and Hephaestos before giving vent to his anguish,[3] or of the long silence of Clytemnestra at the altar, meditating her wrongs and the disasters foreshadowed by the impending return of Agamemnon.[4] Although these silences proceed from the limitations of the form used by Aeschylus, their dramatic effects are most powerful. We have the impression of a tide of inward emotion rising and gathering momentum at the impact of the spoken word, until the floodgates burst and it becomes speech. The dramatic climax, as usual expressed in words, is given tremendous emphasis by means of these pregnant silences. The mute Cassandra, petrified with fear, " trembling like a wild beast in a snare ", has pathetic realism ; that silence too leads up to her trance-like " Otototoi ". Aeschylus' exploitation of silence for dramatic effect, especially

[1] Act I, sc. 3.   [2] Act III, sc. 2.   [3] *Prometheus Bound.*   [4] *Agamemnon.*

in the opening scene of the tragedy, makes him a target for the wit of Aristophanes in *The Frogs*.

> He wants to open with an awful silence—
> The bloodcurdling reserve of his first scene . . .

Aristophanes refers to its use in plays no longer extant, and puts this explanation into the mouth of Euripides :

> The instincts of a charlatan, to keep the audience guessing
> If Niobe ever meant to speak—the play meantime progressing.

But the silence culminated in speech :

> Then after this tomfoolery, the heroine feeling calmer
> Would utter some twelve wild bull words, on midway in the drama. . . .[1]

The immense dramatic superiority of this type of silence over the pause interpolated in the dialogue lies in the fact of its being closely knit with the text. The intensity of the silence increases with the weight of every word spoken by the other characters, and the outburst in which it culminates gains in value not through the mere contrast of silence and speech juxtaposed, but from logical necessity—because such a silence, worked upon by such a dialogue, can end only in speech. We shall see that some of Bernard's most striking effects are achieved by a reversal of this procedure—a gradation of dialogue which can only culminate in an expressive silence.

There is in Sophocles' *Antigone* an example of silence which does not burst into speech. Eurydice, wife of Creon, learns from the messenger that her son Haemon has, in the presence of his father, committed suicide by the side of the dead Antigone. She retires into the house without a word, and her mute suffering later finds its crisis in her self-inflicted death. This is nearer to another modern use of silence, for example that to be found in Bernard's *Martine* and *Le Secret d'Arvers*. With Sophocles, however, this silence remains, as it were, in the background; it is not brought forward, made the main interest of the play and

---

[1] Gilbert Murray's translation.

allowed to speak for itself. It is left to Chorus and Messenger explicitly to comment on its nature and significance. " I know not, but to me at least, a strained silence seems to portend peril, no less than vain abundance of lament." [1]   The incident is of secondary importance in the play, and does not strengthen the fabric in the same way as the impressive silences of Aeschylus.[2]

A third aspect of " silence " arising from the necessity for psychological realism is that emanating from a special kind of dialogue known as " le langage indirect ". The Classics, the Romantics and the late nineteenth-century French dramatists in general have this in common : what their dialogue expresses corresponds exactly with what is passing within the heart and mind of the characters. These characters are not only completely aware of the emotions they are experiencing and the implications of the situation at each progressive stage, but they also possess the literary faculty of fixing these emotions and sentiments in clear and precise terms.

The seventeenth-century dramatists, influenced by the spirit

[1] R. C. Jebb's translation.

[2] The following note by George Thomson in his edition of Aeschylus' *Prometheus Bound* (1932), p. 140, is interesting. He is commenting on Prometheus' silence at the beginning of the drama :

". . . The device is as old as Homer : perhaps the most famous example is the silence of Achilles after the news of the death of Patroclus (*Il.* xviii. 15-77), where the interlude has the effect not merely of relaxing the emotional tension but of making the words of Achilles, with his vow of vengeance—the turning-point in the story—all the more emphatic when at last we hear them. We know that Aeschylus adapted this incident in the Ἕκτορος λύτρα (Schol. in Ar. *Ran.* 911), and the figure of his silent Niobe 'all tears ' has never been forgotten. In his extant plays, we can trace, along with his development of the second actor, the evolution of the silent character. Thus in the *Supplices*, where, in keeping with the practice which was necessary when there was only a single actor, Pelasgus converses with the coryphaeus (240-349), the silence of Danaus has no dramatic value ; but in the *Persae*, where the whole of the πάροδος is designed to lead up to the appearance of Atossa (cp. esp. 64-5, 136-42), the fact that the Messenger addresses himself, not to Atossa (who stands in silence), but to the Chorus, with whom he engages in a dirge, makes Atossa's utterance, when it comes, a second dramatic climax (293-4). This technique is brought to perfection in the prolonged silence of Clytemnestra in the *Agamemnon*. She is seen sacrificing, and is addressed by name (83-4, itself a climax . . .), but does not reply. At the end of the long stasimon which tells the story of the sacrifice of her child, the Elders address to her the question they addressed before—what news ? and at last she speaks. . . . The poet has taken advantage of the climax to enforce upon the minds of his audience a sense of her outraged motherhood (Sheppard, *Camb. Anc. Hist.* vol. v, chap. v)."

of Cartesianism, show a scientific attitude in their use of language. They assume that what relates to man is capable of being noted and defined. The psychology of the Classics is subtle, but the instrument of reason with which they skilfully and delicately probe has its limitations from the point of view of realism. Realism, of course, is not the purpose of the classical dramatists. As Thierry Maulnier indicates in his book on Racine, they aim not at a reproduction of action on the stage, but at an abstract representation of action. With ruthless economy, human experience is selected, reduced to the essential, organized and transmuted into a language as different in kind from the stammering, inconsequential speech of everyday life as music is from the primitive cry or groan. The idea is not to reproduce states of mind but to treat a subject. The intellectual instrument for this purpose is a language hardened, purified, austere, performing with relentless precision its single chosen function : to express meaning. However delicate the psychological nuances in the Racinian tragedy, the firm but flexible instrument of language is equal to the task of expressing them clearly.[1] This extreme clarity and precision of classical utterance is in a sense a distortion of life.

The psychology of the Hugoesque Romantic drama is elementary. The characters are mainly unconvincing variations of the type of " beau ténébreux ", fatal and mysterious, or examples of a violent antithesis of virtue and vice. Vehement, uncomplicated passion is clearly expressed in a lyrical dialogue of great beauty, which does not lack verisimilitude in relation to the type of character presented. But the totality of human experience is falsified through a naïve over-simplification. The subtler theatre of Musset is full of delicate fantasy, but it retains the subjectivity of the Romantics. His heroes represent different aspects of his own personality which he analyses with conscious finesse, and though his language has greater truth, it still shows the traditional close correspondence between the state of mind and the spoken word.

[1] Cf. Thierry Maulnier, Racine (1935), especially ch. 3.

Precision of self-expression in drama continues to modern times. The "well-made plays" of Scribe and Sardou, where character is subordinated to complicated intrigue, necessitate clarity of exposition, and for obvious reasons the problem plays of Dumas *fils* and later of Brieux, the philosophical pieces of Curel, the violent action of Bernstein, the hysterical lyricism of Bataille require a similar clarity of dialogue.

For the dramatists of the *Théâtre de l'Inexprimé* the clear exact expression of what goes on within produces the effect of unrealistic flatness and lack of perspective. When all thought and feeling, whether deep or superficial, is brought to the surface and represented, as it were, on the same plane, all is clarity with no mystery and no roundness of psychology. They proceed from the assumption that even the most enlightened cannot be aware of every one of the motives determining his conduct; accordingly, in real life the spoken word does not and cannot express algebraically all that is in his mind. It cannot even express all that he wishes to communicate, since he is not always aware of his real desires. These, however, can be revealed to the discerning mind not by the actual meaning of the words used, but by the subconscious choice and arrangement of the words and their relation to the situation. This is " le langage indirect".

The theory of " le langage indirect " is elaborated, curiously enough, by Henry Bataille. In his preface to *La Marche nuptiale* entitled "A propos d'art dramatique ",[1] Bataille advocates the use of the Unexpressed in the theatre. For him, human experience, which it is the drama's task to recast and interpret, lies in two worlds, the external world of everyday life and the inner world of thought, feeling and motive. " Le romantisme ignora l'une comme l'autre, la vérité intérieure comme la vérité extérieure; le réalisme ne voulut connaître que la seconde; les psychologues fragmentèrent à l'infini quelques parcelles de la première; quant au symbolisme, lui, il se réfugia dans les abstractions pures, à égale distance de l'une et de l'autre étude." The truth which

[1] Dated July 1907, with some pages added in December 1916.

the drama must seek to convey lies in the relationship between
the world of the soul and the world of outward appearances.
Denied the novelist's resources of direct description, how shall a
dramatist in his imitation of life itself on the stage render to his
audience " les sphères inconscientes et agissantes de l'âme " ?
By using, along with that " direct language " which expresses
in clear terms exactly what is in the mind of the speaker, " indirect
language ", which, instead of conveying a definite and precise
meaning, hints at concealed thoughts and feelings. Thus he
advocates the use of the Unexpressed in the interests of a more
complete realism. " L'homme ne s'exprime entièrement dans la
vie qu'à de rares occasions. Ce qu'il dit n'est généralement qu'un
aspect de lui-même, un rapport momentané de soi avec les êtres
et les événements . . . Il [le théâtre] est elliptique. . . . Par des
cris, des mots, des portes ouvertes sur l'âme, des synthèses mer-
veilleuses et vraies, il conduit le public jusqu'aux ondes obscures
et vivantes de l'être, sans pour cela nuire le moins du monde à la
réalité extérieure et à la vraisemblance orale que nous voulons
complète chez nos personnages." In *Le Masque* [1] he makes
Demieulle say : " Et c'est la vie qu'on puisse entrer dans un
salon et y entendre ' Voulez-vous du café ? ' sans se douter que
ce : ' Voulez-vous du café ? ' veut peut-être dire des choses
charmantes ou infinies." [2] But along with his notion of " le
langage indirect " there exists also in his theories of the drama

---

[1] Act I.

[2] This was no doubt inspired by the following passage in Balzac's *La Cousine Bette* :
" En ce moment Valérie apportait elle-même à Steinbock une tasse de thé. C'était
plus qu'une distinction, c'était une faveur. Il y a dans la manière dont une femme
s'acquitte de cette fonction, tout un langage ; mais les femmes le savent bien ; aussi est-ce
une étude curieuse à faire que celle de leurs mouvements, de leurs gestes, de leurs regards,
de leur ton, de leur accent, quand elles accomplissent cet acte de politesse en apparence si
simple. Depuis la demande : ' Prenez-vous du thé ?—Voulez-vous du thé ? Une tasse
de thé ? ' froidement formulée et l'ordre d'en apporter donné à la nymphe qui tient
l'urne, jusqu'à l'énorme poème de l'odalisque venant de la table à thé, la tasse à la main,
vers le pacha du cœur et la lui présentant d'un air soumis, l'offrant d'une voix caressante,
avec un regard plein de promesses voluptueuses, un physiologiste peut observer tous les
sentiments féminins, depuis l'aversion, depuis l'indifférence, jusqu'à la déclaration de
Phèdre à Hippolyte. . . ." (Balzac, *La Cousine Bette*, édition de Calmann Lévy, pp.
297-8 ; quoted by J.-B. Besançon, *Essai sur le théâtre d'Henry Bataille* (1928), p. 57.)

that of " le lyrisme exact ". By this he signifies not a kind of verbal intoxication, but an accurate representation in words of intense feelings within. He maintains that the lyrical state of mind exists as well as other states, and that it is the duty of the dramatist to give this exact expression. Bataille, passionate by temperament, practised " le lyrisme exact ", and as in the case of Diderot, his theories on the Unexpressed find no place in his dramatic works.

The classical Racine is rich in the suggestion of subconscious motive and desire and hidden feeling, causing, for example, rationalization, or the transference of an illicit emotion to a lawful object—" Mes yeux le retrouvaient dans les traits de son père ".[1] " Il avait votre port, vos yeux, votre langage "[2]—or again dominating and colouring a secondary relationship :

> Cent fois je me suis fait une douceur extrême
> D'entretenir Titus dans un autre lui-même.[3]

In such cases, however, the spoken word is an accurate description of a psychological process, of which the character is fully aware, and indicates that the obsessing passion or desire has been the subject of previous reflection. Racine's theatre deals with the conflict of passions at the moment of their greatest intensity, when they are filling the conscious mind and reflecting themselves clearly in speech.

But another poet of love probes the heart, and watches love take birth and emerge from the most secret recesses of consciousness. " J'ai guetté dans le cœur humain ", says Marivaux, " toutes les niches différentes où peut se cacher l'amour, lorsqu'il craint de se montrer et chacune de mes comédies a pour objet de le faire sortir d'une de ces niches."[4] ". . . c'est tantôt un amour ignoré des deux amants ; tantôt un amour qu'ils sentent et qu'ils veulent se cacher l'un à l'autre ; tantôt un amour timide, qui n'ose se déclarer ; tantôt enfin un amour incertain et comme indécis, un amour à demi né, pour ainsi dire, dont ils se doutent,

---

[1] *Phèdre*, l. 290.   [2] *Ibid.* l. 640.   [3] *Bérénice*, ll. 270-1.
[4] D'Alembert, *Éloge de Marivaux* in *Œuvres*, tome iii (1821), p. 611.

sans être bien sûrs, et qu'ils épient au dedans d'eux-mêmes, avant de lui laisser prendre l'essor." [1]   These vague gropings betray themselves in a form of " langage indirect ".   " Il faut . . . que les acteurs ne paraissent jamais *sentir la valeur de ce qu'ils disent*, et qu'en même temps les spectateurs la sentent et la démêlent à travers l'espèce de nuage dont l'auteur a dû envelopper leurs discours." [2]   In silences, in words let fall dreamily, absent-mindedly, involuntarily, Lélio and his countess betray their growing but unsuspected attraction to each other, and instinct can be seen at work beneath the rational conversation of every day.[3]   Araminte rationalizes her desire to retain Dorante as a steward, although informed by Dubois of his hopeless love.[4] Silvia finds herself defending the supposed valet to her servant Lisette with an inappropriate indignation which ends in tears.[5] Countless examples of the suggestive realism of Marivaux's dialogue could be quoted ; in this he stands out as a striking exception among eighteenth-century dramatists, and Jean-Jacques Bernard readily acknowledges his literary paternity.   Let us note that his " langage indirect " also culminates in precise expression. " Oh! notre amour se fait grand ; il parlera bientôt bon français ", says the wideawake Colombine about her countess in *La Surprise de l'amour.*

As we proceed with the examination of our problem we shall find that in addition to silence and " langage indirect ", other devices are employed in order to convey meaning without direct expression.   In Shakespeare's plays, pathetic fallacy, imagery and symbolism stir the imagination of the listener to complete the text, and allow him an insight into the creative mind of the poet. We have to consider also the sheer verbal music of dialogue, which has its own message, creating atmosphere and rousing emotion.   Racine's dialogue is full of this verbal harmony. Music itself, and décor, can also on occasion convey a meaning

---

[1] D'Alembert, *Éloge de Marivaux* in *Œuvres*, tome iii (1821), p. 584.
[2] *Ibid.* p. 582, d'Alembert's italics.   [3] *La Surprise de l'amour.*
[4] *Les Fausses Confidences.*   [5] *Le Jeu de l'amour et du hasard.*

more effectively than words. All find their place in the works which interest us. But, as I understand it, the *Théâtre de l'Inexprimé* is more than a collection of technical devices ; it embraces those dramatists whose thought and work centre round the Unexpressed, for whom the Unexpressed is a philosophy of the theatre. They are primarily concerned with a problem of dialogue, a dialogue which shall reflect a certain outlook on life, a certain conception of mankind, their notion of reality. And although, as we have seen, aspects of the *Théâtre de l'Inexprimé* exist, sometimes in embryonic form, throughout the history of the drama, it is not until we come to Maeterlinck, and the twentieth-century group, that the Unexpressed constitutes the main pre-occupation of the dramatist. Some of the characteristics of this school will naturally overflow into the works of contemporary dramatists ; it is my intention to confine myself mainly to those writers in whose thought and technique the Unexpressed is inextricably woven.

CHAPTER II

THE FRENCH THEATRE AFTER 1870

I N the introductory chapter I indicated that the *Théâtre de l'Inexprimé* was to grow out of a desire for greater realism, a realism which should not only show the external aspects of human experience, but also penetrate the inner motives and desires, often subconscious, lying behind human conduct.

Never was the theatre farther from reality, even superficial reality, than in the works of Scribe and Sardou, to which Sarcey lent all the weight of his authority. In their " well-made plays ", with their artificial, ingeniously constructed plots, and their arbitrary, optimistic dénouements, truth of character, and hence of dialogue, had to be sacrificed. The Naturalist drama was a reaction against this falsity in art. In the latter part of the nineteenth century the prestige of science, the positivism of Auguste Comte and the determinism of Taine favoured the growth of naturalism in the novel. Unlike those nineteenth-century writers calling themselves " realists ", who endeavoured to give a faithful rendering of life by the amassing of numerous detailed facts, the Naturalists, in addition to documentation, aimed at using the observed facts scientifically, deducing from them the laws to which the human being was subject—those of heredity, environment, instinct—and showing the inevitable workings of these laws with a pessimistic bias. The novel was an excellent medium for the working out of such theories, but the theatre to which Zola, Daudet and others, reacting against " Scribisme ", endeavoured to transfer them, was not so successful. It lacked the process of description, essential to naturalism, and the attempt resulted mainly in melodrama. These plays were not favourably received by the public, still partial to the " well-made play ".

An endeavour to bring truth back into the theatre was made by Henry Becque, whose most important plays were *Les Corbeaux* [1] and *La Parisienne*.[2] Becque was opposed to the Naturalist doctrines of Zola. " Je n'ai jamais eu beaucoup de goût pour les assassins, les hystériques, les alcooliques, pour les martyrs de l'hérédité, et les victimes de l'évolution." [3] But his theatre with its pessimism and its fatalism has a Naturalist bias—*Les Corbeaux* is a representation of human beasts of prey hypnotizing, and battening on their victims. At the same time, although his characters are mediocre, sordid, weak-willed, brutal or pitiable, within their limits they are true, and his dialogue is authentic. He certainly retains some of the unrealistic theatrical conventions —asides, and even monologues—and, as with the traditional theatre, the whole content is in the spoken word. But the truth of his drama is the first important reaction against "Scribisme ".

A more pugnacious assault on " Scribisme " was made by André Antoine with his Théâtre Libre, started on the 30th March 1887. Antoine's most important reform was an attempt to bring realism into the décor, and truth and restraint into the acting. He abolished declamatory gestures and conventional attitudes— the actor, if necessary, could turn his back on the public and even make use of silences. But these silences, imposed by the producer in the interests of a realistic production, were not inherent in the text, and therefore do not concern the subject of our study. His contribution with regard to the dramatic text was to substitute for ingenious intrigue " la tranche de vie mise sur scène avec art ". The success of Antoine's effort imposed naturalism on the French theatre ; the new drama created its own sterile conventions and, emphasizing the seamier side of life, degenerated into the " pièce mufle " and the " comédie rosse ".

The desire for human truth led one realist writer consciously

---

[1] First performed in 1882.   [2] First performed in 1885.
[3] Quoted by Daniel Mornet, *Histoire de la littérature et de la pensée françaises contemporaines* (1927), p. 30.

to practise an economy and precision of style, a condensation of expression, which has a positive, intrinsic value. " Je crois qu'un fait, une idée gagnent à être résumés dans une scène, une phrase."[1] Of Jules Renard, whose dramatic version of *Poil de carotte*[2] is important in the history of the French theatre, J.-P. Sartre says : " Il a créé la littérature du silence,· on sait quelle fortune elle a connu depuis . . .".[3] Jules Renard does not use the methods of the Unexpressed, as we understand them, but the discarding of superfluities in style and the density of his language, the negative aspect, so to speak, of the Unexpressed, represent a turning away from " literature " and a starting-point for experiments with the Unexpressed itself. The sincerity which inspires Jules Renard's economy of language—" Sous aucun prétexte je ne mentirai "[4] —and his preoccupation with timid, unhappy beings who find it difficult to express their desire to be loved and understood, link him in a way with the " silent " dramatists.

Generally speaking, the conditions prevailing in France about this time made for decadence in the theatre, notwithstanding its undoubted technical brilliance. The country, not yet recovered from the shock of " l'année terrible ", suffered, as Paul Bourget expressed it, from " cette reprise inattendue de ce que l'on appelait, en 1830, le mal du siècle ".[5] Her young men, growing up in a climate of moral defeatism, were absorbing from Baudelaire a taste for morbid self-analysis, from Taine a fatalistic philosophy, from Renan a spirit of dilettantism and indifference. Money and the pleasure it could buy became of paramount importance ; the theatre became a commodity for the provision of pleasure, and was tainted with commercialism. It was also infected with " parisianism ", the disease of over-centralization ; it restricted itself mainly to a " mondain " environment and ceased to draw its inspiration from the fresh sources of life. The theatre of the Boulevard flourished. It clung to the " well-made play ", with

---

[1] Quoted by Daniel Mornet, *op. cit.* pp. 178-9.   [2] 1894.
[3] *Situations*, I (1937), p. 294.   [4] Daniel Mornet, *op. cit.* p. 178.
[5] *Essais de psychologie contemporaine*, Preface of 1885.

variations on the theme of the eternal triangle, husband, wife and lover, made classic in Becque's *Parisienne*. Bernstein in his first manner specialized in cynical brutality and violence of action, jolting the nerves and creating a form of unpleasant excitement. Porto-Riche and Bataille lyrically exploited physical love. Brieux, Mirbeau and Donnay dealt with specific questions—money, hygiene, education, feminism—in problem plays. François de Curel produced a theatre of ideas. The subject matter might be stimulating, the plays might be competent and even full of talent, but the wonder and emotion produced by a work of high art were lacking. Never had the drama receded farther from the majestic heights where it had found its beginning. No art is more affected by the moral and intellectual climate of the times than the drama, which, by its very nature, can attain grandeur only when there is a receptive and indeed conditioned public. In ancient Greece, great tragedy dealt with the human being in relation to those fundamental laws of the universe and mankind already recognized by an audience which was thus prepared to wonder and suffer with the hero. In France at the end of the nineteenth century a weary, sceptical public demanded from a commercialized theatre not a poetic and sincere interpretation of life, but entertainment and distraction.

Yet, even while the theatre was developing on these lines, a feeling had arisen, and was slowly growing, that the Naturalists had not succeeded in attaining the whole of truth and reality ; a reaction against the prevalent materialism was setting in. Science, upon which naturalism was based, was losing prestige ; she had not fulfilled the promises people thought she had made. In 1889 Bourget, who had at first believed in science, attacked positivism in *Le Disciple*. Bergson, in his *Essai sur les données immédiates de la conscience*,[1] his *Matière et mémoire*,[2] his *Évolution créatrice*,[3] by introducing new ideas on duration, on the nature of intelligence and intuition, exposed the rigidity of scientific methods, and demonstrated that the conclusions at which they arrived were of

[1] 1889.   [2] 1896.   [3] 1907.

a relative and essentially practical value. Towards 1890 Herbert Spencer's ideas on the Unknowable, set forth in his *First Principles*, were becoming familiar in France. Scientists and philosophers were tending to conclude that the whole of reality might not be contained in material phenomena. And this change of moral climate was causing a definite reaction against the Naturalist writers. In 1883 Brunetière attacked them in *Le Roman naturaliste*; and in 1888 came the famous *Manifeste des Cinq* against the publication of *La Terre*. Moreover, since 1880, foreign writers such as George Eliot, Dostoievski, Tolstoi, Bjoernson, Ibsen, Sudermann and Hauptmann had been exercising an influence on French literature. Antoine had given the works of foreign dramatists in the Théâtre Libre. Even the most strikingly " naturalist " of these did not restrict themselves to physiological truths ; they had succeeded in giving an impression of something intangible, the soul of man, and this found a response in French writers. By 1891 Jules Huret in his *Enquête sur l'évolution littéraire* was concluding that naturalism was dead, or moribund, or on the point of evolving.

The distaste for materialism and positivism, the yearnings towards the strange hidden worlds of the soul, found their expression in the Decadent and Symbolist movements, both deriving mainly from the poetry of Baudelaire. The Decadents, of whom Verlaine was the chief, reacted against the objectivity and hard outlines of the Parnassian school, and endeavoured to express the confused world of emotion, instinct, dream and desire. Their poetry was haunted by the mystery of human personality with its subconscious reserves, and by the mystery of the external world and its affinities with the poet, dimly and uneasily realized. The same mystic truth flowed through the poet's soul as through Nature herself in her various forms—landscape, water, sound and perfume, and the images which surged up from his subconscious were an aspect of his emotion, were the emotion itself. He envisaged poetry as a direct communication between two sensibilities, that of the poet himself and that of the reader. As Daniel

Mornet points out,[1] all French poetry had hitherto conveyed its message through the medium of the intellect, in intelligible language. In the view of the Decadents, the original emotion of the poet was altered, indeed distorted, by this process. That emotion must be rendered by the direct expression of those confused images and symbols which it produced in his consciousness. Reason, the traditional instrument for the knowledge of truth, was replaced by intuition. The intellectual structure of a language based on logical thought was exchanged for a new medium based on emotion, and reflecting in its deliberate lack of precision the confused subconscious origins of elusive dreams and desires, which are impossible to capture and enclose within the confines of the scientific term.

The ideas of Baudelaire regarding the correspondence of the different senses, and accordingly of the objects perceived by those senses—visual beauty, perfume, sound—created an art of haunting loveliness, blurred in outline, full of strange resonances. Of all the arts which this group endeavoured to synthesize, none appealed to them more than music, with its lack of plasticity and, as they imagined, of intellectualism, and with its powerful direct influence upon the emotions. They thus succeeded by a kind of verbal harmony in arousing strange, troubled reactions, which meaning alone could never have produced.

The poetry of the Decadents was subjective and relative.[2] The communication established between poet and reader was based on emotion ; misty autumnal images re-created within the latter the initial uneasy yearnings which had conjured them up in the mind of the poet. A vague attitude of pessimism was common to the members of this group, but no real philosophy of life lay behind their works. The Symbolists, however, aimed farther than the subtle expression of elusive states of mind. They desired to understand through the manifold aspects of the material world the meaning of the universe and to arrive at an absolute truth.

---

[1] *Op. cit.* p. 51.
[2] Cf. Guy Michaud, *Message poétique du symbolisme* (1947), vol. ii, ch. 6.

For Mallarmé, the chief representative of this movement, external phenomena are symbols of a higher system of ideas. While the realist is content to describe these symbols for their own sakes, the true artist must perceive the relationship between them, which is also the relationship of the ideas they represent. In this way he attains a knowledge of true reality. This higher system of ideas constitutes God, and Mallarmé's conception of art has accordingly an idealist and religious basis. As Camille Mauclair puts it,[1] " Le monde n'est qu'un système de symboles subordonné à un système d'idées pures qui sont régies par des lois cosmiques, et dont la réunion constitue la divinité ". External realities are thus instruments whereby pure ideas can be conveyed by the artist to the human mind. In this way, instead of expressing his Hegelian idealism in the logical language of traditional philosophy, Mallarmé, using material phenomena in order to suggest ideas, builds up an elaborate system of analogy.

The Symbolist movement, deriving mainly from Mallarmé, is mystic and universal. Unlike the Decadents, who confine themselves to the expression of elusive individual experience and subconscious tendencies, the Symbolists, aware of relationships between man and the universe, give, as it were, the impression of a collective unconscious, which finds its expression in myth and Wagnerian legend, held by them to be a subconscious product of the race. The notion that external reality in its multitudinous and varied forms is but a manifestation of interrelated primordial ideas leads naturally to the conception of a fusion of all arts, themselves different aspects of these higher ideas ; this is, of course, the aesthetic ideal of Wagner, whose influence on Symbolism in France was considerable.

We shall see that the ideas underlying the Theatre of the Unexpressed begin to germinate in Decadent and Symbolist poetry. The Decadent group reaches towards the subconscious emotions of the individual which by their very nature it is almost impossible to confine in precise descriptive language ; these

[1] *Princes de l'esprit*, " Les Recherches de Mallarmé " (1898), p. 111.

subconscious emotions are the main preoccupation of Bernard. The new poetic language they evolved resulted from their realizing the rigidity of logical language, which deforms the emotion it expresses, an attitude similar to that prompting Bernard's experiments. Intuition, not intelligence, is the instrument of communication, and the message intuitively communicated retains its original purity, unconstricted by the strait-jacket of logical language structure, just as, in the plays of Maeterlinck and Bernard, though by different methods, the emotion is conveyed to the spectator directly and undistorted by description or analysis. We shall note too with what telling effects Maeterlinck uses the verbal music of the Decadents, although for our purpose this element is of secondary importance. In the Symbolist group appears that mystic attitude towards the universe, the idea of a close relationship between human beings and the inanimate world, which forms the basis of Maeterlinck's theories of the Unexpressed. The conception of a cosmic subconscious explains his strange, compelling dialogue ; the symbolism of external objects and the translation of philosophical ideas into significant legend also characterize his work. Finally, the theory common to Decadents and Symbolists that the poet's message should be conveyed by suggestion rather than by description or analysis indicates a form of the Unexpressed. " *Nommer* un objet," says Mallarmé, " c'est supprimer les trois quarts de la jouissance du poème, qui est faite du bonheur de deviner peu à peu ; le suggérer, voilà le rêve." [1]

Suggestion with Mallarmé is, in fact, bound up with a conception of the positive value of silence. Haunted throughout his life by " le Néant ", he ultimately conceives it as being fraught with possibilities, ". . . univers non pas irréel, mais préréel, non pas impossible, mais uniquement fait de possibilités, non pas vide absolument, mais vide de toute *réalité*, de toute réalisation ".[2] The blank paper confronting the poet represents nothingness and

---

[1] Jules Huret, *Enquête sur l'évolution littéraire* (1891), p. 60.
[2] G. Michaud, *op. cit.* vol. i, p. 191.

contains likewise an infinite potentiality of words. The words he writes on it draw their power and significance from that inexhaustible source, and are thus enriched by the symbolic presence of the blank paper in which they are set. The expressed creates in the mind of the poet and reader the idea of a more significant, but elusive, unexpressed. " Je dis : une fleur ! et, hors de l'oubli où ma voix relègue aucun contour, en tant que quelque chose d'autre que les calices sus, musicalement se lève, idée même et suave, l'absente de tous bouquets." [1] This—" la notion d'un objet, échappant, qui fait défaut " [2]—has a positive value greater than that of the expressed, for it remains in the realm of the ideal ; it is the pure idea of which its complement in the expressed, the word, is a pale reflection. Mallarmé carries suggestion to its uttermost limits. His is the poetry of virtuality. As reality is only an imperfect indication of the rich potentialities of " le Néant ", so the true value of the written word lies in the wealth of suggested, unexpressed ideas contained in the symbolic blank which surrounds it. That blank, that silence, holds the real poem. " Tout devient suspens, disposition fragmentaire avec alternance et vis-à-vis, concourant au rythme total, lequel serait le poème tu, aux blancs ; seulement traduit, en une manière, par chaque pendentif." [3] The empty stage in the theatre is charged with similar potentialities from which the evolutions of the human being derive full meaning. When the dancer appears, ". . . le plancher évité par bonds ou dur aux pointes, acquiert une virginité de site pas songé, qu'isole, bâtira, fleurira la figure ". [4] Her movements and figures create out of these bare boards a décor, an atmosphere, a place ; and that elusive creation, not the dancing woman herself, is the quintessence of the art of the dance.

The idea of the fusion of arts to which Symbolism leads raises at once the question of the drama, since the theatre by its nature can use music, painting, dancing, architecture and the spoken

[1] *Divagations* (1897), " Crise de vers ", p. 251.
[2] " La Musique et les lettres ", Taylorian Lecture (1893), *Studies in European Literature*, p. 137.
[3] *Divagations*, " Crise de vers ", p. 247.   [4] *Ibid.* " Crayonné au théâtre ", p. 181.

word. The position of the drama in the Symbolist movement is important for our purpose. Since the Symbolists aim at conveying meaning through methods other than descriptive or analytical language, if they have succeeded in putting their theories into dramatic form, a Theatre of the Unexpressed becomes a possibility.

Although Mallarmé on his own admission rarely went to the theatre, he conducted in the *Revue Indépendante* a " campagne dramatique " in articles which were subsequently published in *Divagations*. Mallarmé's preoccupation with the theatre was a consequence of the Hegelian idealism which, as we have seen, inspired a religious conception of art. For Mallarmé, the idealist and religious attitude must be present both in artist and reader (or spectator). Mallarmé conceives a work of art as something universal, indicating a symbolic relationship of all kinds of phenomena ; it is a ceremonial, a solemn spectacle combining all the arts, in which the spectator actively and religiously participates. This would be achieved in the ideal theatre which, for Mallarmé, is close to the Wagnerian type, a synthesis of the arts, literature, ballet, music, décor. With two differences : unlike Wagner, who subordinates all to music, Mallarmé considers literature, the supreme expression of the human being, as the art which should predominate, and in addition, he attaches more importance than Wagner to the ballet, which he conceives as a kind of writing by the human body on space, expressing something deeper and more significant than the apparent moving picture of a woman dancing, just as the printed characters on a page mean something more than black outlines of letters on a white ground.

The insistence on the active and religious participation of the spectator implies that the latter brings something with him to the theatre. Instead of passively allowing his mind to be distracted by anecdote or psychological analysis, he must co-operate with the actors and endeavour to perceive the ideas of which their performance is an outline and which already exist within him. The aesthetic enjoyment derived from this process is of an intellectual nature ; it is the satisfied perception of relationships and fitness. The essential subject of the ideal Mallarméan drama would be " la confrontation de l'être humain, doué de conscience, avec la nature ".[1]

This religious attitude towards the theatre is exemplified, Mallarmé declares, in that of the ancient Greeks towards their drama or that of the modern Germans towards the Tetralogy. In each case the spectators have within them a totality of legend and belief and they go solemnly to hear its religious evocation. A similar attitude is to be observed in the Catholics at Mass. Mallarmé's ideal theatre is the Ode, singing and celebrating what every man has within him to express, things of which he, linked with the human race over space and time, has inherent foreknowledge.

But for Mallarmé all ends in the Book. As the theatre is to the crowd, so the book is to the reader, in whom we observe the same attitude of active religious participation, the same reaching out to perceive ideas and relationships. As Mallarmé did not actually write for the stage and rarely went to the theatre, it seems that for him the idea of the theatre evolves from the preconceived idea of the book, in other words, that the theatre is the symbol of the book. With regard to the book, Mallarmé draws a careful distinction between the spoken language, which is anecdotal, commercial and utilitarian, and the written language, which in his view is a pattern of black against white, indicating ideas. In a similar way the theatre, according to Mallarmé, is not a realistic representation of human experience in anecdotal form, but a kind of pattern made on a stage with human material, décor, music and dancing, from which ideas emanate.

Just as between book and reader a " lacune " or gap exists, in which something in each fuses together to create a new aesthetic experience, so between actors and spectators there is a similar " lacune ", in which a similar effect is produced by the impact of stage pattern on the audience. As the visual perception of a

[1] C. Mauclair, *op. cit.* p. 125.

photograph is much more direct and simple than the mental perception of ideas which follows the visual perception of the printed characters of the poem, so there is a similar difference between the comprehension of incident or psychological realism on the stage and the comprehension of the type of symbolic drama envisaged by Mallarmé. For the latter, additional mental work must be done by the spectator, and silence or the " lacune " is the element in which that work must take place.

The idea of the silent " lacune " between drama and spectators does not, I think, have much bearing on the subject of this study. Although the traditional drama is anecdotal and psychological, at its best—for example with Shakespeare and Aeschylus —it embraces philosophical ideas which, though more directly expressed than in Mallarmé's ideal drama, still require a certain amount of additional mental work on the part of the spectator. The " lacune " still exists, although it may be relatively small. Actually, when we come to examine the most typical products of the *Théâtre de l'Inexprimé*, we shall see that the dramatists' experiments invariably end in reducing the " lacune ". This is because the writers of this group discard the element of intellectuality which is supreme with Mallarmé. As with the Decadent poets, the aim of the " silent " school is a direct communication of pure emotion, unimpaired by intelligence, a re-creation within the spectator of the emotion experienced by the character.

But the Unexpressed undoubtedly enters into Mallarmé's conception of the theatre. His ideal drama is not anecdotal or psychological description, that is to say, it is not an imitation of life on the stage, but a symbolic structure made with human and other material, indicating abstract ideas. Therefore the dialogue, which is part of the human material, is no more the exact expression of the dramatist's message than the printer's ink on the white page is part of the content of the poem. But since Mallarmé produced no work for the theatre, this ideal drama remains purely hypothetical. How far is it possible to work out in practice the idea of " human writing " on the stage ? In his poetry and prose writings we know that Mallarmé achieves special suggestive effects by a twisting of syntax, a violent change of word order, a condensation of meaning, and a striking use of association and analogy. We must ask ourselves whether, if he had written for the theatre, he would not have produced, in view of the difference of conditions and the multiplicity and diversity of the audience, a different type of language. Only by examining the works he admires can we assess his theories and their influence on the drama of the Unexpressed. Their influence on the Symbolist movement as a whole was of course inestimable.

We cannot take into account what he says of the mime and the dance. He views both as a kind of pattern outlined in space by the human body, suggesting ideas and therefore producing in the spectator aesthetic sensations of the highest quality. But they are not the drama, although, with Mallarmé's quasi-Wagnerian conception of the drama, they may be separate elements of it. For the same reason we cannot consider separately what he says with regard to the suggestive power of music and décor.

We must therefore consider the Wagnerian type of drama, admired by Mallarmé, with a view to detecting whether it has a relationship to or an influence on the Theatre of the Unexpressed. Desiring to give expression to the eternally human, man's inner life, his soul in its essential nature, unaffected by circumstance or accident, Wagner finds his inspiration in legendary figures which he attempts to invest with a universal significance. Words which convey intellectual truths are inadequate to express the mysteries he wishes to communicate, and at a certain point music is necessary to give them full and direct interpretation. As Ernest Newman indicates,[1] the orchestra utters the unspeakable, that is to say, that which is unutterable through the organ of understanding, and the music with its recurring themes gives us remembrance of emotion and foreboding of what is to come. With Wagner, music indicates a wealth of experience which does not normally find direct expression in words, and his use of the

---

[1] *Wagner as Man and Artist* (1925), p. 207.

leitmotiv is of great dramatic interest. But, as Mallarmé observes, the music submerges the spoken word. I have already indicated that I consider the spoken word to be the basic material of drama. For all his theories, what Wagner produces is not drama, but a special type of opera, and we must at present limit ourselves to a consideration of his libretto. This libretto, taken by itself, is clear, direct expression more or less in the traditional manner. When a message is conveyed indirectly, it is through the medium of the music. A good example [1] comes at the end of the *Valkyrie*. Brünnhilde, condemned by Wotan to sleep until wakened by a man who will claim her for his wife, falls on her knees and begs that only the most fearless of heroes shall have this privilege. The Siegfried theme in the music prophesies who it will be, but if one takes the libretto alone, the full significance of her utterance arises only from the fact that the audience already knows the legend, and not by virtue of a deliberate or subconscious choice of words. Wagner's libretto is essentially anecdotal—a man pulling a sword out of a tree, or a conjugal altercation between a pair of Teutonic gods—and there is the degree of incidental symbolism we find in Ibsen. His use of legend constitutes a kind of living and moving metaphor, in effect no more characteristic of the " unexpressed " than the poetic imagery of Victor Hugo.

With regard to the dialogue, therefore, Wagner's is not a Theatre of the Unexpressed, but the composer interests us in so far as he contrives to separate and underline the different elements of the drama with which the Theatre of the Unexpressed, using its own characteristic methods, is especially concerned. The effects of verbal music, which his dialogue achieves by the devices of alliteration, assonance and onomatopoeia, are attained by Maeterlinck through different methods, but we are not mainly concerned with this factor which is common in varying degrees to all poetic drama. More significant to us are the importance

---

[1] Used by Dorothy Knowles in discussing Wagner's leitmotiv, *La Réaction idéaliste au théâtre depuis 1890* (1934), p. 53.

he attributes to intuitive knowledge, as opposed to that obtained through the intelligence ; his suggestive use of the leitmotiv to indicate subconscious thought or desire ; the idea of a collective or racial subconscious embodied in characters such as Wotan and Brünnhilde ; the rich symbolism of external objects such as the Rhinegold or Siegfried's sword.

The influence of Wagner on the French Symbolist movement was immense. The *Revue Wagnérienne*, founded in 1885, was one of the many famous literary reviews which played such an important part in the establishment of Symbolism. Most of the dramatic experiments of the Symbolists were consciously or unconsciously influenced by Wagner's theory and practice, and we must consider whether their work is in any way related to the Theatre of the Unexpressed.[1]

Édouard Schuré was interested in the possibilities of incorporating music into the drama in order to bring out its inward meaning. Rejecting, however, his master's " music-drama ", where music dominated and overshadowed the dramatist's thought, he conceived the notion of the " drame parlé avec musique intermittente " ; the music " s'ingénierait à rendre les plus délicates nuances, les phénomènes les plus profonds et les plus élevés de la *vie intérieure*. La musique jointe à la pensée serait alors l'interprète de l'*inspiration consciente* ",[2] and in his drama *La Roussalka*[3] the music of Chevillard was used for this

---

[1] Although the expression Symbolist Drama appears in most works of criticism concerned with the French theatre and with Symbolism, so far the term does not seem to have been satisfactorily defined and limited. I do not know of any work confined to the study of the Symbolist Drama as such, and an attempt at a proper definition would entail a long discussion and detailed examination of plays beyond the scope of this book. G. Woolley is of the opinion that the term translates " plutôt un idéal qu'une réalité, comme, d'ailleurs, la création dramatique des Symbolistes est restée une conception assez vague qui n'a jamais été réalisée " (*Richard Wagner et le symbolisme français* (1931), p. 141). Among the authors most frequently named by critics discussing from their varying viewpoints the Symbolist Drama are Maeterlinck, Claudel, Villiers de l'Isle-Adam, Verhaeren, van Lerberghe, Laforgue, Quillard, Schuré, Dujardin, Péladan, Remy de Gourmont and Saint-Pol-Roux. These are the names I have in mind when referring here to the Symbolist Drama. The strong influence of Ibsen's plays, given in translation, is generally noted, and many critics by implication include his later works in that group.

[2] *La Genèse de la tragédie* (1926), p. 117.

[3] Performed 21st Mar. 1903 by Lugné-Poe at the Œuvre.

purpose. Schuré's dialogue is, however, violently romantic, and therefore in the traditional style of the " expressed ".

Although by music Schuré, like Wagner, succeeded in conveying something to the audience without the intermediary of words, the use of music in the drama, even when subordinated to the text, cannot be considered as coming within the scope of our subject. I hold the view that the drama is essentially a literary form, and that the arts of décor, and on occasion music, which may be associated with it, must be subsidiary. They can never equal it in importance or merge with it ; they may, however, predominate if the play is inadequate. With Wagner the music predominated ; later with Gaston Baty the décor submerged the text. In the type of play envisaged by Schuré, the music is to all intents and purposes a kind of décor, and however good the décor may be, the finest type of drama is complete in itself. What message is not contained in the actual meaning of the words should be conveyed by their arrangement, by the special use the writer makes of them. As pure stone is the medium of the sculptor, as pure sound is the medium of the composer, so the medium of the dramatist is the unadulterated text. An art form requiring more than one type of creative mind—Wagner, who wrote his own text was an exception to the rule—is on the way to degeneration. The cinema play, for example, when concocted by a multitude of collaborators, rarely rises above the good second-rate, and the only inspired work in this medium is produced by a single purposeful mind thinking in terms of the camera alone.

Édouard Dujardin, the founder of the *Revue Wagnérienne*, was a " fervent wagnérien " who endeavoured to translate his master's theories into terms of the dialogue itself. Like the " music-dramas " of Wagner, his plays have a minimum of action and are full of long speeches in melodious, rhythmic style. He attempts to work the leitmotiv into the language itself, the sound of the words providing the element of music. In *Antonia*,[1]

---

[1] First performed 20th Apr. 1891.

he achieves striking effects by the repetition of theme sentences and phrases, or, within the sentence unit itself, by the repetition of vowels, consonants or syllables considered appropriate by their sound to the idea or emotion expressed. Mallarmé admires Dujardin's dramatic verse. " Ce tissu transformable et ondoyant pour que, sur tel point, afflue le luxe essentiel à la versification où, par places, il s'espace et se dissémine, précieusement convient à l'expression verbale en scène. . . ." [1] He goes on : " Voici les rimes dardées sur de brèves tiges, accourir, se répondre, tour-billonner, coup sur coup, en commandant par une insistance à part et exclusive l'attention à tel motif de sentiment, qui devient nœud capital ". The type of verbal leitmotiv used by Dujardin does not, however, enter into our conception of the *Théâtre de l'Inexprimé*, since it is used to enhance meaning in a dialogue of direct expression. By the Unexpressed is understood that which is deliberately left unsaid, either in significant pause or in dialogue so worded that the avoidance of the essential subject of com-munication is made clear to the audience. The effects of Dujardin to which Mallarmé draws our attention are from this point of view similar to those of music itself in the Wagnerian drama.

Paul Claudel's " théâtre de l'immobilité " [2] shows a strong Wagnerian influence. Without attempting Dujardin's intricate experiments in verbal music, Claudel produces a rhythmic and liturgical dialogue of great power and beauty. The music of his verse is produced the right way, that is to say, it proceeds naturally from the surge of religious inspiration, just as the sound of waves is a function of the mass of the water. Claudel's dialogue, how-ever, with its prolonged unrealistic incantation, represents exactly what the *Théâtre de l'Inexprimé* attempts to avoid.

The drama of Villiers de l'Isle-Adam (who knew Wagner and visited him at Triebschen in 1868 [3]) has, in common with that of the other Wagnerians, long, almost static scenes, in which

[1] *Divagations* (1897), " Crayonné au théâtre ", p. 216.
[2] The term is used by J.-R. Bloch in *Destin du théâtre*.
[3] Villiers de l'Isle-Adam, *Chez les passants*, *Œuvres complètes*, vol. xi, p. 98 *et seq.*

a small number of characters participate, interminable monologues, rhythmic periods, and, though his style inclines to grandilo-
quence, a majestic verbal music. The love scene near the end of
Axël has been likened to that in *Tristan and Isolde*, and the
symbolism of the treasure in the same play to that of the Rhinegold
in the Tetralogy. As in the case of the other Symbolist dramatists I have mentioned, his allegorical characters, his lack of
realism, and his tendency to verbosity show a type of drama
essentially opposed to that of the Unexpressed. In his work,
however, we may detect the germ of certain ideas characteristic
of the *Théâtre de l'Inexprimé*. Maeterlinck acknowledges a great
debt to him. " Tout ce que j'ai fait, c'est à Villiers que je le dois,
à ses conversations plus qu'à ses œuvres, que j'admire beaucoup
d'ailleurs." [1]

Deeply influenced by Kant, Hegel and Schopenhauer, and
reacting violently against the positivist theories of the age,
Villiers' whole work is a statement of his philosophy of idealism,
and his drama is a perpetual antithesis of the ideal and material
worlds. In *La Révolte*, silence is the element in which the aspiring
soul learns to know the Ideal. " Je vais renouer avec le Silence,
c'est mon vieil ami ", says Élisabeth, the prototype of the idealist,
planning to break away from her materialistic husband.[2]   Returning in defeat, she admits that four years of second-rate existence have caused her to deteriorate. " Je ne comprends plus
les exaltations de l'Art ni les apaisements du Silence." [3]   In
silence the hero through meditation is to learn to renounce the
material world and surrender to the eternal law. " Regarde
plutôt les cieux ! " says Maître Janus to Axël, "Où point de cieux
point d'ailes ! — Transfigure-toi dans leur silencieuse lumière ;
songe à développer dans la méditation, à purifier, au feu des
épreuves et des sacrifices, l'influx infini de ta volonté ! à devenir
un adepte dans la Science des forts ! à n'être plus qu'une intelligence affranchie des vœux et des liens de l'instant, en vue de la

Loi suréternelle." [1]   In *Elën* there is a Maeterlinckian suggestion of the communion of souls and their linking with the spirit flowing through the universe.   " Nous nous sentions gagner par le profond, par le mystérieux Silence ; nous nous étions déjà connus peut-être, et quelque chose se touchait au fond de nos destinées : le fluide inexpliqué du Commencement enveloppait notre mémoire de ses vagues foudres; autour de nous le vent froid se plaignait à voix basse dans les branchages desséchés." [2]   And in *Le Nouveau Monde* there is a trace of another Maeterlinckian idea, that of love breaking down barriers of reserve between human beings and enabling one to read into the heart of another. "Je t'aime tant que tes soucis les plus cachés, — ceux que tu n'oses me dire à moi-même, — je les devine ! " [3]   In *Axël* Villiers makes a distinction which Maeterlinck is later to elaborate between different qualities of silence.   " Par exemple," says Axël disdainfully to the materialistic Kaspar, " il est fort concevable que vous préfériez l'Or (dût-il n'être que fictif) à tous les silences, — puisque le Silence ne représente rien pour vous, qu'un bâillement.   En effet, ce mot, vide quand vous usurpez le droit de le prononcer, n'a pas (bien que de mêmes syllabes) l'ombre d'une parenté avec celui que j'ai proféré tout à l'heure.   C'est en vain que vous essayez de les confondre en une même valeur. . . ." [4]

The occasional technical use of silence is interesting from the purely dramaturgical point of view.   Villiers' work has been described as a transition between Romanticism and Symbolism. His plays were all written before 1890 ; *Elën* and *Morgane* date back as far as 1865 and 1866 respectively [5] ; *La Révolte* was first performed in 1870 ; *Le Nouveau Monde*, according to the author's preface, was written in 1875.   As for *Axël*, although it was published at least in part in 1872, according to G. Kahn the idea goes back to 1862. [6]   There are in Villiers' drama striking elements of Hugoesque Romanticism, and they, rather than the

[1] *Œuvres complètes*, vol. iv, p. 198.   [2] *Ibid.* vol. viii, p. 251.
[3] *Ibid.* vol. vii, p. 95.   [4] *Ibid.* vol. iv, p. 160.
[5] Remy de Gourmont, *Promenades littéraires, 1904-13*, 2ᵉ série.
[6] Dorothy Knowles, *op. cit.* pp. 78-9.

Symbolist aspect of his work, appear to be the basis of most of his " silent " effects. *Elën, Morgane* and *Le Nouveau Monde* contain silences or suggestions of silence not unlike those in the drama of Hugo : the breathing-space, as it were, after a torrent of lyricism, or the melodramatic halt before a sensational un-masking, which the ebb and flow of Romantic dialogue natur-ally demands. In the first section of *Axël* the prolonged silence of Sara before her laconic " Non ", and the silence before she finally disposes of the loquacious Archdeacon, form striking Romantic antitheses to the interminable flow of words on the part of her interlocutors. Incidentally, there is in *Morgane* a type of brooding taciturn Romantic hero. Sergius is " un original auquel le silence a porté à la tête ". Mistress Andrews of *Le Nouveau Monde*, haunted by an atavistic curse, is also intended to be such a character. " J'ai voulu, ainsi, créer le type d'une âme étrange, ténébreuse et amère, d'une fille de race, hantée de mélancolie, de silence et de fatalité." [1] It will be interesting to note in *Le Jardinier d'Ispahan* Bernard's treatment of a similar character, obsessed by a problem of heredity and working for the destruction of her rival's love, although this play is not among his most characteristic works.

It is, however, mainly with the dramatic content of the silence that the *Théâtre de l'Inexprimé* is concerned, and in this respect Villiers' silences are comparatively flat. We need not dwell on the " regards ineffables " which we find, for example, in *Elën*.[2] They are quite unlike those of Jean-Jacques Bernard which derive such force from the movement of the preceding text. In *La Ré-volte* there is an interesting " scène muette ", to mark the passage of time between Elisabeth's departure and her return. After appropriate music the hours strike between rather long silences, and through devices astonishingly similar to those used in the modern cinema, Villiers contrives to give the impression of time passing. The scene produces an effect of strangeness, set as it is

---

[1] *Avis au lecteur, Œuvres complètes*, vol. vii, p. 86.
[2] *Œuvres complètes*, vol. viii, p. 252.

in the midst of a text of overpowering verbosity. The most striking silences are, however, those of Sara which have already been noted in the discussion of *Axël*.

Although *Axël* was ultimately performed in 1894, Villiers had never intended it for the stage, and had classed it among his philosophical works. But as he elected to express his ideas in dramatic form, it is from the dramatic point of view that Sara's silences must be considered. In the opening scenes of the play solemn preparations are being made to receive the young girl into a religious order. As the impressive ceremonial slowly proceeds, and the Archdeacon addresses her in an eight-page monologue, punctuated only by the sound of the bell and the singing of the nuns, Sara is mute. Finally, when the fateful question is put, she utters a monosyllabic " Non ". From the purely dramaturgical point of view, however, she might equally well have uttered a monosyllabic " Oui ". Impressive though the silent tableau is with its striking antithesis, nothing fruitful is created in it. Although some hints of Sara's rebellious character are given by the Abbess, and references are made to a mysterious parchment which is to prove the key to a fabulous treasure, the " Non " is not adequately foreshadowed and the audience does not fully realize till afterwards the reasons for her choice. That choice, the act of will which is the highlight of this scene, is not shown to ripen in the silence, either through significant hints thrown out in foregoing dialogue from the character now mute, or through the perceptible impact of the speech of the others on the sustained silence. The author deprives himself of the effective and legitimate weapon of suspense, so well adapted to the use of the Unexpressed. Instead of sitting tense with expectation wondering when the blow will fall, the audience is suddenly jerked out of its equanimity by a melodramatic " coup dè théâtre ". A similar impression is created in the final scene of mime at the end of the first section. After a steady flow of exhortation from the Archdeacon which takes up five pages of text, Sara, without uttering a word, seizes an axe, and forces the old man to descend into the funeral vault which she closes behind him, flings a pilgrim's cloak over her dress, leaps to the window, and lets herself out and down with the aid of a funeral cloth which she has knotted round the bar. All this athleticism is disconcerting after the static scene preceding it, and the flat silence of a mimed action which has not, so to speak, been projected by the dialogue, does not blend harmoniously with the rest of the play. It is as if a different art form were suddenly interpolated. Sara's silences might have additional point if we felt they were consistent with a reserved character, but this is belied by a tidal wave of monologue towards the end of the play, and we are almost persuaded that she has been saving her lungs for the benefit of her lover.

We must not, however, omit one example of a moving and realistic silent effect. In Part II[1] Axël, who has disdained to defend his refusal to do anything about the buried treasure, starts as he sees the troubled distress and conflicting doubts in the minds of his aged retainers. They cannot believe that their master's honour is tarnished, but their simple minds find it difficult to resist Kaspar's plausible arguments. After an inward struggle, Axël condescends, for their sake alone, to speak. Unfortunately, the effect of this brief scene is swamped by the torrent of grandiloquent argumentation which follows.

With regard to the dialogue itself, although, as we have said, it is verbose and clearly expressed in the traditional style, there is some indication of the type of idea which the methods of the *Théâtre de l'Inexprimé* are so well adapted to convey. In a long speech to Kaspar Axël says :

> . . . Tous ces mots, si captivants à cause des intrinsèques images qu'ils sont censés contenir et magnétiquement effluer, — oui, c'est vrai ! tu les as prononcés ! — les enveloppant même des élégances d'emprunt de ta manière, acquise au frôler des courtisans.
>
> Mais, sous le voile de ce dont il parle, nul ne traduit, n'évoque et n'exprime jamais que lui-même.
>
> Or, conçues par toi, imbues de ton être, pénétrées de ta

[1] *Œuvres complètes*, vol. iv, pp. 149-50.

voix, par ton esprit reflétées, les choses de ces paroles, à leur
ressortir de ta nature et de toi proférées, ne m'arrivaient, in-
carnées en l'intime de ta présence, que comme autant d'effigies
de toi-même — frappées en des sons neutres d'une vibra-
tion toujours étrangère à leur sens, et le démentant.

Car ces choses, fictivement incluses en des mots qui, par
eux-mêmes, ne peuvent être, jamais, que virtuels, — ne me
semblaient plus, songées par toi, que d'une *prétendue* identité
avec celles, — du même nom, — dont la vivante illusion
verbale m'eût peut-être charmé.   Comment, en effet, les
reconnaître !   Sèches, répulsives, inquiétantes, glacées, —
hostiles, dès lors, à ces noms mêmes qu'elles avaient l'air
d'usurper sur ta langue pour m'abuser, — je ne ressentais
d'elles, en tes dires dénués de leurs images *réelles*, qu'une
odeur de cœur désséché, qu'une impression de cadavérique
impudeur d'âme, que le sourd avertissement d'une constante
arrière-pensée de perfidie.   Et ce triple élément, constituant, à
mes yeux, l'air interne, exclusivement pour toi respirable, de
ton hybride, ambiguë, éteinte et tortueuse entité, tes paroles ne
résonnaient que . . . comme des vocables troubles, ne tra-
duisant que l'atrophie, innée en toi, des choses mêmes dont ils
prétendaient me suggérer le désir.   En sorte que, sous les
capiteux voiles de ta causerie ainsi brodée de ces beaux mots-
spectres, sache que toi seul, — morne et chatoyant convive !
— m'est apparu.[1]

The whole passage raises the question of the relationship of
the spoken word to the state of mind of the speaker.   The
difference between what is said and what is meant or felt is the
starting-point of the dramatists of the Unexpressed, but whereas
they convey this to the spectator through silence or the deliberate
avoidance of the essential thought in a carefully worded dialogue,
in *Axël*, it is not the arrangement of Kaspar's words but his
attitude in uttering them that makes clear his duplicity of character, to which Villiers subsequently draws our attention by the
analytical language of Axël.

The passage quoted leads us to consider the importance which
Villiers attaches to the intrinsic creative power of the Word.

[1] *Œuvres complètes*, vol. iv, pp. 144-6.

" Tout verbe, dans le cercle de son action, crée ce qu'il exprime. Mesure donc ce que tu accordes de volonté aux fictions de ton esprit." [1] Remy de Gourmont states that Villiers explained to him the mystery of transubstantiation in accordance with this principle, and believes that he took literally the formula of Thomas Aquinas : " Verba efficiunt quod significant ".[2] This aspect of Villiers' philosophy is opposed to the ideas of the dramatists of the Unexpressed who hold the view that words distort the purity of truth, whose real element is silence.

Apart from Maeterlinck, Villiers alone of the Symbolist dramatists appears to show definite traces of a dramatic use of the Unexpressed, but his use of it in relation to the *Théâtre de l'Inexprimé* is extremely elementary. His work, in common with that of other Symbolist writers for the theatre, illustrates the paradoxical fact that the Symbolist movement, with its doctrine of suggestion rather than analytical statement, its endeavours to convey truth by means other than logical language, generally produces a drama whose dialogue seems to be contrary in spirit to its philosophy. One reason for this lies in the difference between the nature of drama and that of poetry, which is the Symbolist medium *par excellence*. With poetry we have the individual reader concentrating on the printed word. With the drama we have a multiplicity of spectators contemplating a three-dimensional stage on which the complicated elements of space, architecture and colour, and the human body with voice, gesture and movement all have a place. In poetry the special effects of suggestion, the fusion of music, colour and speech, are achieved within the medium of the language itself. The contemplative reader is in a position to respond to the subtle and delicate overtones of the single word unit, with its inwardly heard music, its wealth of association, its half-remembered linguistic history, and its intimate appeal to the rich store of conscious and subconscious personal experience. He is also in a suitable state of mind for

---

[1] *Œuvres complètes*, vol. iv, p. 88.
[2] *Promenades littéraires, 1909-13*, vol. ii, pp. 6-7.

perceiving the suggestive effects of unusual syntactical forms and difficult analogy. In the theatre, apart from the broader appeal necessitated by the diversity of the spectators, the attention of the audience, instead of being focused on the single element of the spoken word, radiates, as it were, over body, movement, voice, architecture. Each of these, being a unit of the manifold whole, must of necessity retain its simplicity, since there are limits to what the human attention can cope with. We may compare the language of Symbolist poetry to the composite material of a small, richly inlaid box whose beauty is appreciated by a close scrutiny ; that of the Symbolist drama resembles more the pure marble of an architectural masterpiece viewed from a distance in relation to site, surrounding landscape and space itself. Owing to the exigencies of the theatre, Symbolism on the stage almost invariably produces an uncomplicated type of dialogue, whose rhythmic and melodious effects are closely bound up with meaning.

Another reason for the absence of the Unexpressed in the Symbolist drama is that the latter generally takes the form of allegory.[1] The characters, who are unreal abstractions, loquaciously represent ideas, the language in which these ideas are accurately expressed corresponds closely to them, and the whole message of the dramatist is conveyed in the meaning of the words. In " le langage indirect ", that special type of dialogue, which, as was indicated in the first chapter, is peculiarly characteristic of the *Théâtre de l'Inexprimé*, the message is conveyed less by the actual meaning of the words than by their subconscious choice and arrangement. I shall endeavour to show that this kind of dialogue, which figures largely in the work of Bernard, is usually the result of a rationalized subconscious emotion experienced by a convincingly real individual. The spectator appreciates that emotion by temporarily identifying himself with the stage

---

[1] Cf. P. Martino, *Parnasse et symbolisme* (1925), ch. 11, " Le Théâtre symboliste ", p. 199. " L'allégorie dont ils [les poètes Symbolistes] usaient communément est volontiers parleuse."

character, experiencing the emotion, and going through a similar process of rationalization, while at the same time retaining a detached judgment. Thus, all that is in the character is not contained in the meaning of the words; the language, besides having meaning, indicates by its arrangement hidden reserves in the character; the appreciation of the message on the part of the spectator is largely emotional, and is the result of psychological realism on the stage. In Symbolist allegorical drama the character embodies an abstract idea, and is no more capable of indicating hidden reserves of emotion than an algebraic sign. The function of such characters on the stage is to demonstrate through speech and action a relationship with a system of ideas, and this relationship is perceived by a rapid intellectual process similar to that which serves to interpret the meaning of a graph. Any dramatic force the Unexpressed may have is bound up with emotion, with psychological realism and character represented in depth. The *Théâtre de l'Inexprimé* represents deep but simple emotion through " le langage indirect ". The Symbolist allegorical drama attempts to convey complex relationships of an intellectual nature, which have to be expressed in clear language.

A certain type of " symbolic " drama must, however, be considered separately—that of Ibsen, which reconciles realism of character and action on the stage with philosophical meaning. There is nothing in *The Wild Duck*, *The Master Builder*, *John Gabriel Borkman*, to which one could take serious exception on the grounds of probability, yet from the Ibsen drama we can sense action on a higher plane of ideas. A somewhat different conception of drama seems to lie in Mallarmé's idea of *Hamlet*. For him it is the drama *par excellence*. Behind the living, thinking, hesitating prince he sees the eternal, detached, ideal Hamlet, not contained in the actual words of the dialogue, but, as it were, a precious and elusive by-product of the genius of Shakespeare. In both cases, however, we have to do with an element common in varying degrees to all great tragedy. No work of art worthy of consideration is produced by the realism of Madame Tussaud's waxworks. In all art forms genius imposes that hint of meaning or mystery which relates the work to our inner lives. The working out of ideas behind the realistic action in an Ibsen play is certainly more systematic than in conventional drama, and the spectator is perhaps made unduly conscious of the controlling mind of the author. In the *Théâtre de l'Inexprimé* we are concerned with dialogue as it relates to the characters, with the implications of what is left unsaid as they affect those characters who interest us as specimens of humanity similar to ourselves, who exist for the time being in their own right, and whose poignant reality leaves no room for their inventor in the mind of the spectator.

Maeterlinck appears to be the sole Symbolist poet who really succeeds in making dramatic use of the Unexpressed,[1] and this can be accounted for by the element of realism in his plays. His theories of the " tragique quotidien " spring from the desire to perceive the truth underlying the simple experiences of everyday life. The special kind of dialogue in which the Unexpressed figures is realistic, being the authentic form of expression for the strange, subnormal and not unreal characters he likes to portray. The subtle effects of suggestion are achieved through methods appropriate to the theatre. Although the dialogue is musical, it retains on the whole its simplicity and meaning, and the " unexpressed " is revealed by selection and arrangement of language, instead of by the subjection of that medium to the strange alchemy of the Symbolist poem.

As long as the commercial theatre held sway in Paris—and as far as the French drama was concerned, Paris, to all intents and purposes, was France—there was little hope of a hearing for the new idealists. There were, however, men of imagination who decided to make a stand against the " Boulevard " by creating theatres of their own for the regeneration of dramatic art. Among

---

[1] Edmond Sée says that in *La Vie muette*, first performed at the Œuvre, 27th Nov. 1894, Maurice Beaubourg " mit en pratique la théorie du Silence, ou du dialogue tacite, depuis fort en honneur parmi les jeunes écrivains dramatiques d'après-guerre " (*Le Théâtre français contemporain*, 1933 edition, p. 94). This play is an obvious and very feeble imitation of Maeterlinck, and need not therefore claim our attention.

the most notable of these enterprises, from our point of view, was the Théâtre d'Art of Paul Fort, started in 1890, which gave poetic and Symbolist plays, and also readings of poetry and prose. Its programme included two " silent " plays by Maeterlinck, *L'Intruse* [1] and *Les Aveugles*. [2] The work of the Théâtre d'Art was continued by the Théâtre de l'Œuvre, started in 1893 by Lugné-Poe. The task he imposed upon himself was to make known to the French public the great foreign dramatists and the plays of the young idealists. In his own words, his aim was " de faire du théâtre *de quelque façon que ce soit* ŒUVRE D'ART, ou tout au moins de *remuer des Idées* ". [3] Antoine had already introduced foreign dramatists to France—Ibsen, Turgeniev, Hauptmann— but played with a naturalistic bias. Lugné-Poe presented plays by Ibsen, Bjoernson, Hauptmann, Strindberg, from the idealist standpoint. As for French and French-speaking writers, he was to give the public Maeterlinck, Rachilde, Henri de Régnier, Verhaeren, Claudel. Lugné-Poe had also been associated with " Les Escholiers ", a club founded in 1886 by pupils of the Lycée Condorcet, which, although not exclusively theatrical, by its aims and by performances of plays, made an important contribution to the renewal of the French theatre.

Continuing the tradition of the Théâtre d'Art, which had been the first to play Maeterlinck, Lugné-Poe gave as the opening performance of the Œuvre *Pelléas et Mélisande*, [4] which the Théâtre d'Art had found impossible to play, repeated *L'Intruse* the following month, and gave the first performance of *Intérieur*. [5]

It is interesting to note that as far back as 1893 the possibilities of exploiting silence dramatically had presented themselves to Lugné-Poe. " Un temps, je songeais à créer un théâtre où s'associeraient poésie et silences, mais j'en concevais les difficultés. L'histoire est assez plaisante car, encore impressionné des silences si bien exploités au Théâtre Libre, des silences si émouvants dans

---

[1] First performed 21st May 1891.   [2] First performed 11th Dec. 1891.
[3] *La Plume*, 1st Sept. 1893, dossier du Théâtre de l'Œuvre, quoted by Dorothy Knowles, *op. cit.* p. 172.
[4] 17th May 1893.   [5] 15th Mar. 1895.

le théâtre de Maeterlinck, de l'effet dramatique qu'on pouvait en tirer (n'était-ce pas le temps où le Théâtre Funambulesque était à son apogée avec Félicia Mallet, Courtès, Paul Clerget), j'essayai d'intéresser quelques amis . . . mais Faguet, mon maître, me répondit par une plaisante lettre qui me découragea rapidement." [1]

Émile Faguet had written : " Votre idée me séduit beaucoup, d'autant plus qu'elle permettrait aux auteurs de n'avoir pas de talent et que c'est par le temps qui court une condition qui s'impose à l'art dramatique. C'est à ce point que je ne sais pas si c'est pour que les auteurs n'aient pas besoin de talent que vous avez eu cette idée, ou parce qu'ils n'en ont point que l'idée vous est naturellement venue." He points out that Lugné-Poe is re-echoing the dramatic theories of Diderot, and goes on : " Un seul point m'inquiète. Je crois qu'il faudrait supprimer complètement les paroles. Dès qu'on parlera un peu l'impression sera qu'on ne parle pas assez. Le genre mixte sera très difficile, et je croirais assez volontiers impossible à constituer."

The time was not yet ripe for a " school of silence ". The " silent " dramatists writing after 1918 took as their starting-point a desire for deeper psychological realism. Lugné-Poe's efforts were directed towards the establishment of an idealist theatre, and he welcomed the work of Maeterlinck as a type of idealist drama. It is, however, through the incidental realism in his plays that the Unexpressed emerges as a force of considerable dramatic power.

---

[1] *Le Sot du tremplin* (1930), pp. 223-4.

CHAPTER III

MAURICE MAETERLINCK: I

M AURICE MAETERLINCK was born in Ghent in 1862, of old Flemish stock. He early lost the faith inculcated by the Jesuits of the Collège de Sainte-Barbe. His distaste for Law, which he was obliged to study, and the oppressive atmosphere of provincial family life seem to have contributed to that uneasiness of spirit which, with the subtle influence of the misty Flemish landscape, made him fruitful soil for the ideas of mystic philosophers. In 1886 Maeterlinck went to Paris to complete his legal education. At the Brasserie Pousset in Montmartre he used to see Villiers de l'Isle-Adam, whose influence he warmly acknowledged, Saint-Pol-Roux, Mikhael, Quillard, Darzens and Mendès.[1] His stay in Paris also gave him the opportunity of meeting Mallarmé.[2] Maeterlinck tells Huret the names of the main writers who influenced his work : in philosophy, Kant, Carlyle and Schopenhauer " qui arrive jusqu'à vous consoler de la mort " ; in literature, Shakespeare, Swinburne, Baudelaire, Laforgue, Edgar Allan Poe, Rossetti and William Morris. He also mentions the painters Burne-Jones and Puvis de Chavannes, whose idealized characters people his theatre. His essays show the influence of Ruysbroeck l'Admirable and Novalis, whose work he translated, and of Jakob Boehme, Swedenborg and Emerson, whose ideas harmonize with his mystic philosophy.

In common with the other Symbolists, Maeterlinck holds that one mysterious spirit flows through the universe and through the beings that people it. The true nature of the individual is

---

[1] J. Huret, *Enquête sur l'évolution littéraire* (1891), p. 128.
[2] J. Bithell, *Life and Writings of Maeterlinck* (1913), p. 12.

perceived only when outer trappings are discarded and the mysterious vital essence is revealed in all its purity, and, as it is common to all, by allowing it to operate freely, human beings may communicate directly and intuitively with each other and with the universe. What interests Maeterlinck in man is not mind, character or heart, for him relatively superficial aspects, but that which he calls the soul. By soul he seems to signify the special manifestation of the universal spirit as it appears in the individual and is tinged with his personality, relating him at the same time, through its fundamental nature, to other individuals and to the whole universe. The mystic ideal is communion of souls, the keen sense of the unity behind external phenomena which inspires an active desire to participate in the harmony of the universe.

Silence is the element in which this mystic communion takes place. As the universal spirit is hidden deep, it can be perceived only when the superficialities of everyday life are laid aside. Human speech is regarded as one of these superficialities. Its function is utilitarian and the message it conveys is of ephemeral importance. It may be used to disguise or conceal the essential thought. It may assume undue importance, and the mundane matters which it introduces into the human consciousness may blot out the light of the spirit. He quotes Carlyle. " La parole est trop souvent, non comme le disait le Français, l'art de cacher la pensée, mais l'art d'étouffer et de suspendre la pensée, en sorte qu'il n'en reste plus à cacher." [1]

[1] *Le Trésor des humbles* (1896), p. 10.
The passages from Carlyle, quoted by Maeterlinck in French translation in the essay " Le Silence " (*Le Trésor des humbles*, i), are as follows :
" SILENCE and SECRECY ! Altars might still be raised to them (were this an altar-building time) for universal worship. Silence is the element in which great things fashion themselves together ; that at length they may emerge, full-formed and majestic, into the daylight of Life, which they are thenceforth to rule. Not William the Silent only, but all the considerable men I have known, and the most undiplomatic and unstrategic of these, forbore to babble of what they were creating and projecting. Nay, in thy own mean perplexities, do thou thyself but *hold thy tongue for one day* : on the morrow, how much clearer are thy purposes and duties ; what wreck and rubbish have those mute workmen within thee swept away, when intrusive noises were shut out ! Speech is too often not, as the Frenchman defined it, the art of concealing Thought ; but of quite

Words never serve for the most vital kind of communication between human beings.

> Les lèvres ou la langue peuvent représenter l'âme de la même manière qu'un chiffre ou un numéro d'ordre représente une peinture de Memlinck, par exemple, mais dès que nous avons vraiment *quelque chose à nous dire,* nous sommes *obligés* de nous taire ; et si, dans ces moments, nous résistons aux ordres invisibles et pressants du silence, nous avons fait une perte éternelle que les plus grands trésors de la sagesse humaine ne pourront réparer, car nous avons perdu l'occasion d'écouter une autre âme et de donner un instant d'existence à la nôtre ; et il y a bien des vies où de telles occasions ne se présentent pas deux fois. . . .
>
> Nous ne parlons qu'aux heures où nous ne vivons pas, dans les moments où *nous ne voulons pas* apercevoir nos frères et où nous nous sentons à une grande distance de la réalité.[1]

Maeterlinck concedes that words, besides being utilitarian, may effectively concern themselves with the profound things of life, and indeed he can scarcely do otherwise in view of the quantity of them which he, like Carlyle, uses in praise of silence. But they are the instruments of reason, and while reason is useful for superficial truths, only intuition can reach the fundamental mysteries. " Dès que nous exprimons quelque chose, nous le diminuons étrangement." [2]

Words do not express the real nature of things, and the most precious essence of truth eludes them.

stifling and suspending Thought, so that there is none to conceal. Speech too is great, but not the greatest. As the Swiss Inscription says : *Sprechen ist silbern, Schweigen ist golden* (Speech is silvern, Silence is golden); or as I might rather express it : Speech is of Time, Silence is of Eternity.

" Bees will not work except in darkness ; Thought will not work except in Silence ; neither will Virtue work except in Secrecy. . . ."—*Sartor Resartus*, Book III, ch. 3 (Oxford, Clarendon Press, 1913), pp. 156-7.

" The noble silent men, scattered here and there, each in his department ; silently thinking, silently working ; whom no Morning Paper makes mention of ! They are the salt of the Earth. A country that has none or few of these is in a bad way. Like a forest which has no *roots* ; which had all turned into leaves and boughs ;—which must soon wither and be no forest. . . . Silence, the great Empire of Silence : higher than the stars ; deeper than the Kingdoms of Death ! . . ."—*Heroes and Hero-worship*, Lecture vi (Oxford, Clarendon Press, 1910), pp. 203-4.

[1] *Le Trésor des humbles*, p. 11.   [2] *Ibid.* p. 61.

Et dans le domaine où nous sommes, ceux-là mêmes qui
savent parler le plus profondément sentent le mieux que les
mots n'expriment jamais les relations réelles et spéciales qu'il
y a entre deux êtres. Si je vous parle en ce moment des choses
les plus graves, de l'amour, de la mort ou de la destinée, je
n'atteins pas la mort, l'amour ou le destin, et malgré mes
efforts, il restera toujours entre nous une vérité qui n'est pas
dite, qu'on n'a même pas l'idée de dire, et cependant cette
vérité qui n'a pas eu de voix aura seule vécu un instant entre
nous, et nous n'avons pas pu songer à autre chose. Cette
vérité, c'est *notre vérité* sur la mort, le destin ou l'amour ; et
nous n'avons pu l'entre-voir qu'en silence.[1]

As an iridescent soap bubble disintegrates at the touch, so the
nature of death, love and destiny vanishes at the gross impact of
the spoken word, and what the word contains is something other
than those elusive forces.

Maeterlinck distinguishes between passive silence " qui n'est
que le reflet du sommeil, de la mort, ou de l'inexistence ", and
active silence, in which the communion of souls takes place.[2] The
joy of this communion can be known by even the most wretched
of beings, and most of us, he says, have experienced it twice or
thrice in our lives. Silence, according to Maeterlinck, comes out to
meet the soul at special moments—at departure or return, in the
midst of great joy, in the presence of death or misfortune. Here
we see the starting-point of a dramatic use of silence, the suggestion of movement, the rich potentialities of silence and its association with human crisis.

The dramatic theories emerging from Maeterlinck's mystic
conception of silence are contained in the famous essay *Le
Tragique quotidien*.[3] For Maeterlinck the truly tragic is found
not in violent external adventure but in everyday life. The task
of the drama is not to represent conflict between human beings,
desires, passion and duty. Its real subject is " ce qu'il y a d'éton-
nant dans le fait seul de vivre ". In *Macbeth, Hamlet, King Lear*,
it is not the violence of action but the sense of the infinite mystery

---

[1] *Le Trésor des humbles*, p. 22.   [2] *Ibid.* p. 13.   [3] *Ibid.* pp. 161 *et seq.*

of life emanating from the plays that constitutes their grandeur. This mysterious emanation, instead of being incidental to the drama, should, according to Maeterlinck, be shifted to the foreground and made the main concern of the dramatist. " Ce qu'on entend sous le roi Lear, sous Macbeth, sous Hamlet, par exemple, le chant mystérieux de l'infini, le silence menaçant des âmes ou des Dieux, l'éternité qui gronde à l'horizon, la destinée ou la fatalité qu'on aperçoit intérieurement sans que l'on puisse dire à quels signes on la reconnaît, ne pourrait-on, par je ne sais quelle interversion des rôles, les rapprocher de nous tandis qu'on éloignerait les acteurs ? " [1]   A good painter will not paint Marius and the Cimbri or the assassination of the Duke of Guise, because the psychology of victory or murder, according to Maeterlinck, is elementary ; " le vacarme inutile d'un acte violent étouffe la voix plus profonde, mais hésitante et discrète, des êtres et des choses ". Rather will he represent " une maison perdue dans la campagne, une porte ouverte au bout d'un corridor, un visage ou des mains au repos ; et ces simples images pourront ajouter quelque chose à notre conscience de la vie . . .".[2]

This conception of the tragic underlying the repose of everyday life leads to the idea of a static theatre, from which external violence of movement is to be eliminated. Such a theatre already exists, says Maeterlinck, in the tragedies of Aeschylus. *Prometheus Bound*, *The Suppliants*, the *Choephoroe* before the murder, are practically immobile ; even the psychological interest is reduced to a minimum, and the real subject is the situation of man in the universe.

The substance of these tragedies appears not in the acts but in the words. The words, however, do not contain that substance ; they merely indicate it. The real content of the tragedy is revealed beneath the language of the characters.

> . . . il faut qu'il y ait autre chose que le dialogue extérieurement nécessaire. Il n'y a guère que les paroles qui semblent d'abord inutiles qui comptent dans une œuvre. C'est en elles

[1] *Le Trésor des humbles*, pp. 162-3.   [2] *Ibid.* p. 165.

que se trouve son âme. A côté du dialogue indispensable, il y a presque toujours un autre dialogue qui semble superflu. Examinez attentivement et vous verrez que c'est le seul que l'âme écoute profondément, parce que c'est en cet endroit seulement qu'on lui parle. Vous reconnaîtrez aussi que c'est la qualité et l'étendue de ce dialogue inutile qui détermine la qualité et la portée ineffable de l'œuvre. Il est certain que, dans les drames ordinaires, le dialogue indispensable ne répond pas du tout à la réalité ; et ce qui fait la beauté mystérieuse des plus belles tragédies se trouve tout juste dans les paroles qui se disent à côté de la vérité stricte et apparente.[1]

Just as the phenomena of everyday life conceal deep mysteries, so the spoken word, itself such a phenomenon, conceals the wordless speech of the spirit. Maeterlinck's conception of the " hidden dialogue " is quite different, as we shall see later on, from that of Jean-Jacques Bernard and of Denys Amiel. Amiel represents a tacitly and consciously acknowledged secret of a superficial nature, a kind of painful drawing-room game between sophisticated people. Bernard goes deeper and examines emotion sunk into the subconscious of the individual. For Maeterlinck the hidden dialogue reveals a subconscious of a different nature. It is the cosmic subconscious of the Symbolists, a mysterious spiritual force within the individual linked with those existing behind the whole universe. The meaning of the word " psychology " is not the same for Maeterlinck as for the post-1918 writers. For him psychology is the knowledge of Psyche, the soul. For them it is the study of the working of human personality. By Freudian standards the psychology of victory or murder may be extremely complicated. When Maeterlinck states, however, that it is elementary, he means that the motives behind victory or murder are related to the more superficial aspects of human life and nowhere touch the deep, pure spirit which flows through all men, even criminals.

Il s'agit . . . d'une psychologie tout autre que la psychologie habituelle, laquelle a usurpé le beau nom de Psyché,

[1] *Le Trésor des humbles*, pp. 173-4.

puisqu'en réalité elle ne s'inquiète que des phénomènes spirituels les plus étroitement liés à la matière. Il s'agit, en un mot, de ce que devrait nous révéler une psychologie transcendante qui s'occuperait des rapports directs qu'il y a d'âme à âme entre les hommes et de la *sensibilité* ainsi que de la *présence extraordinaire* de notre âme.[1]

In Maeterlinck's view the soul remains unsullied by the acts of the body. " Je puis commettre un crime sans que le moindre souffle incline la plus petite flamme de ce feu."[2]   And man's conscious and subconscious life is for him uncomplicated :

> . . . plus on descend dans la conscience de l'homme, moins on y trouve de conflits. On ne peut descendre très avant dans une conscience qu'à la condition que cette conscience soit très éclairée ; car il est indifférent de faire dix pas ou mille au fond d'une âme plongée dans les ténèbres, on n'y trouvera rien d'imprévu, rien de nouveau, les ténèbres étant partout semblables à elles-mêmes. Or, une conscience très éclairée a des passions et des désirs infiniment moins exigeants, infiniment plus pacifiques, plus patients, plus salutaires, plus abstraits et plus généreux qu'une conscience ordinaire.[3]

The beauty and the mystery of the subconscious lies in the " sagesse occulte " possessed by the finest type of human being. This deep wisdom may fall to the humblest peasant, to a beggar, to a little child.

It is not our task to discuss the validity of Maeterlinck's theories, which interest us only in so far as they relate to his Theatre of the Unexpressed. His conception of the human subconscious leaves no room for the dramatic development of inward conflict resulting from the Freudian psychology of Bernard. In Maeterlinck's plays the conflict, or rather the opposition, is that of the human being and external fatalities ; the will of the victims is paralysed by the sinister unseen forces and they know themselves to be condemned from the start. Death is the in-

---

[1] *Le Trésor des humbles*, p. 37.   [2] *Ibid.* p. 150.
[3] *Le Double Jardin* (1904), pp. 122-3.

visible protagonist. " La présence infinie, ténébreuse, hypó-
critement active de la mort remplit tous les interstices du poème." [1]
Death is " ce troisième personnage, énigmatique, invisible mais
partout présent ", indispensable in any great work of dramatic
art.[2] Love is the other unseen force in Maeterlinck's drama. At
first it is overshadowed by Death, but subsequently it gains
supremacy, and we shall see how, as it does so, the nature of
Maeterlinck's drama changes.

Maeterlinck's idea of the " tragique quotidien " leads us to
expect a degree of realism which, as I have tried to show, is
indispensable for a Theatre of the Unexpressed. The characters
and setting of *L'Intruse*, *Les Aveugles* and *Intérieur* are not inconsistent with reality. And even in the " legendary " pieces, there
is, within a restricted field, a realism of character which enables
Maeterlinck to produce powerful effects of silence. The characters, though symbolic, and to a certain extent stylized, have no
connection with the allegorical abstractions of numerous Symbolist plays. These abstractions proceed from an intellectual
approach ; the truths which the Symbolists wish to convey are,
as it were, surveyed in a detached manner from a higher plane.
But Maeterlinck lives and feels his mystic truths which, he senses,
are present within him as they are present in all nature. His
dramatic representation of these truths is accordingly a reproduction of life and nature. In the interview with Huret, Maeterlinck
distinguishes between two kinds of symbol : that of the allegory,
the symbol " a priori ", the symbol " de propos délibéré ", which
starts from the abstraction and which the poet endeavours to
invest with some humanity, and his own, the unconsciously
created symbol, which emerges from a work rooted in nature.
The poet should be " passif dans le symbole " ; he is " plus ou
moins puissant, non pas en raison de ce qu'il fait lui-même, mais
en raison de ce qu'il parvient à faire exécuter par les autres, et par
l'ordre mystérieux et éternel et la force occulte des choses ! ".[3]

[1] Preface to *Théâtre* (1911), vol. i, p. iv.   [2] *Ibid.* p. xvi.
[3] J. Huret, *op. cit.* pp. 124-6.

Maeterlinck's temperament leads him to feel truths rather than apprehend them intellectually, and so it is with his characters. The presence of cosmic forces and their silent hostility to the individual, which preoccupied the poet during his first period, are conveyed by the emotional reactions of the strange beings that people his stage, and those reactions are so intense and so compelling that the truth of the characters, shadowy though they be, is powerfully impressed on the spectator. And thus, without descriptive or analytical language, through sheer authenticity of emotion and realism of character, Maeterlinck succeeds in communicating philosophical truths.

The representation of ideas through emotion also produces in the so-called " static theatre " a degree of dramatic movement, since there is generally a progression and heightening of fear as the presence of Destiny is felt to approach more closely. This silent dramatic " dynamism " is threefold : it is in the advance of the invisible fatalities, in the growth of fear which that relentless advance creates in the stage character, and in the active imagination of the spectator, who, under the influence of the contagious emotion, reconstructs the idea of the advancing fate. In Maeterlinck's " théâtre de l'attente " [1] an element of movement is subtly implied. The characters (and the spectators) subconsciously know what they are waiting for, hence subconsciously they anticipate the change from uncertain immunity to certain destruction.

Le Trésor des humbles, the book of essays containing Maeterlinck's dramaturgy of the Unexpressed, was published in 1896 after the eight " silent " plays had appeared. In *Le Maeterlinckianisme*,[2] Maurice Lecat emphasizes the influence of Georgette Leblanc who was to be Maeterlinck's companion for many years. It was she who had written the words, " Nous ne nous connaissons pas encore, nous n'avons pas encore osé nous taire ensemble ", which appear in his essay on Silence.[3] But it is obvious from the

---

[1] The phrase is used by Guy Michaud in *Message poétique du symbolisme* (1947).
[2] 1937-9.   [3] *Le Trésor des humbles*, p. 19.

very earliest dramas that the idea of silence was working and developing within the poet.

Two early non-dramatic works already foreshadow Maeterlinck's dramas. In the story *Le Massacre des innocents*,[1] while Spanish soldiers massacre the children before their parents' eyes, their chief, who does not understand the language of the peasants, stands mute and impassible. In this sinister figure, before whose servants the peasants are dazed and completely passive, Lecat sees a representation of Fate silently destroying its unresisting victims, a theme used often in the later works.[2] *Serres chaudes*[3] is a collection of strange Decadent poems with an atmosphere of morbid uneasiness, melancholy and ennui. They contain in fleeting symbols images which reappear in the décor of the plays, and sometimes a whole Maeterlinckian scene is latent in a single line :

Princesses abandonnées en des marécages sans issues . . .[4]

Ils sont pareils à des prisonniers qui n'ignorent pas que tous les geôliers se baignent dans le fleuve,
Et qui entendent faucher l'herbe dans le jardin de la prison.[5]

Toutes les filles du roi sont dans une barque sous l'orage ! [6]

The first play, *La Princesse Maleine*,[7] presents on the stage itself the actions of violence and horror which the dramatist was to condemn later on in *Le Tragique quotidien*. Murders are committed and blood flows copiously as in *Macbeth*, *Hamlet* and *King Lear*, which Maeterlinck was in a sense imitating. The Romantic stock - in - trade is drawn upon : comets, thunderstorms, an eclipse, a cemetery, a fool, ravens and swans, poison and seven nuns with Latin orisons. In spite of all the bric-à-brac, however, the idea of a static drama suggests itself, since the real

---

[1] Published 1886 in *La Pléiade*.
[2] Maurice Lecat, *Le Maeterlinckianisme* (1937), Premier Fascicule, pp. 29-30.
[3] 1889. J. Bithell hints that Maeterlinck was indebted to Whitman for the form of some of the *Serres chaudes*.   [4] P. 75, " Regards ".
[5] P. 62, " Cloche à plongeur ".   [6] P. 47, " Hôpital ".
[7] Dated 1890 in *Théâtre*, vol. i, but appearing in a first edition for private circulation in 1889.—J. Bithell, *op. cit.* p. 30.

significance of the play lies not in the external action but in the paralysed non-resistance of the characters as Fate in the shape of Death relentlessly advances.

At the betrothal feast of Princess Maleine and Prince Hjalmar a violent quarrel breaks out between the royal fathers, giving rise to war. Maleine's father and mother perish, their land is laid waste, Maleine escapes with her nurse from an old tower to join Hjalmar who, thinking she is dead, has listlessly allowed himself to be betrothed to Uglyane, whose mother, Anne of Jutland, a monster of wickedness, has amorous designs on both Hjalmar and his father. Maleine is received unrecognized as an attendant to Uglyane. When her identity is discovered, Anne attempts unsuccessfully to have her poisoned, and then, with the unwilling assistance of the old king whom her depravity has reduced to a state of dotage, strangles her in her bedroom. Hjalmar stabs the guilty queen and takes his own life. The aged king survives in a state of imbecility, prattling inconsequentially about his breakfast salad.

In his reverberating article in *Figaro* [1] Octave Mirbeau did not hesitate to compare Maeterlinck with Shakespeare. *Macbeth* and *Hamlet* were undoubtedly in Maeterlinck's mind when he wrote the play. " Quand j'ai écrit la *Princesse Maleine*, je m'étais dit : ' Je vais tâcher de faire une pièce à la façon de Shakespeare pour un théâtre de Marionnettes '." [2] Mirbeau's comparison is of course grossly exaggerated. The resemblances to Shakespeare are superficial. But there is a peculiar streak of individual genius in *La Princesse Maleine*, and it is bound up with the implications of the term *Théâtre de Marionnettes*. Unlike Shakespeare, whose theatre centres on man, Maeterlinck, in accordance with the theories later outlined in *Le Trésor des humbles*, shifts to the foreground the invisible forces which move the universe, and their place in the drama is so disproportionately great that the characters dwindle in comparison into wraiths and shadows. As J. Bithell puts it, the real actors are behind the scenes : the forces

[1] 24th Aug. 1890.   [2] J. Huret, *op. cit.* p. 129.

that work the strings of the puppets.[1] Nevertheless, as I have already indicated, although the characters, helpless before all-powerful and inexorable Fate, move and act with the automatism of marionettes, they are not unreal. Maeterlinck's legendary princesses give the impression of charming but slightly sub-normal creatures of instinct, childlike and elusive, akin to the timid, wide-eyed animals of the woods where they wander in a state of semi-somnambulism.

Maeterlinck conveys the idea of advancing doom by realisti-cally representing the sense of horror with which the subnormal character becomes intuitively aware of it. Fear, the natural weapon of self-defence, is intensified in a weak person, half conscious of her own inadequacy to deal with life. A state of anxiety is progressively intensified as Death draws nearer and the helplessness of the individual becomes more and more apparent. The contagion of anguish reaches the spectator who, temporarily identifying himself with the character, becomes emotionally aware of the horror and relentlessness of death. In this way, without having recourse to descriptive or narrative language, Maeterlinck impresses an idea on our minds with tremendous force.

When the material object of fear is close at hand the characters maintain a kind of paralysed silence. Maleine, wandering in the woods with the nurse and confronted by unpleasant men, or raged at by her father for remaining loyal to Hjalmar, becomes almost dumb with fear, and her mute horror before she begs for mercy from the king and queen who are about to murder her is one of the most harrowing things in drama. But long before the emotion has attained such a pitch of intensity the sentiment of vaguely impending disaster is insidiously suggested to the audience. Like the sheep that Yniold sees on their way to slaughter,[2] Maeterlinck's victims seem to sense dimly the presence of the unseen forces to which they are appointed to be sacrificed. Such perceptions are animal and intuitive. The characters are

---

[1] *Op. cit.* p. 37. [2] *Pelléas et Mélisande*, Act IV, sc. 3.

E

too weak-willed and too unintellectual to attempt to conquer those uneasy feelings by the normal procedure of analysing the situation and reasoning with themselves. Hence the vague sense of anguish emerges in a dreamy iterative dialogue, wondering repetitions of half thoughts, echoing and dying.

This repetitive dialogue may be associated with Maeterlinck's ideas on the " tragique quotidien ". As the mystery underlying external phenomena is a state of spiritual purity, with the result that ideal dramatic action is reduced to a minimum and the drama is " static ", so in language, anecdote, intellectual meaning and logical shape are eliminated, with the result that language is reduced almost to a pure cry. It *is*, rather than it represents, the sheer emotional reaction to mysterious presences sensed intuitively. The mind, if indeed we can talk about mind in connection with Maeterlinck's attractive little moron, does not choose to organize this reaction into a shapely sentence. The character is not telling us about her emotion but visibly experiencing it. The realism of primitive naked fear is so compelling that the audience can scarcely fail to be directly affected by this most contagious of emotions. The process of communication is accordingly similar to that employed in Decadent poetry, but the methods of realization are different. The medium of the language is undistorted ; the unit is not the word with its associations and overtones but the recurring sentence :

> MALEINE. J'ai peur !
> HJALMAR. Allons plus loin . . .
> MALEINE. Quelqu'un pleure ici . . .
> HJALMAR. Quelqu'un pleure ici ? . . .
> MALEINE. J'ai peur.
> HJALMAR. Mais n'entendez-vous pas que c'est le vent ?
> (. . . . . .)
> MALEINE. Oh ! vous avez jeté de la terre sur moi !
> HJALMAR. J'ai jeté de la terre sur vous ?
> MALEINE. Oui, elle est retombée sur moi !
> HJALMAR. Oh ! ma pauvre Uglyane !
> MALEINE. J'ai peur !

HJALMAR. Vous avez peur auprès de moi ?
MALEINE. Il y a là des flammes entre les arbres.
HJALMAR. Ce n'est rien ; — ce sont des éclairs, il a fait très chaud aujourd'hui.
MALEINE. J'ai peur ! oh ! qui est-ce qui remue la terre autour de nous ?
HJALMAR. Ce n'est rien ; c'est une taupe, une pauvre petite taupe qui travaille.
MALEINE. J'ai peur ! . . .[1]

The elimination of anecdote and intellectual meaning, the concentration on sentences reflecting directly a state of consciousness and the constant repetition of those sentences not only have a kind of hypnotic effect on the nerves of the spectator but make him unduly aware of the element of the human voice, which, besides intensifying the impression of human reality, also has the power of haunting music.[2] Maeterlinck, said to be no musician—he was insensible to the beauty of Debussy's rendering of *Pelléas et Mélisande*—excels in verbal music, which is achieved not through experimenting with the medium or from the rhythmic sweep of logically developed thought, but through this pure element of the human voice, whose sounds, enclosed in the unit of the sentence, recur like the sound of breaking waves. The quality of these repeated phrases, with their cumulative effect on the listener, may be less elusive than that of the subtle suggestion in Symbolist poetry, but Maeterlinck's device is singularly well adapted to dramatic use, and to the direct communication of human anguish. Verbal music, which exists in all great dramatic poetry, is not, properly speaking, an instrument of the Unexpressed. In the case of Maeterlinck, however, its intimate association with the pure quality of the human voice, the cry of anguish, does serve to intensify the strong emotion through which, without direct expression, the poet seeks to convey his truths.

Unfortunately this kind of repetitive dialogue may have the

---

[1] Act II, sc. 6.
[2] James Huneker notes that Maeterlinck's characters are "voice or nothing". *Iconoclasts* (1905), p. 386.

defects of its qualities, and we occasionally find passages which might have been extracted from an infant's reading book.

> MALEINE. Mais cependant . . . je vois la mer.
> LA NOURRICE. Vous voyez la mer ?
> MALEINE. Oui, oui, c'est la mer ! Elle est verte !
> LA NOURRICE. Mais alors, vous devez voir la ville. Laissez-moi regarder.
> MALEINE. Je vois le phare.
> LA NOURRICE. Vous voyez le phare ?
> MALEINE. Oui. Je crois que c'est le phare . . .
> LA NOURRICE. Mais alors, vous devez voir la ville.
> MALEINE. Je ne vois pas la ville.
> LA NOURRICE. Vous ne voyez pas la ville ?
> MALEINE. Je ne vois pas la ville.[1]

Maeterlinck himself, coming back to his early plays, was not insensible to what he calls " beaucoup de naïvetés dangereuses . . . ces répétitions étonnées qui donnent aux personnages l'apparence de somnambules un peu sourds constamment arrachés à un songe pénible ",[2] but he suggests that they convey the tone of the atmosphere and of the countryside. They may well be, as many critics point out, the language of the taciturn peasants among whom Maeterlinck lived. The landscape of many of the earlier plays is predominantly Flemish. Maeterlinck adds, " . . . ce manque de promptitude à entendre et à répondre, tient intimement à leur psychologie et à l'idée un peu hagarde qu'ils se font de l'univers ". His timid, withdrawn, absent-minded children seem to be listening all the time to a tale of other-worldly mysteries, and their attention must be continually refocused to the things of everyday life.

Hjalmar, a pale shadow of Shakespeare's Hamlet, is, however, something like a normal thinking human being. He does not speak out what is in his heart, not because he is unaware of what is happening, but because the horror of it paralyses speech. Suspecting Anne's illicit love for his father, and later her incestuous love for himself, he is consciously reticent.

---

[1] Act I, sc. 4.   [2] Preface to *Théâtre* (1911), vol. i, pp. i-ii.

HJALMAR. J'ai entrevu aujourd'hui les flammes de péchés auxquels je n'ose pas encore donner un nom!

ANGUS. Je ne comprends pas.

HJALMAR. Je n'ai pas compris non plus certains mots de la reine Anne, mais j'ai peur de comprendre!

ANGUS. Mais qu'est-il arrivé?

HJALMAR. Peu de chose; mais j'ai peur de ce que je verrai de l'autre côté de mes noces. . . .[1]

The unlawful desire of the queen for her stepson is not directly expressed, but both she and he are aware of it. " Pourquoi donc êtes-vous si froid? Avez-vous peur de moi? Vous êtes presque mon fils cependant; et je vous aime comme une mère — et peut-être plus qu'une mère; — donnez-moi votre main." [2] The feeling does not break out into a clearly expressed admission as in *Phèdre*, nor is it deeply submerged in the subconscious as in *Le Printemps des autres* by Bernard. This particular form of the Unexpressed, the masking of an unacknowledged secret between two people, is relatively superficial, both by the standards of Maeterlinck, for whom the finest quality of silence contains mystic truth, and by those of Bernard, whose purpose is to probe deeply into the recesses of the human heart. The monstrous wickedness of Anne may be considered as a manifestation of the powers of evil in the universe, and the psychological realism of the scene between her and Hjalmar may be regarded as incidental. In any case, the cumulative effect of muted forebodings such as those expressed by Hjalmar is powerfully disturbing to the listener.

The device of pathetic fallacy is employed in *La Princesse Maleine* for the purpose of enhancing without direct expression the sense of impending disaster. Comets, tempests and thunderbolts are liberally borrowed from Shakespeare. As the horrible crime is committed, the wind howls and the hail knocks against the windows with millions of fingers, working on the imagination of the king and increasing his terror to the point of madness. The

---

[1] Act II, sc. 3.   [2] Act II, sc. 2.

idea of a close correspondence between nature and man is bound up with Maeterlinck's Swedenborgian mysticism, and not only is his use of the natural elements more systematic than in Shakespeare, but their significance in the scheme of the universe is disproportionate in comparison, inasmuch as Shakespeare tends to subordinate them to man.   Unlike Lenormand and Gantillon, Maeterlinck does not produce the impression of a single external force—the Simoon, the Cyclone, the tropical heat—bringing about a deterioration in human character.   There is rather a development of Victor Hugo's ideas on exact locality, the "personnage muet", expressed in the Preface to *Cromwell*[1] : "Le lieu où telle catastrophe s'est passée en devient un témoin terrible et inséparable".   Maeterlinck goes farther than this and represents the active participation of inanimate nature in a cosmic scheme where human beings are included.   In quiet moods he uses pathetic fallacy with a strange personal poetry.   Hjalmar embraces Maleine : " ici le jet d'eau, agité par le vent, se penche et vient retomber sur eux . . .".   " Quelqu'un pleure ici ", says Maleine.   When Hjalmar discovers that Maleine has come to his trysting place instead of Uglyane," le jet d'eau sanglote étrangement et meurt ".[2]   The qualities attributed to nature may also be a projection of man's imagination.   " Allez une nuit dans le bois du parc près du jet d'eau ; et vous remarquerez que c'est à certains moments seulement, et lorsqu'on les regarde, que les choses se tiennent tranquilles comme des enfants sages et ne semblent pas étranges et bizarres ; mais dès qu'on leur tourne le dos, elles vous font des grimaces et vous jouent de mauvais tours." [3]

In *La Princesse Maleine* the sinister power of death was associated with the physical form of Queen Anne.   In *L'Intruse* [4] death is in effect the invisible Third Person who moves silently through the Maeterlinckian drama.   A family sits waiting for the father's sister, a nun, while the mother lies ill in the next room, and the baby she has brought into the world is unnaturally

[1] 1827.   [2] Act II, sc. 6.   [3] Act III, sc. 2.   [4] 1891.

silent. Strange forebodings trouble the mind of the almost
sightless grandfather, and are gradually communicated to the
other members of the family. In the end they realize what they
had dimly felt, that the visitor they awaited was Death, silently
announced by the black-robed Sister who had entered the sickroom by unseen ways.

The theme is similar to that of *Les Flaireurs* by Charles van
Lerberghe,[1] and Maeterlinck, acknowledging his debt to that
author, says that *L'Intruse* is the daughter of *Les Flaireurs*.[2]
But there is no similarity in treatment. In *Les Flaireurs* a girl
watches over her dying mother, and the " flaireurs ", one after
the other, knock at the door ; first the man with the water, then
the man with the linen, then the man with the coffin. Although
van Lerberghe's intention is to produce a crescendo of horror by
purely symbolic action—since in strict realism the gruesome
visitors would surely have postponed their appearance until after
the old woman had passed away—the total effect with loud
bangings, cries of terror, and death rattles is more reminiscent of
the Grand Guignol. According to Jules Lemaître,[3] " ce n'est
point là un appareil pour suggérer l'idée de la chose, c'est la chose
elle-même en avance de quelques heures sur la réalité. Il est
radicalement impossible de savoir si c'est un ' symbole ', ou si c'est
la reproduction fidèle d'une regrettable erreur de l'Administration
des Pompes funèbres."

In *L'Intruse* Maeterlinck contrives to suggest the coming of
Death with a realism infinitely more subtle. Death is personified
by a moving Presence, invisible, but sensed by the spectators
through its effects in passing on surrounding objects. The swans
are suddenly afraid, the fish dive in the pond, and, as the Presence
seems to enter the room, the lamp is dimmed. The pattern of
these incidents suggests for us the complement of an invisible
form as definitely as the shape of a background encloses the chief

---

[1] First published 1889 (Maurice Lecat, *op. cit.*).
[2] *Livre d'art*, dossier du Théâtre d'Art, quoted by Dorothy Knowles, *op. cit.* p. 163.
[3] Feuilleton du *Journal des Débats*, 13th Jan. 1896.

figure of a drawing. These background incidents, and the significant details creating a strong impression of supernatural powers at work, could, as in the symbolic plays of Ibsen, plausibly be explained by natural causes. It is not beyond the bounds of possibility that the carpenter should be plying his saw and the gardener his scythe; it is not altogether unlikely that the nightingales should stop singing or that the oil in the lamp should give out, that the glass door should be open, letting in a chill wind, that the daughters should be unable to shut this door because " something " is lodged there. This is the " tragique quotidien ", aided, to be sure, by a certain arbitrary selection and arrangement of incident and detail, subdued, strange and disturbing.

The scene takes place in modern times but the theme is eternal. The characters are stylized : they are not given names, and are referred to as the Grandfather, the Father, the Three Daughters, but the universality of the theme and the intensity of their emotional responses impress us with a deep sense of reality. The décor is realistic. The " tragique quotidien " is manifest in the symbolic objects of everyday life which participate mystically in this drama of expectation. The lamp which grows dim and finally goes out signifies human life coming to an end; the old Flemish clock ticking in the silence marks the relentless passing of time ; the doors mask the Unknown. " Victor Hugo a dit que rien n'est plus intéressant qu'un mur derrière lequel il se passe quelque chose. Ce mur tragique est dans tous les poèmes de M. Maeterlinck, et quand ce n'est pas un mur, c'est une porte ; et quand ce n'est pas une porte, c'est une fenêtre voilée de rideaux. . . ." [1] There are four doors shown : two of them are significant, the door of the sick woman's room concealing the mystery of death, and that leading to the room where the child lies, a symbol of life beginning anew.

The presence of the invisible intruder is sensed by the human being who, because of his physical limitations, is most closely in

[1] Jules Lemaître, *Impressions de théâtre*, 8e série, pp. 153-4—article dated 18th June 1893.

contact with spiritual realities. The absence of physical vision in the aged man develops more strongly this faculty for spiritual perception.

> L'Oncle. Mais il n'est pas absolument aveugle ?
> Le Père. Il distingue les grandes clartés.[1]

The blindness theme, which reappears in other plays, finds its origin here. Blindness for Maeterlinck symbolizes the enigma of the physical world and the bewilderment of the human being searching in vain for meaning in life ; it gives rise to a " hidden dialogue " of poignant irony :

> L'Aïeul. Il est arrivé quelque chose ! Je suis sûr que ma fille est plus mal ! . . .
> L'Oncle. Est-ce que vous rêvez ?
> L'Aïeul. Vous ne voulez pas me le dire ! . . . Je vois bien qu'il y a quelque chose ! . . .
> L'Oncle. En ce cas, vous voyez mieux que nous.[2]
>
> L'Aïeul. Il ne faut plus essayer de me tromper ; il est trop tard maintenant, et je sais la vérité mieux que vous ! . . .
> L'Oncle. Mais enfin, nous ne sommes pas aveugles, nous ! [3]

This close communion with things of the spirit makes the old man falter when confronted with earthly realities. Thinking at first that his fears are groundless, the father invites him to enter the sickroom and confirm that nothing is amiss. " Non ; non, pas maintenant . . . pas encore . . ." is his troubled reply. And when at length the truth is known, and they silently enter the death chamber, " l'aveugle, resté seul, se lève et s'agite à tâtons, autour de la table, dans les ténèbres. . . . 'Où allez-vous ? — Où allez-vous ? — Elles m'ont laissé tout seul ! ' " It is as if the grandfather lived on a higher spiritual plane. When forcibly transported to earthly reality and confronted with physical truths, he is uneasy, out of his element, and cannot respond to their message.

Another recurring idea can be detected, that intuition in

---

[1] *Théâtre*, vol. i, pp. 217-18.   [2] *Ibid.* p. 227.   [3] *Ibid.* p. 237.

women is more highly developed than in men, and that women are closer to spiritual truth. The aged man rails at the men whom he accuses of keeping a horrible secret from him, but speaks tenderly to his three granddaughters : ". . . Je sais bien que vous m'apprendriez la vérité, s'ils n'étaient pas autour de vous ! . . ." [1] But the deepest occult knowledge is in the child. In *Le Trésor des humbles* the author speaks of " la sagesse inconsciente de cet enfant qui passe . . . l'enfant qui se tait est mille fois plus sage que Marc-Aurèle qui parle ".[2] Here it is the wordless crying of the child behind the closed door that marks the appearance of death. This conception of the unconscious wisdom of the child, similar to that of Wordsworth in the *Ode on Intimations of Immortality*, constantly appears in Maeterlinck's work.

The silent advance of the unseen Presence is marked not only by outward physical signs but also by the progressive intensification of the emotion of fear. Vague uneasiness develops by gradations into anguish ; the contagion of the old man's anxiety spreads to the other characters and to the audience. Again fear is conveyed in a hypnotic, repetitive dialogue, enhanced by double meaning and the implied symbolism of blindness. Dreamy, murmuring dialogue also indicates close harmony between the human beings and nature, and their intense awareness of what is happening around them. The strange death warnings of nature are communicated to us through the half dreaming commentaries of the characters. They see, without consciously perceiving, the significant behaviour of the swans and the nightingales ; they hear the sounds of the saw and the scythe, because they are attuned to a certain mood ; and they say what they see and hear as spontaneously and as automatically as a pool reflects objects, or an instrument responds to touch. The direct impact of external objects on the senses, the fleeting impressions, unorganized and unshaped by reason, are re-echoed in broken phrases which convey a sense of primitive mystery.

---

[1] *Théâtre*, vol. i, p. 237.   [2] *Le Trésor des humbles* ; "Novalis", p. 143.

Towards the end of the play the hypnotic dialogue is punctuated by deep silences. The lamp has gone out, the light is gone, and the sound motif is developed. The profound silence makes the old man conscious of the ticking of the clock ; his sense of hearing becomes more and more acute as his anguish increases ; he hears the falling of the leaves on the terrace, the girl clasping her hands, and even senses the trembling of her sisters; and when midnight strikes, it is to him as if he hears the invisible Intruder rising. At this point the child starts crying for the first time since its birth, steps are heard in the sick woman's room, and after a deathly silence the Sister of Charity appears and announces the news by the sign of the Cross.

In *Les Aveugles* [1] the static drama reaches its utmost limits. As Jules Leclerq points out,[2] there is in *L'Intruse* a degree of dramatic conflict between the old grandfather and the rest of the family, who at first fail to share his vision. But in *Les Aveugles* " tous ont une même perception : c'est un *chœur*, non pas une scène ". In addition, the interest is no longer the approach of Death, for Death is already there in the midst of the unfortunates.[3] Movement and progression, even on the spiritual plane, are eliminated, and there is entire dramatic immobility until the moment of discovery. Twelve blind people living in a home on an island have walked abroad under the guidance of an aged priest to enjoy the air and sunshine before the onset of winter. The priest has left them for a time, and they await his return so that he may lead them home. As he fails to come, fear descends on them and increases to anguish until the dog takes them to the priest and they find that he is dead. They imagine they can hear footsteps. Nobody replies to their questionings, but the baby, the only sighted creature amongst them, starts to cry, and the sound of its voice tells them that it is turning its face towards the invisible Presence as it moves past. " Il suit toujours le bruit

[1] 1891.
[2] *Mercure de France,* January 1892. Quoted by D. Knowles, *op. cit.* p. 154.
[3] Cf. M. Lecat, *op. cit.* Premier Fascicule, p. 39.

des pas (. . .) Il se retourne pour voir (. . .) Il faut qu'il voie quelque chose d'étrange." Once more it seems—but the suggestion is more vague than in *L'Intruse*—that Death is personified by an unseen force.

As in *L'Intruse*, death is announced by the crying of a child. Doubtless Maeterlinck intends to signify the eternal renewing of life and nature ; the winter of death is followed by the springtide of childhood. The incident also develops the Wordsworthian idea of the " sagesse occulte " of the child. In *L'Intruse* the child, who has been strangely silent throughout the long watch, cries out with fear at the approach of death. The blind grandfather, who had sensed it, put his vague forebodings into broken phrases, but the child, who knew and understood, was incapable of expressing that knowledge otherwise than by a wordless cry. The newly-born child is nearer to nature and truth than experienced age. Spiritual knowledge is blotted out by earthly experience which itself deteriorates through the rigidity of the spoken word. The child, incapable of self-expression, possesses knowledge too deep for words, while the more man is versed in words, the farther he has moved from fundamental truths. In *Les Aveugles*, the child, the only one with sight and knowledge, is unable to tell the others what it sees, while the blind people who can express themselves in words can only guess vaguely at realities beyond their conception. Animals, bereft as they are of speech, have often a sure instinct and a true knowledge denied to man. The flock of sheep which the blind man watches over never fail to find their way back to the home of their own accord, guided by the light in the tower. But for the dog which, as in *La Princesse Maleine*, reveals the presence of death, the blind would still be groping for their guide.

As with *L'Intruse*, the " action " of *Les Aveugles* never crosses the bounds of possibility. Here, however, the symbolism is more marked and systematic. The blind, led by the priest, represent humanity under the guidance of religion, but religion too is groping its way, and, having lost its divine inspiration, is a

lifeless formality, no longer capable of giving humanity a lead.
Physical blindness symbolizes here not only the hopelessness of
our quest for truth, but also the impossibility of our knowing
one another. Humanity's frustration is echoed in Golaud's
despairing cry : " Ah ! misère de ma vie ! . . . Je suis ici
comme un aveugle qui cherche un trésor au fond de l'océan ! . . .
Je suis ici comme un nouveau-né perdu dans la forêt. . . ." [1]
The symbolism is elaborated in the distinction made between
various types of blindness : there are those who once had sight
and dimly remember what they saw, those who were born blind,
and one who can sense a line of light between his lids. In addition,
the differences of attitude and temperament have deep significance. One is resigned to his condition and shows no desire to
change it. He is content to remain within the precincts of the
home or to sit beside a warm fire. Another wants to go into the
open. "J'aime mieux sortir à midi; je soupçonne alors de grandes
clartés ; et mes yeux font de grands efforts pour s'ouvrir." [2]
The young girl, who once could see, still hopes and yearns for
the gift of sight to be restored. " Mes paupières sont fermées,
mais je sens que mes yeux sont en vie. . . ." [3]

The idea that intuitive understanding is deeper in women
than in men is also developed. The girl and the old woman
reproach the others for failing to understand the priest :

> LA JEUNE AVEUGLE. Vous ne l'écoutez pas quand il parle !
> LA PLUS VIEILLE AVEUGLE. Vous murmurez tous quand il
> parle ! " [4]

It is the blind girl who smells the flowers when the others can
smell only the earth.

In both *L'Intruse* and *Les Aveugles* the meaning is conveyed
by the accumulation of significant detail, creating an oppressive
atmosphere of fear, and communicated by the same repetitive and
groping speech. " J'ai peur. . . ." " J'entends que vous vous penchez vers moi. . . ." "J'entends le bruit de vos cheveux. . . ."

---

[1] *Pelléas et Mélisande*, Act III, sc. 5.   [2] *Théâtre*, vol. i, p. 265.
[3] *Ibid.* p. 272.   [4] *Ibid.* p. 257.

The physical blindness develops acutely the sense of hearing ; the slightest variations detected in the human voice reveal nuances of attitude and behaviour. " J'entendais qu'il souriait trop gravement ; j'entendais qu'il fermait les yeux et qu'il voulait se taire. . . ." [1] This unnatural concentration of the auditive faculties works on the nerves of the audience in whom the initial state of uneasiness is re-created. The subjectivity of human perceptions and the emotional reaction to external phenomena are stressed by the monotonous repetition of the hearing motif. " J'entends que vous vous penchez vers moi ", not " Vous vous penchez vers moi " ; " J'entends que vous brisez des tiges vertes ", not " Vous brisez des tiges vertes ".

The double meaning arising from the symbolism of blindness is, as we indicated, more systematically developed than in *L'Intruse*, and produces a continuous " hidden dialogue " of impressive beauty and ironical pathos. Yet there is no suggestion of arbitrariness or artificiality. The simple realism of the characters and the intensity of their anguish give the work the stamp of human truth.

Les Sept Princesses [2] is less successful as a drama of the Unexpressed. It was regarded as unplayable, but was performed by Ranson's marionettes in 1891.[3] The " action " takes place on a terrace behind glass windows. The king and queen gaze with misgivings into the hall with marble steps on which the seven princesses lie sleeping. The prince who has come to claim Ursule, the fairest of them, cannot enter the hall from the terrace as the door will not open. He penetrates into the room through subterranean passages, past ancestral tombs, only to find that Ursule has died in her sleep.

The main characters are silent throughout the play, and their silence is brought out by the commentary of those on the terrace. Here, instead of speech impinging on silence, as happens in the famous silences of Aeschylus, we have a deep, unbroken silence impinging on speech. The poet attempts to convey the same

---

[1] *Théâtre*, vol. i, p. 256.   [2] 1891.   [3] D. Knowles, *op. cit.* p. 283.

feeling of anguish as in his other plays, but the effectiveness of his method is impaired by the puerility of the dialogue, which is worse than anything in *La Princesse Maleine* :

> LE PRINCE. Où sont mes sept cousines ?
> LA REINE. Ici, ici ; attention, attention . . . n'en parlons pas trop haut ; elles dorment encore ; il ne faut pas parler de ceux qui dorment. . . .
> LE PRINCE. Elles dorment ? . . . Est-ce qu'elles vivent encore toutes les sept ? . . .
> LA REINE. Oui, oui, oui ; prenez garde. . . . Elles dorment ici ; elles dorment toujours. . . .
> LE PRINCE. Elles dorment toujours ? . . . Quoi ? Quoi ? Quoi ? . . . Est-ce que ? . . . toutes les sept ! . . .

And eventually :

> Je vois ! Je vois ! je vois ! je les vois toutes les sept ! . . . Une, deux, trois (*il hésite un moment*), quatre, cinq, six, sept. . . . Je ne les reconnais presque pas. . . . Je ne les reconnais pas du tout. . . . Oh ! qu'elles sont blanches toutes les sept ! . . . Oh ! qu'elles sont belles toutes les sept ! Oh ! qu'elles sont pâles toutes les sept ! . . . Mais pourquoi dorment-elles toutes les sept ?

This strange, remote fairy tale is pointless without a metaphysical significance, yet the symbolism is so obscure that any interpretation must be subjective. Dorothy Knowles suggests [1] that Maeterlinck opposes the world of reality (the terrace) to an ideal world (the hall where the princesses sleep). To possess his dream, man must have known death (symbolized by the subterranean tombs), but, nevertheless, when he grasps his dream, it vanishes ; the princess no longer lives. The ship which we see moving off in the distance is action and life departing, never to return. Camille Mauclair, she continues, compares this play to a passage in Schopenhauer where the world of ideas is likened to a fortress without doors, round which a warrior wanders in vain, since it is only through a subterranean passage that it can be entered.

[1] *Op. cit.* p. 284.

G. Hulsman, on the other hand, submits this interpretation :
" Our heart is this palace, and in this palace lies our soul, a
beautiful sleeper. It sleeps, and dreams, and waits for the coming
of the ideal hero who shall awaken it out of its slumber and
cherish it with the warmth of his love. And these seven princesses are the different qualities of the human soul. . . .
Ursula, the middle sister, is Psyche, that is the real self, the
deepest, the essential in our being. This real self is unconscious
and unknowable. Let the ideal come, no ideal man can unveil
the deepest. It is dead to us." [1]

Some critics see the play merely as a theatrical transposition
of a painting in the style of Burne-Jones, a sort of fairy tale without deeper significance, represented on the stage for its intrinsic
beauty. It is difficult to believe, however, that the selection of
strange details is purely arbitrary. There is undoubtedly a
suggestion of some deeper philosophical meaning. The dramatic
imagery is consistent with that found in Maeterlinck's other
" silent " plays, where constantly there reappears the impenetrable barrier between the known and the unknown, the wall, the
door, the window, mentioned by Lemaître, an effective concrete
expression of humanity's frustration in the presence of the unknowable and the unattainable. The diversity of interpretations
shows the fundamental weakness of the play. Maeterlinck's
deliberate and excessive vagueness reduces the work to an
exasperating literary riddle. The Unexpressed ceases here to be
eloquent and merely serves to bemuse the spectator. The lapse,
however, is temporary. In subsequent works the Unexpressed
is again to be used with considerable dramatic effect.

[1] *Karakters en Ideeën*, quoted by J. Bithell, *op. cit.* p. 59.

CHAPTER IV

MAURICE MAETERLINCK : II

ERHAPS the most haunting and pathetic of Maeterlinck's
" silent " dramas is *Pelléas et Mélisande*.[1] Here Maeterlinck
uses the triangular situation and the violent action which he
condemns in *Le Trésor des humbles*, and these on the stage as-
sumed an intrinsic importance which, despite their symbolic
significance, gave the piece at its " première " " de furieux airs
de vieux mélo ".[2] But the beauty of the Unexpressed comes out
in the reading. As we have seen, Maeterlinck's " silent " theatre
is of two kinds. *L'Intruse*, *Les Aveugles* and *Intérieur* give us
the " tragique quotidien " : in a realistic setting the mystery of
everyday life is impressed upon the spectator by an atmosphere
emotionally created, the " action " is static, and the crisis or
violent incident which releases this atmosphere never takes place
before our eyes. The " legendary " pieces are in some respects
nearer to the usual type of Symbolist play : in a setting and period
remote from everyday life, despite the realism of emotion and
even character, the philosophical idea must to a certain extent be
" exteriorized " in the form of anecdote and often violent action.
Maeterlinck's aim is to concentrate the attention of the audience
on the symbolism of the action, and he blames the human element
of the actor for destroying " la densité mystique de l'œuvre d'art ".
Something of Hamlet is dead to us the day we see him die on
the stage. Hence his conception of a *Théâtre de Marionnettes* :

> La scène est le lieu où meurent les chefs-d'œuvre, parce
> que la représentation d'un chef-d'œuvre à l'aide d'éléments

[1] 1892.
[2] *Le Petit Parisien*, 18th May 1893, " P. G.", quoted by Dorothy Knowles, *op. cit.*
p. 176.

F

accidentels et humains est antinomique. Tout chef-d'œuvre est un symbole et le symbole ne supporte jamais la présence active de l'homme qui s'y agite. Le symbole du poème est un centre ardent dont les rayons divergent dans l'infini, et ces rayons, s'ils partent d'un chef-d'œuvre absolu comme ceux dont il est question en ce moment, ont une portée qui n'est limitée que par la puissance de l'œil qui les suit. Mais voici que l'acteur s'avance au milieu du symbole. Immédiatement se produit, par rapport au sujet passif du poème, un extraordinaire phénomène de polarisation. Il ne voit plus la divergence des rayons, mais leur convergence ; l'accident a détruit le symbole, et le chef-d'œuvre, en son essence, est mort durant le temps de cette présence et de ses traces. . . .

Il faudrait peut-être écarter entièrement l'être vivant de la scène. . . . L'être humain sera-t-il remplacé par une ombre, un reflet, une projection de formes symboliques ou un être qui aurait les allures de la vie sans avoir la vie ? . . .[1]

Of Maeterlinck's masterpiece Mallarmé says :

Pelléas et Mélisande sur une scène exhale, de feuillets, le délice. Préciser ? Ces tableaux, brefs, suprêmes : quoi que ce soit a été rejeté de préparatoire et machinal, en vue que paraisse, extrait, ce qui chez un spectateur se dégage de la représentation, l'essentiel. Il semble que soit jouée une variation supérieure sur l'admirable vieux mélodrame. Silencieusement presque et abstraitement au point que dans cet art, où tout devient musique dans le sens propre, la partie d'un instrument même pensif, violon, nuirait, par inutilité.[2]

While hunting the wild boar in the woods, Golaud discovers a fugitive princess weeping by the fountain, and takes her home to be his wife. A spiritual love grows up between Mélisande, the princess, and Golaud's half-brother, Pelléas. Seeking to avert Destiny, these troubled children embrace for the last time beneath the trees in the darkness before Pelléas takes his departure. Their long shadows in the moonlight betray them to Golaud, who silently stabs Pelléas and pursues his wife. The next morning Golaud and Mélisande are discovered before the door. Golaud has

---

[1] *La Jeune Belgique* (1890), tome 9, p. 331.
[2] *Divagations* (1897), " Crayonné au théâtre ", pp. 220-1.

slightly wounded Mélisande and has tried to kill himself. It is Mélisande who is to die after giving birth to a child, " une toute petite fille qu'un pauvre ne voudrait pas mettre au monde . . . une petite figure de cire . . .". The conflict in this wistful fairy tale is that of spiritual and earthly love, and Mélisande seems to be the human soul caught up in this mortal struggle. The greater unseen power of Death is all-conquering ; Pelléas and Mélisande are sacrificed, while Golaud, its instrument, like blind, frustrated humanity, is left to mourn.

Despite the dreamlike atmosphere and the legendary setting of the tale, there are touches of authentic psychological realism. There is a strange human reality about this timid little princess who tells lies to her husband out of fear, and who says to her lover: "Non; je ne mens jamais; je ne mens qu'à ton frère . . .". At the Fontaine des Aveugles, Mélisande, playing with the ring Golaud has given her, lets it fall into the water. The action betrays her antipathy to her husband and her regret at having married him ; the ring is the symbol of her marriage ; the loss of the ring, subconsciously willed, is the blotting out of the marriage which she would rather had never existed. It is rare to find in the shadowy characters of Maeterlinck such indications of repressed personal desire. For him the human subconscious, a manifestation of an all-pervading cosmic unconscious, usually reveals itself in an instinctive foreknowledge of destiny. The incident may of course have a more general significance and its touch of individuality may be fortuitous. Dorothy Knowles' interpretation is as follows : " La bague d'or . . . semble être, sous forme tangible, le bonheur de Golaud, petit jouet entre les frêles mains de Mélisande. L'anneau glisse d'entre ses doigts et tombe dans l'eau ; avec lui sombrent tous les espoirs de Golaud, les liens qui l'attachaient à Mélisande, irréparablement rompus ; c'est à Pelléas qu'appartient maintenant la petite princesse." [1]

It is possible that the author, who deliberately blurs the out-lines of any realistic scenes he represents, may have had this

[1] *Op. cit.* p. 176.

symbolism in mind. The meaning of other scenes scarcely leaves room for doubt. In the first, reminiscent of Shakespeare, dark deeds are foreshadowed. The bustling servants try in vain to clean the entrance to the castle, and the porter says to them : " Oui, oui, versez l'eau, versez toute l'eau du déluge ; vous n'en viendrez jamais à bout . . .". The flock of sheep going to the slaughter and sensing their doom represents to Yniold the fate awaiting the forlorn lovers.

The reticent scenes in this play are convincing and realistic. In Act III, scene 1, before the flowering of their love, Pelléas and Mélisande have sat quietly in the dusk exchanging banal phrases. Golaud's little son enters with a lamp and, holding it up to their faces, he sees that they have been weeping. Words could not have conveyed the pathos of these shy, frustrated children, and indeed, at this stage of their love, would for them have been unnatural. On another occasion Golaud discovers Pelléas embracing Mélisande's hair as she leans out of her window to him. Instead of storming at them in the style of a romantic villain, he laughs nervously and exclaims : " Quels enfants ! Quels enfants ! " He is an unsubtle man of action, and his mind works slowly. It is as if he does not want to see the meaning of their action. We watch the doubts slowly forming in his mind, and tormenting him as they increase. He holds little Yniold up to the window to spy on the lovers ; only the child's cry of pain as his father's hand tightens convulsively on him tells us the full measure of Golaud's anguish.

Scenes of crisis are enacted with complete silence on the part of the character on whom our attention is fixed. Golaud's suspicions are developing into certainties. He leads Pelléas through sinister underground caves, pervaded by the deadly odour of a subterranean lake. When they reach the edge of the abyss his voice becomes troubled and his hand trembles as he holds the lantern. But in the end they leave the place in silence.[1] The mute terror of Mélisande when Golaud in anguish and fury

[1] Act III, sc. 3.

seizes her by the hair and drags her along on her knees has a sickening effect of horror.[1] Golaud watches in silence the long shadows of Pelléas and Mélisande at their tryst by the Fontaine des Aveugles, and when the lovers sense his presence and embrace desperately, he rushes upon them, kills Pelléas and pursues Mélisande without uttering a word.[2] All these silences, except perhaps the last, which has a flavour of " mélo ", are consistent with character and highly convincing. Unlike the silences of Jean-Jacques Bernard, which also appear at a stage where traditional drama uses the tirade, they do not relax the tension by resolving the situation. They serve to stress a significant state of mind, and their cumulative effect is one of painful oppression.

Maeterlinck's conception of a kind of racial subconscious reveals itself in the intuitive foreknowledge on the part of simple folk of disasters to come. The servants of the castle, although present in few scenes, perform to some extent the functions of a chorus. Already in the first scene, vainly trying to clean the castle entrance, they have set the key of the strange music of the drama. Now,[3] Mélisande is lying ill, and they are assembled in a basement room, awaiting her death.

> UNE VIEILLE SERVANTE. Vous verrez, vous verrez, mes filles ; ce sera pour ce soir. — On nous préviendra tout à l'heure. . . . (. . .)
> QUATRIÈME SERVANTE. Nous saurons bien quand il faudra monter . . .
> CINQUIÈME SERVANTE. Quand le moment sera venu nous monterons de nous-mêmes. . . .

The children are playing noisily in front of the air-hole. "Ils se tairont d'eux-mêmes tout à l'heure", says one of the servants. "Le moment n'est pas encore venu", says another. A little later the children's voices are still and they huddle before the air-hole. The moment has come and the servants silently go out. Once more it is the child who is nearest to the truth. Into the room where Mélisande lies dying and Golaud tries in vain to know for

---

[1] Act IV, sc. 2.   [2] Act IV, sc. 4.   [3] Act V, sc. 1.

certain what for him is the most important truth—whether the
lovers have been " guilty "—these women steal silently and stand
along the walls, waiting. When the moment comes they suddenly
fall on their knees.

> ARKËL (*se tournant*). Qu'y a-t-il ?
> LE MÉDECIN (*s'approchant du lit et tâtant le corps*). Elles
> ont raison. . . .[1]

For materialistic man, silence is a baffling, impenetrable
barrier. The eternal silence of Mélisande brings anguish and
frustration to Golaud, who now will never know the lovers'
secret. But, for the wise, silence is the element in which they
enter into close communication with the great mystery of death.

The double meaning running through the dialogue enriches
this play with a haunting sadness :

> ARKËL. Tu as du sang sur le front — qu'as-tu fait ?
> GOLAUD. Rien, rien . . . j'ai passé au travers d'une haie
> d'épines. . . .[2]

> MÉLISANDE [*dying*]. Est-ce vous, Golaud ? Je ne vous
> reconnaissais presque plus. . . . C'est que j'ai le soleil du soir
> dans les yeux. . . .[3]

We find, too, words and phrases which, though not necessarily
of dramatic significance, bring out like a recurring theme in a
symphony the mood and inspiration of the piece. " Si j'étais
Dieu, j'aurais pitié du cœur des hommes." [4] ". . . Elle ne
pouvait pas vivre. Elle est née sans raison . . . pour mourir ;
et elle meurt sans raison. . . ." [5] ". . . C'était un petit être si
tranquille, si timide et si silencieux. . . . C'était un pauvre petit
être mystérieux, comme tout le monde. . . ." [6]

Alladine et Palomides, *Intérieur* and *La Mort de Tintagiles*
were published in 1894 as " trois petits drames pour marionnettes ".

---

[1] Act V, sc. 2.   [2] Act IV, sc. 2.   [3] Act V, sc. 2.   [4] Act IV, sc. 2.
[5] Act V, sc. 2.

[6] Act V, sc. 2. A. Bailly quotes these three passages, among others, as being more
significant than those directly governing the action ; they reveal for a brief instant
" l'abîme de la destinée " (*Maeterlinck* (1931), pp. 27-8).

Alladine et Palomides develops the philosophical idea of *Pelléas et Mélisande* and foreshadows that of *Aglavaine et Sélysette*. Palomides renounces spiritual love, embodied in Astolaine to whom he had been betrothed, for Alladine, who is earthly love in its fairest form ; yet in some way his soul still worships the highest. " Je t'aime aussi . . . plus que celle que j'aime ", he tells Astolaine. Astolaine, who is a symbol of perfection, lets him go. Her father, the sage Ablamore, who is in love with Alladine and is infuriated by Palomides' treatment of his daughter, has the lovers bound and taken into the subterranean vaults of his castle. When they see stones being dislodged in the wall they imagine Ablamore is coming to kill them, and let themselves drop into the sea. It was really Astolaine coming with the sisters of Palomides to save them. They are rescued from the shallow water and lie dying in adjoining rooms, their voices communing as they slip out of life. This time earthly love is conquered by death and spiritual love is left to mourn, frustrated.

Earthly love experiences disillusion before the sacrifice. When they have loosened their bonds, the cave seems to the lovers to be radiant with a strange beauty. But with the dislodging of the stones, the crude light of day floods in, revealing the sinister squalor of reality. The foreshadowing of a kind of expressionistic technique is interesting here. The inner processes of the mind are " exteriorized " by scenic effects, and thought is made, so to speak, concrete to the spectator. Similar devices are used in *Joyzelle*, where on the stage a wilderness of weeds and rank grass is visibly transformed by the power of love into a garden of wonderful flowers. In the same way some aspect of the human being is " exteriorized " in the form of a living creature. The lamb which is inseparable from Alladine seems to be a concrete representation of her soul, as later, in *Joyzelle*, the fairy Arielle embodies the hidden desires of Merlin. This expressionism is not out of keeping with Maeterlinck's drama, since, in the way he uses it, it serves to emphasize the participation of nature and human beings in the universal scheme.

In a sense, too, it conveys ideas without the medium of speech. But fundamentally it is opposed to the theories of the " tragique quotidien ", since the physical shapes in which it endeavours to enclose elusive truth must in their own way have as confining and as distorting an effect as the spoken word.

As I have already indicated, Maeterlinck's mysticism implies that souls can communicate directly and wordlessly, not only with nature, but also with each other. We are all manifestations of the same eternal spirit, and, purified of the dross of civilization, we are like calling to like. The idea of the direct communication of souls would not appear to be in contradiction with that of the isolation of human beings, so poignantly symbolized in *Les Aveugles*. Spiritual love alone can reveal souls to one another, and Golaud will never fathom the meaning of Mélisande's dying words because his love is too earthly. In silence full communion is attained. In *La Princesse Maleine* Hjalmar trysts Uglyane in a wood at night. " Je veux la voir enfin en présence du soir. . . . Je veux voir si la nuit la fera réfléchir. . . . Est-ce qu'elle aurait un peu de silence dans le cœur ? " [1] Pelléas and Mélisande have exchanged their love long before it has been put into words. Even on a lower spiritual plane souls quest after one another. When Golaud's horse shies in the forest at the very moment when Mélisande drops his ring in the fountain, the coincidence could be interpreted as a direct message picked up by his uneasy spirit. This wakefulness of instinct, this uneasiness of soul, is present in Alladine. At the beginning of the play, her immediate instinctive attraction to Palomides is betrayed in a torrent of chatter which conceals more than it expresses and strikes Ablamore as strange. " Toi qui ne parlais pas, comme tu parles ce soir." Later the old man wishes to show her the flowers he has planted for her.

> ALLADINE. Non, pas ce soir. . . . Si vous le voulez bien . . . j'aime bien y aller avec vous . . . l'air est très pur et les arbres . . . mais pas ce soir. . . . (*Se blottissant en*

[1] Act II, sc. 6.

pleurant contre la poitrine du vieillard) Je suis un peu souf-
frante.

    ABLAMORE. Qu'as-tu donc ? Tu vas tomber. . . . Je vais
appeler. . . .

    ALLADINE. Non, non . . . ce n'est rien. . . . C'est
passé. . . .

    ABLAMORE. Assieds-toi. Attends. . . .

    (*Il court à la porte du fond et l'ouvre à deux battants. On
voit Palomides assis sur un banc, en face de cette porte. Il
n'a pas eu le temps de détourner les yeux. Ablamore le regarde
fixement, sans rien dire, puis rentre dans la chambre. Palomides se lève et s'éloigne dans le corridor en étouffant le bruit de
ses pas. L'agneau familier sort de l'appartement sans qu'ils
s'en aperçoivent.*) [1]

There is an affinity between this scene and the final scene of
Bernard's *L'Ame en peine*, where the woman's troubled awareness of her twin soul's proximity behind the barrier of the door is
used with similar dramatic effect. Bernard uses his scene as a
climax. For Maeterlinck it is an episode in the story. The
tension of the situation is diminished by the expressionistic
device of the lamb which, as it goes out, seems to represent the
yearning of Alladine's soul towards the departing Palomides.

In *Alladine et Palomides* we begin to perceive tendencies of
Maeterlinck's unrealistic second manner, a growing self-consciousness on the part of the characters, who endeavour to
analyse and define this power of communion between souls.
Astolaine is Maeterlinck's ideal woman in direct contact with
spiritual truth. Her personality is radiant with the purity of this
truth and awakens a deep response in the souls surrounding her.
All this is expressed somewhat garrulously by Palomides :

    . . . Il y eut des soirs où je vous quittais sans rien dire,
et où j'allais pleurer d'admiration dans un coin du palais, parce
que vous aviez simplement levé les yeux, fait un petit geste
inconscient ou souri sans raison apparente, mais au moment
où toutes les âmes autour de vous le demandaient et voulaient
être satisfaites. Il n'y a que vous qui sachiez ces moments,

<hr>

[1] Act II, sc. 1.

parce que l'on dirait que vous êtes l'âme de tous, et je ne crois pas que ceux qui ne vous ont pas approchée puissent savoir ce que c'est que la vie véritable. . . ."

And so on.[1]

Astolaine and Ablamore, close to each other as loving father and daughter can be, have not needed words to talk to one another. When Astolaine from the highest motives denies that she now loves Palomides, Ablamore knows instinctively that she is not speaking the truth. With a long-windedness characteristic of Maeterlinck's " sages " he elaborates on the theme of direct communication :

> . . . Tu sais bien que je n'ai pas compris ce que tu viens de dire et que les mots n'ont aucun sens quand les âmes ne sont pas à portée l'une de l'autre. Approche-toi davantage et ne me parle plus. (*Astolaine se rapproche lentement.*) Il y a un moment où les âmes se touchent et savent tout sans que l'on ait besoin de remuer les lèvres. Approche-toi. . . . Elles ne s'atteignent pas encore, et leur rayon est si petit autour de nous ! . . . (*Astolaine s'arrête.*) Tu n'oses pas ? — Tu sais aussi jusqu'où l'on peut aller ? C'est moi qui vais venir. . . . (*Il s'approche à pas lents d'Astolaine, puis s'arrête et la regarde longuement.*) Je te vois, Astolaine. . . .
> ASTOLAINE. Mon père ! . . . (*Elle sanglote en embrassant le vieillard.*)
> ABLAMORE. Tu voyais bien que c'était inutile. . . .[2]

The exchange of eloquent looks is a favourite device of the *Théâtre de l'Inexprimé*. With Bernard they are usually part of a closely knit pattern of psychological action revealed in the fore-going dialogue. In the loose episodic drama of Maeterlinck the interest is watered down by the flood of words poured out by the venerable sage, a ridiculous old bore who, incidentally, has to hold back his long white beard in order to kiss his sleeping betrothed. The loquaciousness of Ablamore is inexhaustible, and the symbolic scene where he enters abruptly and drags Alladine away from Palomides without saying a word loses all

---

[1] Act II, sc. 4.   [2] Act III, sc. 1.

effectiveness ; the audience is merely stupefied to see the old man disappear for once without seizing an opportunity to exercise his voice.

In *Intérieur* we have another illustration of the " tragique quotidien ". As in *Les Sept Princesses*, the principal characters on whom our attention is concentrated are not heard to utter a word. They are, as it were, in a separate world, cut off from our own by windows of glass, on the other side of which the speaking characters, by their comments, bring out the meaning of their existence. Only the physical viewpoint is different. We looked directly into the world of the princesses, while the other characters gazed in from the far terrace. The people of *Intérieur* are seen from the garden through the windows of a house, spiritualized by the distance, the soft light and the filmy glass. The family sits in quiet content while the old man outside in the garden discusses with the Stranger how he can break the news that one of the daughters has been found drowned. His distress increases as the inevitable hour draws nearer. The villagers are approaching in a procession with the girl on a litter, and the crowd is now at the windows. He must tell them. He is seen to enter the house. The breaking of the news is silently enacted behind the lighted windows. It seems that the mother has guessed before the words were spoken. The distressed family rush into the garden to the drowned girl, now revealed by the moonlight. Then all are gone but the Stranger who had first discovered the girl's body, and who remains at the windows—perhaps a symbol of death. In the house the child whom the mother had carefully laid on the chair sleeps on. "L'enfant ne s'est pas éveillé !" says the Stranger. Death has taken his toll, but life, symbolized by the child, is eternally renewed.

The title of the play suggests that Maeterlinck has in mind a dramatic treatment of a Flemish interior painting, and desires to bring out the pathos of everyday life. We are reminded of the passage in *Le Trésor des humbles* where he praises the quietist school of painting which speaks with " la voix plus profonde, mais hésitante et discrète des êtres et des choses ". But finding impossible a direct transposition of such quietude on to the stage, Maeterlinck is obliged, in spite of his theories, to have recourse to an external act, violent in nature, which, however, has taken place before the curtain rises. The drowning is perhaps accidental, perhaps willed ; characteristically, the author leaves us in doubt. Unlike the paintings, whose tragedy comes from within, this tragedy arises from the impact of this external act on the family. The drama is one of ironic situation. Our pity and awe are roused by the sight of the tranquil, contented domesticity of a family, ignorant of a horrible impending reality of which we have knowledge, and we await the tragic revelation in painful suspense.

The characters in this play appear to be situated on two different planes : the silent members of the family inside the house, their movements, as it were, slowed down and spiritualized by the distance, and, outside in the garden, the old man, the Stranger, and the crowd, who, like a chorus, watch the others and comment on the meaning of their actions. At the tragic moment the silence of the members of the family does not flow from their nature or mood but is contrived by the stage illusion of distance. For the people in the house by no means dispense with speech. Speech is the instrument used by the old man in order to communicate his gruesome tidings. Their physical remoteness alone prevents us from hearing what is said. The silent revelation is effected here by a trick of perspective, and we have the vague impression that the " coward's way out " has been chosen. We have two visible sets of actors on different physical planes, one conveying a message through the spoken word, another using the totally different art of mime. There is an inharmonious blend of disparate elements, and the play seems somehow out of focus. The impression may be compared to that once made in a ballet, where at a certain point the *premier danseur* startled the audience by bursting into poetry, while the saltatory efforts of the *corps de ballet* froze into picturesque attitudes.

The *Théâtre de l'Inexprimé* excels in rendering two planes of action through the single medium of the spoken word and its complementary silences. The symbolism of the barrier between human beings would not have lost in intensity, and greater poignancy would have been attained, if the people in the house had not been visible to the spectators, and if the words of the chorus had been allowed directly to stimulate our imagination. The scene where Golaud holds up Yniold to the window would have been infinitely less moving if the lovers had been visible to the audience. A certain sharpness of outline, absent from that effective scene in *Pelléas et Mélisande*, is introduced into the dialogue by the embodiment of the shadowy members of the family in living though silent actors. For all its shortcomings, *Les Sept Princesses* is an organic unity. The silence of the Princesses is the realistic silence of sleep, and sleep and death are fraught with a deeper meaning. Here the apparent silence of the family, which is no silence at all, is in the nature of a " tour de force ", and has no real significance in the play.

The true drama comes from the irony of the situation. " Ils se croient à l'abri . . . ils ont fermé les portes ; et les fenêtres ont des barreaux de fer. . . . Ils ont consolidé les murs de la vieille maison ; ils ont mis des verrous aux trois portes de chêne. . . . Ils ont prévu tout ce qu'on peut prévoir. . . ." [1] The true pathos is in the old man who expresses in stammering cries humanity's despair at the inevitability of fate, and its anguish at the thought of the soul's isolation. The girl had let slip some words which, too late, the old man realized might have meant something. " On ne voit pas dans l'âme comme on voit dans cette chambre. Elles sont toutes ainsi. . . . Elles ne disent que des choses banales ; et personne ne se doute de rien. . . . On vit pendant des mois à côté de quelqu'un qui n'est plus de ce monde et dont l'âme ne peut plus s'incliner ; on lui répond sans y songer : et vous voyez ce qui arrive. . . . Elles ont l'air de poupées immobiles, et tant d'événements se passent dans leur cœur. . . ." [2]

[1] *Théâtre*, vol. ii, p. 184.   [2] *Ibid.* p. 181.

La Mort de Tintagiles is another variation on the theme of the ruthlessness and inevitability of death. Little Prince Tintagiles has been summoned from across the sea to the island where his grandmother, the queen, reigns, dreaded and unseen, in the tower of a dark, crumbling palace built in a valley. His sisters Ygraine and Bellangère, troubled by vague fears, guard him fiercely and lovingly. One night as he sleeps between them, clutching their tresses in his little hands, and even between his teeth, three veiled servants of the queen enter like the Fates, cut the hair, and bear him off, still clinging to the shorn tresses. Ygraine follows the trail of the golden hair—the weaker Bellangère has fainted—and after mounting innumerable steps, reaches an impenetrable iron door with hair caught in it. Against this door she beats in frenzy while the pleading Tintagiles is overtaken by a mysterious, implacable Presence. His strangled body is heard to fall behind the door. After " un long silence inexorable ", Ygraine shrieks out in rage and defiant despair : " Monstre ! . . . Monstre ! . . . Je crache ! . . ." and sinks down, sobbing, before the door.

As in *L'Intruse*, Death is personified by an unseen and silent Presence. As the sisters sit wakefully guarding the child with old Aglovale, a key grinds in the lock, the door opens of its own accord, and the sword which Aglovale places across it is shattered to bits. They push vainly against the door which continues to open slowly. Only a cold light penetrates. Tintagiles utters a cry of deliverance, and the door closes. The departure from realism makes this scene less effective than the similar one in *L'Intruse*. There the old grandfather feels the cold air entering through the glass door which has been left open. The girls try in vain to shut it. Perhaps the damp has swollen the wood, perhaps there is something lodged between the leaves of the door. The sense of the supernatural behind an ordinary incident of everyday life is more subtly conveyed.

The audience's feelings are harrowed to the utmost by the suggestion of the silent Presence behind the heavy door in the tower. Tintagiles has escaped " her " for a moment, but knows

" she " is coming. For all his pleading and for all Ygraine's frantic efforts, the door back to this life cannot be opened. Death, kept at bay by watchful humanity, falls upon us when we are off our guard. It is the horror more than the mystery of it that obsesses Maeterlinck here. In *L'Intruse* and *Intérieur* Death stole noiselessly in ; here the invisible silent monster imperiously claims her victim. The play works up to a crescendo of horror, which terminates in a violent fortissimo. This ending is un-aesthetic and out of keeping with Maeterlinck's usual quiet style. The audience is left, as it were, on the crest of a wave. The deep human need to relax the tense nerves and readjust the mind before leaving the theatre is unsatisfied, and one misses the limitations of the Greek stage which, by imposing a quiet termination, responded to that need. The dialogue, starting with vague fore-bodings, becomes in the end a cry of animal terror. Our hair rises and our blood is effectively curdled, but we do not respond to this play as to high tragedy, where all is lost save human dignity.

Symbolic themes of earlier plays recur in *La Mort de Tin-tagiles*. The inexorable door is the barrier between this life and the next, between the known and the unknown. Ygraine's lamp seems to signify human hope ; its light still burns despite the wind in the dark stairs, but it is dashed to pieces against the relentless door. The motif of long tresses with their live and gleaming sinuosities suggests, as Lemaître hints, a relationship between the human being and the plant world.[1] The hair may also symbolize a living bond between souls, as when Pelléas embraces the flowing tresses of Mélisande, leaning from her window. In *Intérieur* the tresses of the sisters behind the windows seem to quiver in response as the Stranger talks of the drowned girl's hair. In *La Mort de Tintagiles* the sisters' golden locks symbolize the strong bond of love between them and their little brother, which is severed only by the instruments of Death. Aglavaine's tresses reflect her " soul ". ". . . Et puis tu verras,

---

[1] *Impressions de théâtre*, 8e série, p. 143.

elle a des cheveux singuliers ; on dirait qu'ils prennent part à toutes ses pensées. . . . Ils sourient ou ils pleurent selon qu'elle est heureuse ou triste, alors même qu'elle ignore si elle doit être heureuse ou s'il faut qu'elle soit triste. . . ." [1]

In the previous plays Death paralyses the human will, and the victims resign themselves without a struggle. Here for the first time Death is defied—significantly, by a woman. Men have always bowed down in terror before the dread Queen, and the aged Aglovale knows that his efforts will be unavailing and that his sword will break. Deep instinctive love gives a woman the courage to pit herself against Destiny, although her efforts to avert the sacrifice are doomed from the start. The theme of love is henceforth developed, and a change takes place in the nature of Maeterlinck's theatre.

In 1896 appeared *Le Trésor des humbles*, containing Maeterlinck's meditations on silence and the nature of the drama, and showing the strong influence of Novalis, Emerson, Carlyle and Ruysbroeck. The content and even the style of the essays find their way into the later plays. The influence of the actress Georgette Leblanc, who inspired much in these essays, and for whom, moreover, Maeterlinck appears to have been writing parts, cannot be discounted, and the fabric of his Theatre of the Unexpressed begins to disintegrate. That peculiar dramatic vein of other-worldly mysticism dries up. With the exception of the pleasant fairy tales *L'Oiseau bleu* [2] and its sequel *Les Fiançailles*, [3] the plays from *Aglavaine et Sélysette* are either wordy allegories or pieces more or less in the traditional style. The author inclines more to the essay form, and produces works such as *La Sagesse et la destinée*, [4] *La Vie des abeilles*, [5] *Le Temple enseveli*, [6] *Le Double Jardin*, [7] *L'Intelligence des fleurs*, [8] *La Mort*, [9] *L'Hôte inconnu*. [10] The power of Death begins to diminish before the increasing power of Love, under whose inspiration the human will makes

---

[1] *Aglavaine et Sélysette*, Act I.   [2] 1909.   [3] 1921.   [4] 1898.
[5] 1901.   [6] 1902.   [7] 1904.   [8] 1907.
[9] 1913—English edition, 1911.   [10] 1917—English edition, 1914.

some effort to assert itself. The silences of death, pain and destiny advance towards us from the depths of events. But we can go to meet the silences of love.[1] A new conception of Fate appears in *La Sagesse et la destinée*, dedicated to Georgette Leblanc, and greatly influenced by her. True wisdom may enable the human being to move out of the shadow of destiny, inner fatality no longer exists, and a measure of freedom is conceded to the human will. With the elimination of the passive, receptive attitude, with the appearance of the human will as a positive factor, Maeterlinck's " theatre of silence " finally vanishes.

Love and Death still contend in *Aglavaine et Sélysette*.[2] Maeterlinck says that he had wanted Love to triumph, but Death was too strong for him.[3] Aglavaine, the widow of Sélysette's brother, comes to stay in the castle of Sélysette and her husband Méléandre. Aglavaine, intended to be a woman of deep understanding, finds in Méléandre a twin soul, and they begin to love one another with a higher spiritual love. As for Sélysette, " Pourquoi ne monterait-elle pas en même temps que nous vers l'amour qui ignore les petites choses de l'amour?". The purely spiritual nature of their love does not prevent Aglavaine and Méléandre from frequently kissing one another, and the naïve and spiritually unawakened Sélysette who discovers this—for they never attempt to conceal their love—is jealous and dismayed. Under the tuition of Aglavaine, Sélysette tries to raise herself into the rarefied atmosphere in which her husband and sister-in-law now move, in order that the three may live together in the perfect concord of pure love. In the process of acquiring self-knowledge, Sélysette finds a kind of happiness, and much unhappiness. She solves the problem by falling from her tower, and to the last persists in trying to make the others believe that the fall was accidental.

> Qui était Aglavaine ? [asks A. Poizat] Tout simplement ce qu'on appelle aujourd'hui la femme moderne, une grande esthète, une divinité à bouleverser les cabarets artistiques, une

---

[1] *Le Trésor des humbles*, p. 24.   [2] 1896.   [3] Preface to *Théâtre*, vol. i, p. xvii.

nouvelle déesse-Raison, une matérialisation quasi-surnaturelle du faux-beau, du toc intellectuel. Tous les propos que fait tenir Maeterlinck à Aglavaine sont d'un creux, d'un faux, d'un emphatique qui déconcertent. . . . On dirait que le sphinx a parlé à Maeterlinck par la bouche de M. Homais ou que les tables tournantes lui ont tout expliqué.[1]

Poizat's words are not too severe. Aglavaine is an intolerable and pretentious bore, and if we accept the characters as realistic, the situation is false and unpleasant. Aglavaine explains to Sélysette why she kisses Méléandre so often. " Parce qu'il y a des choses qu'on ne peut dire qu'en s'embrassant. . . . Parce que les choses les plus profondes et les plus pures peut-être ne sortent pas de l'âme tant qu'un baiser ne les appelle. . . ." This is the utter limit of fatuousness, and one's sympathy is all for the bewildered little Sélysette. If we treat the play as purely symbolic, its meaning is obscured by the confusion of different types of love. Love between husband and wife is different in kind from the spiritual love of the mystic. Gentle Sélysette, rising to true spiritual love, would have found not unhappiness but an enhancement of her earthly love. Whatever Maeterlinck's intentions may have been, the result is the conventional triangular drama, expressed in the pretentious style of the quack spiritualist healer.

The underlying idea is similar to that in *Alladine et Palomides*, that earthly love in itself is not strong enough to conquer death. The new element is the striving of earthly love to attain spirituality. The work is unconvincing because two of the characters, Aglavaine and Méléandre, are neither the dream children of the " legendary " plays, nor flesh-and-blood man and woman. They are the mouthpieces of the author, abstractions, analysing themselves and paraphrasing in shapely sentences the essays in *Le Trésor des humbles*. The theories of direct communication are self-consciously expressed instead of being implied, and their value is diluted by the interminable flow of " literature ". Except in the case of Sélysette and perhaps the minor characters of

[1] Quoted by M. Lecat, *op. cit.* Premier Fascicule, p. 56.

Méligrane and Yssaline, the author abandŏns realism, with the result that his theatre, still " silent " in theory, becomes garrulous in practice, and begins to resemble the main body of unplayable Symbolist pieces.

> Je t'en prie [says Aglavaine to Sélysette], ne tente pas de fuir au moment où tout ce qu'il y a de plus grave dans ton être voudrait venir à moi. . . . Crois-tu que je n'entende pas les efforts qui se font ? . . . Crois-tu que nous serons jamais plus proches l'une de l'autre ? . . . Ne mettons pas des petits mots d'enfants, des petits mots pareils à des épines entre nos pauvres cœurs. . . . Parlons comme des êtres humains, comme de pauvres êtres humains que nous sommes, qui parlent comme ils peuvent, avec leurs mains, avec leurs yeux, avec leur âme, quand ils veulent dire des choses plus réelles que celles que les paroles peuvent atteindre. . . . Crois-tu que je n'entende pas que ton cœur déborde ? . . . Serre-toi contre moi dans la nuit, laisse-moi t'entourer de mes bras ; et ne t'inquiète pas si tu ne peux répondre . . . quelque chose parle en toi que j'entends aussi bien que toi-même. . . .[1]

Again, in the same scene:

> C'est que tu n'écoutais pas, Sélysette. Vois-tu, ce n'est pas avec les oreilles qu'on écoute ; et ce que tu entends à présent, ce n'est pas avec tes oreilles que tu l'entends vrai-ment; car au fond, tu n'entends pas ce que je dis, tu entends simplement que je t'aime. . . .

And so it goes on.

If words are useless to express realities, one wonders why Aglavaine produces such a steady flow of them. But for her paradoxical verbosity there would, of course, be no play, for consistently to act in accordance with their theories, Aglavaine and Méléandre would be moving about the stage in inarticulate beatitude, each exuding an aura of spiritual truth. What more than anything sets this play into the class of " théâtre de l'exprimé " is the fact that not only is every single thought and idea put into words, but we have no feeling of spiritual reserves, no hidden

---

[1] Act II, sc. 2.

depths, no subconscious. In the plays of Bernard, on the few occasions when the characters express to one another their ideas on direct communication, that is not the case. Julien in *Martine*, Pierre in *La Louise are* more than what they say, and what they say with regard to direct communication is imposed on them by the emotion of the situation. Only in Francine of *Nationale 6*, an inferior play, do we detect a similar self-conscious enjoyment of beautiful experiences, and nothing Francine says is quite so bad as this sort of thing : " Il ne faut jamais faire attendre des moments comme ceux-ci. Ils ne reviennent pas deux fois. . . . J'ai vu ton âme, Sélysette, parce que tu m'as aimée malgré toi tout à l'heure. (. . . .)

". . . viens, partons. . . . Il ne faut pas s'attarder trop longtemps aux endroits où notre âme a été plus heureuse qu'une âme humaine ne peut l'être. . . ." [1]

Of the principal characters, the only truly " silent " person, the only one who *is* more than what she says, is Sélysette. Child-like, naïve, unawakened, her intuition is truer and quicker than that of the self-conscious Aglavaine. " Ne lis pas si vite ", she says as Méléandre reads Aglavaine's letter containing her joyous anticipation of meeting him again. " Je sais que je ne suis pas belle ", she sighs, after listening to his praise of Aglavaine. The little phrases which escape her lips come straight from the heart. In Sélysette lingers still some of the magic of Maeterlinck's little princesses.

From now onwards Maeterlinck's dramatic work develops into a Theatre of the Expressed. *Ariane et Barbe-Bleue* [2] and *Sœur Béatrice* [3] are allegories described by the author as libretti for opera. In *Joyzelle* [4] we have a rhetorical style similar to that of Aglavaine and unrealistic melodramatic asides. Nothing is left unsaid, and the hero, besides speaking all his thoughts, also translates into words everything that comes within the field of his vision. The expressionistic devices already mentioned tend to fix and confine elusive truths in a manner contrary to that of

---

[1] Act. II, sc. 2.   [2] 1901.   [3] 1901.   [4] 1903.

the " silent " theatre. The fairy tales *L'Oiseau bleu* [1] and *Les Fiançailles* [2] both continue the tendency to " exteriorize " philosophical ideas. The latter has interesting expressionistic touches, for example, the presentation of Destiny as a huge menacing Shape which dwindles in the course of the play into a feeble infant in arms, and the materialization of the hero's ugly thoughts in the form of fantastic shapes. In *La Puissance des morts* [3] the author uses the dream technique which, like expressionism, renders concrete and tends to oversimplify half-conscious desires. In one striking scene, where all the lighting is directed on the convulsions of the dying money-lender's clutching hand, truth is conveyed without verbal expression, but this cinematic concentration on visual detail is a superimposed effect, and not an organic part of the play.

Other familiar works by Maeterlinck such as *Monna Vanna, Marie-Magdaleine, Le Bourgmestre de Stilmonde* are in the style of the conventional theatre. The silent rôle of Prinzivalle in the final scene of *Monna Vanna* [4] is without dramatic significance. One has the impression that Maeterlinck simply does not know what to do with him at that particular stage. *Marie-Magdaleine* [5] abounds in statuesque tableaux, but the silences spring neither from character nor from the impetus of events, and they are never adequately prepared. Maeterlinck had indeed abandoned his early ideas on the drama. In *Le Double Jardin* he was already emphasizing the importance of action in the theatre. [6] Many years later, in a letter to B. H. Clark, he minimizes the significance of the " silent " theatre, which he dismisses as a theory of his youth. [7]

Maeterlinck's *Théâtre de l'Inexprimé* consists in effect of the eight plays from *La Princesse Maleine* to *La Mort de Tintagiles*, written between 1889 and 1894. In these plays he endeavours to communicate philosophical truths through the medium of the

[1] 1909.   [2] 1921.   [3] 1927.   [4] 1902.   [5] 1913.   [6] 1904, p. 119.
[7] Barrett H. Clark, *A Study of the Modern Drama* (1925), p. 163.

Unexpressed. Abstract ideas may be conceived and worked out in silence, but it is impossible to convey them from one person to another without verbal expression. Using the medium of the spoken word, Maeterlinck may render his thoughts by sustained symbolism, as in *Les Aveugles*. He succeeds in presenting his analogies in dramatic form, because he lives his philosophy and thinks not in a logical way but in striking visual images. This is apparent even in his essays : for example, ". . . l'âme est comme un dormeur qui, du fond de ses songes, fait d'immenses efforts pour remuer un bras ou soulever une paupière ".[1] His mysticism makes life its starting-point ; his language is capable of containing hidden dialogue in so far as it is realistic.

But Maeterlinck conveys his ideas most powerfully without even the indirect verbal expression of symbolic language. He is most effective when he communicates not the truth itself, but the intensity of feeling produced by this truth. Realistically represented on the stage, this emotion is passed on to the audience, who reconstruct its initial cause. It is the intensity of emotion contained by Maeterlinck's Unexpréssed that renders the medium so eloquent.

Two kinds of emotion are connected with Maeterlinck's philosophical ideas : fear at the prospect of death or inscrutable destiny, joy at the realization of spiritual love. Of these only the first is really dramatic. Its gradations from vague uneasiness to intense anguish are varied and complex ; it is capable of visible development ; it is to a high degree contagious, stirring up disquieting and primitive responses in the hidden depths of the spectator ; and it implies hostility, and therefore, in a way, conflict, the very essence of drama. While fear holds sway, Maeterlinck's drama cannot really be described as static. If it is static in the anecdotal or psychological sense, there is a compelling " dynamism " of emotion, even in plays like *L'Intruse* and *Les Aveugles*.

The real static drama arises when spiritual love takes the

[1] *Le Trésor des humbles*, p. 34.

ascendancy. As long as human love occupies a subordinate
place in the drama, Maeterlinck can depict with moving realism
love scenes of wistful beauty. Those between Pelléas and
Mélisande, and Alladine and Palomides, must rank high in
European literature. Incidentally, while the growth of such love
may be indicated by the Unexpressed, the emotion invariably
reaches a climax of subdued lyricism. There is no analysis ; the
characters are simply conscious that the feeling is there, and
express it in a pure cry. But when love is conceived as a mysterious guiding force of the universe, equal in power to death,
its spiritual significance for a man of Maeterlinck's temperament
can be conveyed only by the emotional reaction it arouses in the
individual. The state of mystic joy which it creates comes from
a sense of harmony with the universe, life's problems are solved,
there is no tension, no conflict, and consequently no drama.
The author is then obliged to create a " situation ", as in *Aglavaine et Sélysette*, and the drama, such as it is, is achieved by
conventional methods. There is little opportunity for the
dynamic development of mystic joy, and far from being contagious, the type of beatitude represented by Aglavaine leaves
the normal spectator completely cold.

Fear is naked, primitive, common to all ; it is the instinctive
weapon of self-defence implanted by nature, and the most urbane
and civilized of human beings cannot root it out. Mystic joy is
acquired through a process of purification and elimination of the
conflicting desires which are the substance of the human being
and therefore the substance of drama. Mystic joy, given to few,
cannot awaken the mass response which the drama requires.
Fear can be expressed realistically and dramatically in complete
silence by attitude. The terrified silence of Maleine before her
angry father, the mute terror of Mélisande before Golaud,
besides containing the pure force of the emotion itself, are
also full of the conflict, or rather—as happens in Maeterlinckian
drama—the opposition of personalities. The fear which emanates
from the stammering dialogue is enhanced by the suggestion of

invisible hostile forces, which would vanish if defined in words. But attitude and gesture do little to interpret the silence of mystic beatitude. Aglavaine and Méléandre, who frequently kiss one another, are obliged to " exteriorize " the content of their blissful silences, and explain away in a copious flow of unequivocal words any doubtful interpretation of an act inspired by the noblest of motives. With the true static drama, which is the drama of long-windedness, Maeterlinck's Theatre of the Unexpressed disappears.

The naked realism of fear gives Maeterlinck's theatre its element of human truth, which constitutes the dramatic force of the Unexpressed. The dialogue, whether it consists of broken, stammering phrases, as in the early plays, or of language of grave beauty with a double meaning running through it, is authentic. The characters too are rendered convincing, in spite of their pale shadowiness, in spite of their elementary psychology. Maeterlinck desires to remove all external contingencies in order that his work may have a lasting and universal significance. " Pour faire des œuvres durables, ne faut-il pas justement s'élever au-dessus de son époque, se dégager des accidents de la civilisation, des contingences de l'actualité immédiate ? "[1] Consequently his characters are stylized, usually in legendary or idealized modern settings. They bear names reminiscent of a remote Arthurian age, or else they are unnamed—the Father, the Daughter, the Child—representing some fundamental aspect of humanity. Another factor accounting for the lack of complexity in Maeterlinck's characters is his own peculiar notion of the subconscious. The Freudian psychology of Jean-Jacques Bernard is rich in silent dramatic conflict. By Maeterlinck, even such a deeply probing psychology would be accounted superficial and indeed wrongly designated, since it does not penetrate to the soul, as he conceives it, and reveal the primordial essence of man, the mysterious, all-pervading spirit of which man and nature are manifestations. The resolution of man and the universe into

---

[1] J. Huret, *Enquête sur l'évolution littéraire* (1891), p. 121.

their most primitive and elemental substance eliminates inner conflicts and complexities, and, without the interest of normal psychological nuances, these remote " souls " in human shape would fail to arouse much response in an audience, if their transparency were not suffused with the live emotion of fear.

Full dramatic development of the emotion of fear is rendered possible by the attitude of passive resignation on the part of the characters. A philosophy of utter and total determinism is implicit in these eight " silent " tragedies. There is no question, as in the fatalistic Greek drama, of a defiant will doomed in advance ; there is no question of retribution for sin or overweening pride. Maeterlinck's *Théâtre de l'Inexprimé* centres on the ruthless and inexorable forces of Fate and Death, before which the human will dwindles into nothingness. It is a complete slaughter of the innocents.

The exercise of the will implies an element of logical reasoning which is inconsistent with Maeterlinck's intuitive and emotional methods. When the individual makes an effort to conquer fear, he is bound, to some extent, to analyse the situation and reason inwardly, using unexpressed words in a logical manner. Such inward reasoning could not be conveyed to an audience except by direct verbal expression. We have also seen that, according to Maeterlinck, a silent, passive attitude is necessary before the individual can attain mystic truth. This can be achieved only by eliminating the lively intellectual element of verbal expression. With such an attitude, induced by native temperament, Maeterlinck confronts the problems of existence, and he insensibly transfers it to his characters, rendering them peculiarly susceptible to the horror of death, which seems to have obsessed him in his earlier years. Not only do the characters refrain from exerting themselves against the sinister, invisible forces, but they may even exult in the sensation of their own ruin, as Mélisande does when she knows that all is lost. The discounting of reason, moreover, gives free rein to the imagination and Fate assumes such gigantic proportions that all conception of an alternative is blotted out. It is only when Maeterlinck conceives the possibility of love as a superior guiding force that an alternative is presented, necessitating a choice ; the will is developed under love's more positive inspiration, and, the initial fear still persisting, the situation created by the presence of the two forces is analysed in the tremendous flood of words characteristic of Maeterlinck's second manner.

The limitations imposed on Maeterlinck's theatre by the methods of the Unexpressed are obvious. The elimination of the intellect, and the elementary psychology resulting from his mysticism, deprive his drama of richness and variety. He is obliged to concentrate on the narrow field of pure emotion, and since his preconceived dramaturgy discounts anecdotal and psychological action, he achieves dramatic development through the Unexpressed only when fear predominates. When he deliberately deprives himself of direct verbal expression to communicate his philosophy, the ideas expressed by pure emotion and suggestive atmosphere are of necessity few and simple ; death is horrible, death is relentless, resistance is hopeless. And as there are limits to the variations on a single theme, the possibilities of Maeterlinck's particular kind of *Théâtre de l'Inexprimé* soon exhaust themselves. At the same time, the restricted means of the Unexpressed impress these simple ideas on the emotions and nerves of the audience with a strange intensity, rarely equalled by traditional methods.

The Unexpressed as used by Maeterlinck produces a type of drama not satisfying to the human spirit. It is decadent. It concentrates on one aspect of life, instead of viewing life as a whole. It is a theatre for marionettes, which, says Lemaître, " sentent les ficelles sombres qui les tirent ".[1] Man is of little account in Maeterlinck's theatre. He is submerged by the invisible forces of the universe. Maeterlinck goes so far as to say that the presence of human beings on the stage is undesirable since it destroys the symbol. " L'être humain sera-t-il remplacé

---

[1] *Op. cit.* 8ᵉ série, p. 144.

par une ombre, un reflet, une projection de formes symboliques ou un être qui aurait les allures de la vie sans avoir la vie ? " [1] This is the very suicide of drama, as surely as the application of sealing-wax instead of paint to the canvas would be the suicide of painting. The living actor is, and always has been, with the best dramatists, the basic material of the drama. The theatre by its nature must centre round man. Whatever the philosopher's view of man may be—and to me Maeterlinck's philosophy seems inadequate—if he selects the drama as his medium of communication, he must bear in mind the fact that the drama, using human material on the stage, is essentially a humanistic art form. That material can be used to the full only when all human potentialities are drawn upon. By eliminating intellect and the will, and narrowing down the field of emotion, Maeterlinck deprives himself of rich sources of beauty, and produces a depressive effect similar to that of the musician who limits himself to the five black keys of the piano, instead of drawing on its entire range of notes.

[1] *Vide supra, La Jeune Belgique* (1890), tome ix, p. 331.

CHAPTER V

THE FRENCH THEATRE AFTER 1918

THE real cleavage between the nineteenth and the twentieth centuries came with the 1914–18 war, and, as might be expected, this tremendous cataclysm reacted on the French theatre. Its immediate effect was to bring to a head the vulgarity, triviality and bad taste of the commercial theatre which proceeded to make money by exploiting emotions which the stress of the times should have rendered sacrosanct, and by providing a new public of permissionnaires, foreign allies and nouveaux riches with rubbish and pornography. An important factor also against the production of good dramatic work during the war was the unnatural and exalted state of mind of that part of the public normally receptive to it. Strain, anxiety, grief and a desperate unquestioning patriotism affected for the time being people's critical balance. Thus, for example, a competent comedy of middle-class life such as Paul Géraldy's *Noces d'argent* [1] met with hostility because of its rather cynical presentation of a French family. Moreover, most of the young French writers, in whose hands the salvation of the drama lay, were in the trenches, many never to return.

The 1914–18 war had, however, more far-reaching effects on the French theatre. It precipitated movements and tendencies which were already existing and growing. The social conditions and comfortable system of morals which made the " Boulevard " possible were no longer acceptable to men who had been through the horrors of trench warfare. The old society was cracking ; the stable values in which the drama finds its roots were shifting.

[1] First performed 5th May 1917.

A new idealism and yearning for poetry appeared, tempered by a pacifist love of humanity. There was a desire to escape from the ugliness and sordidness of everyday life. A new materialism which Benjamin Crémieux calls " le taylorisme et le fordisme " [1] was penetrating into French life. Crémieux compares the ethics resulting from it with those implicit in Taine's dictum that vice and virtue are products like vitriol and sugar, and notes a parallelism between the reactions against post-1870 positivism and post-1918 " Americanism ". While ﹀the Romantics of 1830 escaped across time into the past, across space into lands of distant enchantment, these avenues had no more mystery for a period in which, as J.-R. Bloch points out, scientific inventions and scholarly research had conquered both space and time. [2] Life had seared these younger writers too deeply for them to be able to divorce themselves entirely from reality, and their escape took the form of what J.-R. Bloch calls the " fuite à l'intérieur ". Instead of studying human behaviour in relation to a recognized social and ethical code imposed from without, dramatists were beginning to find rich material in the individual as complete in himself. Pirandello [3] examines the mystery of human personality. His theme is the subjective value and therefore purely relative truth of human nature, which is the form imposed upon life by the fallible consciousness of each individual, and his tragedy is that which arises from man's recognition of the fact that the idea he has formed of his own personality does not correspond with reality. The theories of Freud—his stressing of the unconscious, with its influence on the conscious, and of inner conflicts and repressions—had important effects on the new drama. The plays of H.-R. Lenormand centred round the Freudian conception of the unconscious and we shall see how Freudian theories are implicit in some of the plays of the post-1918 *Théâtre de l'Inexprimé*. Bergsonism, which had " broken the chains " of

[1] *Inquiétude et reconstruction* (1931), p. 148.
[2] Cf. J.-R. Bloch, *Destin du théâtre* (1930), p. 53 *et seq.*
[3] First presented to the Parisian public in 1922 by Charles Dullin with *La Volupté de l'honneur.*

pre-war youth, was now in the ascendant. Bergson's theories of intuition were in tune with post-war tendencies, and his philosophy was interpreted in such a way as to support them. We shall see, too, the part played by intuitive knowledge in the works we are examining.

This new attitude began to inspire fresh efforts on the part of the experimental theatres. There was a revival of the Théâtre Libre under Pierre Veber. The Œuvre renewed its activities with Lugné-Poe. Jacques Copeau, Gaston Baty, Charles Dullin, Louis Jouvet and the Pitoëffs were to infuse new life into the drama. Although there was an element of intellectual snobbery in the audiences of these special theatres, the intrinsic value of the productions was such that a genuine response was awakened in the public who were beginning to tire of the superficial " well-made plays". In the end, to retain their clientèle, the "Boulevard" began to put on the works of some of the authors from the experimental theatres.[1]

Two of the " animateurs " of the French theatre are especially interesting from our point of view. Jacques Copeau had opened the Vieux Colombier in 1913 in an attempt to combat the pre-war industrialization which was ruining the drama. His reforms were mainly concerned with acting and décor, in both of which he was opposed to the naturalism of Antoine. Just as a dramatic text should not aspire to be reportage of real life, but must be concentrated, and one might even say deformed, for scenic purposes, so the representation of life on the stage must not mechanically conform to the movements of everyday life, but must have a rhythm and a pace suited to the optics of the theatre. Ramón Fernández in *Molière et Copeau* says that with Copeau the theatre takes on once more " son étrangeté, son indépendance vis-à-vis du réel et de la littérature ".[2] The décor was consciously simplified in order to bring out the value of the text and the rhythmic

---

[1] Cf. T. H. Dickinson, *The Theatre in a Changing Europe* (1938), No. IV, " The French Post-War Theatre ", by Edmond Sée.

[2] Quoted by Marcel Raymond, *Le Jeu retrouvé* (1943), p. 30.

action to which it gave rise. Marcel Raymond quotes the words of a workman overheard one day in a café talking of the economy of stage properties in the Vieux Colombier. " Il y a des fois où ils n'ont même pas de chaises. Ils s'assoient par terre. Alors, comme il n'y a rien, ça fait que *tu vois les mots*. . . ." [1] The theatre of Jacques Copeau was therefore anti-realist and " theatrical ", not in the false style of the nineteenth century " cabotins ", against whom Antoine had revolted, but in a new poetical sense. Copeau was reviving the best traditions of the commedia dell' arte ; his was " un théâtre de mots et de gestes ".[2] Although he produced *Le Paquebot Tenacity* by Vildrac, one of the plays in which we are especially interested, any direct influence he might have had as a theorist on contemporary dramaturgy would tend away from the *Théâtre de l'Inexprimé*, since his conception of the producer's task was fundamentally the presentation of a text, as it were, in bold relief, the focusing of the audience's attention on the spoken word.

The theories of Gaston Baty, however, must claim our attention, since the post-1918 *Théâtre de l'Inexprimé* was so intimately associated with his name that many thought that he had directly inspired it. A man of culture, with a university training and a Catholic background, Baty had absorbed the ideas of Gordon Craig, Adolphe Appia, Georg Fuchs, Stanislavski and Meyerhold, which were circulating in France,[3] and evolved his own philosophy of the theatre, which was indeed for him a world, an outlook on life. In his view the theatre was essentially a fusion of all arts, text, décor, music, rhythm and plastic art, into a glorious new act of beauty, one might say of adoration. This was, he maintained, the true tradition of Aeschylus and the *mistere*. The classical theatre, where all is contained in the text, was for him an impoverishment, a distortion—he speaks of the " hypertrophie de l'élément verbal "—having its origin in the

[1] Marcel Raymond, *Le Jeu retrouvé*, p. 43.   [2] *Ibid.* p. 42.

[3] In 1910 Jacques Rouché had published *L'Art théâtral moderne*, analysing the achievements of these men. He himself was to take over the direction of the Théâtre des Arts a short time later.

humanism of the Reformation, and reaching its height in the Cartesian seventeenth century. The drama was an interpretation of life and life was greater than " l'individu analysable, l'homme tel que l'ont inventé les humanistes ".

. . . L'homme en vérité dépasse de toutes parts ce schéma de l'homme. Sa vie consciente est toute baignée de vie inconsciente ou consciente seulement à demi. Il n'est pas seulement l'idée claire qu'il a de lui-même, mais ses rêves obscurs, sa mémoire endormie, ses instincts refoulés ; dans l'ombre de son âme habitent les ancêtres, l'enfant qu'il a été, les autres hommes qu'il aurait pu être. Tout cela n'affleure qu'à peine, par éclairs, dans le champ de sa conscience ; cette vie obscure conditionne cependant son autre vie. Elle est une matière presque inexploitée et combien riche !

Les groupements humains ont une vie propre, différente de celle des individus qui les composent. Aussi bien qu'un caractère personnel, les communautés sont des entités dramatiques ; le métier, la cité, la classe, la nation, la race. Non point réunion de plusieurs êtres ; chaque fois un être nouveau, polycéphale, existant en soi.

Mais l'univers, ce n'est pas seulement les hommes ou les groupements humains. Il y a autour d'eux tout ce qui vit, tout ce qui végète, tout ce qui est. Et tout ce qui est, est matière dramatique : les animaux, les plantes, les choses. Toute la vie quotidienne et son mystère : le toit, le seuil, le banc, la porte qui s'ouvre et se ferme, la table avec l'odeur du pain et la couleur du vin, et la lampe, et le lit, et ce battement au cœur de l'horloge. Il y a des personnalités inanimées : l'usine, le navire, la ville, la forêt, la montagne ; il y a tout le merveilleux mécanique, la machine construite par l'homme, mais qui ensuite "marche toute seule". Il y a les grandes forces de la nature : le soleil, la mer, le brouillard, la chaleur, le vent, la pluie, plus puissantes que l'homme et qui l'oppriment, l'accablent, transforment son corps, usent sa volonté, repétrissent son âme.

Nous voici déjà loin de la dramaturgie du "coucheront-ils ?". Le royaume que doit conquérir le théâtre nouveau s'étend bien au delà, jusqu'à l'infini. Après l'homme et son mystère intérieur, après les choses et leur mystère, nous touchons à des mystères plus grands. La mort, les présences invisibles, tout ce qui est par delà la vie et l'illusion du temps. Fléau des balances où s'équilibrent le bien et le mal. Ce qu'il faut de douleur pour racheter le péché et sauver la beauté du monde. Tout, jusqu'à Dieu.

This extract quoted by Paul Blanchart [1] is from an article, *Le Théâtre sera sauvé*, which was inserted in several programmes of the Théâtre Montparnasse, which Baty took over in 1930. Although unsigned, the style is unmistakably that of Baty, and the substance is, in any case, an exact résumé of his theories, and indeed a synthesis of the tendencies which had been developing before the 1914–18 war, and which were strongly evident in the post-war writers. In this rich passage we can detect traces of Bergson, who had revolted against the " esprit de géométrie " which had hitherto dominated philosophy and attached import-ance to memory and ancestry, the strong influence of Freud, with his theories of the unconscious, something of the unanimistic ideas of Jules Romains and some echoes of Maeterlinck.

The theatre, Baty asserted, had lost the richness and beauty of life through concentrating at different periods on one only of its many aspects—psychological analysis in the Classical age, poetry with the Romantics, truth with the Realists and mystery with the Symbolists. These elements must be fused in order to achieve his aim : " rethéâtraliser le théâtre ", and for this purpose it was necessary to " orchestrate " colour, line, plastic art, music and rhythm, text and silence. Each must play its part, none must predominate. Thus human experience would be recorded, but man would have his true place in the scheme of things, and man himself would be complete in all aspects ; mystery of the instinct and the unconscious would be there as well as clarity of intellect, Dionysos as well as Apollo. Baty accordingly takes as his emblem *la Chimère*, not the Greek mythological monster, but the bird-woman of the Nordic tales, " symbole ", he writes, " d'un art épris d'universalité et d'équilibre, qui se voudrait

[1] Paul Blanchart, *Gaston Baty* (1939), pp. 65-6.

H

harmonieux au point de concilier, de réconcilier en lui les puissances que des habitudes séculaires ont artificiellement dressées l'une contre l'autre, l'esprit et la matière, le surnaturel et la nature, l'homme et les choses ".[1]

In the phrase " Sire le Mot " Baty expresses his contempt for " literature " in the drama.   Here are his views on the relation of the text to the theatre :

> Le texte est la partie essentielle du drame.   Il est au drame ce que le noyau est au fruit, le centre solide autour duquel viennent s'ordonner les autres éléments.   Et de même qu'une fois le fruit savouré, le noyau reste pour assurer la croissance d'autres fruits semblables, le texte, lorsque se sont évanouis les prestiges de la représentation, attend dans une bibliothèque de les ressusciter quelque jour.
>
> Le rôle du texte au théâtre, c'est le rôle du mot dans la vie. Le mot sert à chacun de nous pour se formuler à soi-même et communiquer éventuellement aux autres ce qu'enregistre son intelligence.   Il exprime directement, pleinement, nos idées claires.   Il exprime aussi, mais indirectement, nos sentiments et nos sensations, dans la mesure où notre intelligence les analyse ; ne pouvant donner de notre vie sensible une transcription intégrale et simultanée, il la décompose en éléments successifs, en reflets intellectuels, comme le prisme décompose un rayon de soleil.
>
> Le domaine du mot est immense puisqu'il embrasse toute l'intelligence, tout ce que l'homme peut comprendre et formuler. Mais au delà, tout ce qui échappe à l'analyse est inexprimable par la parole.[2]

These views are similar to those held by the dramatists of the *Théâtre de l'Inexprimé*, but it would be erroneous to conclude that Baty is the originator of the group which formed after 1918. Jean-Jacques Bernard and Denys Amiel, its two main representatives, were on the reading committee of *Les Compagnons de la Chimère*, and Baty produced the " classics " of this school, *Martine* and *L'Invitation au voyage* by Bernard and *Le Voyageur*

---

[1] Paul Blanchart, *Gaston Baty*, p. 86.
[2] *Le Théâtre sera sauvé*, quoted by Paul Blanchart, *op. cit.* p. 73.

by Amiel. But he denies being the founder of a school. "L'ins-piration s'accommode mal de l'a-priorisme des théories. Les œuvres que nous jouons n'ont pas été faites pour *la Chimère* ; c'est *la Chimère* qui a été faite pour elles." [1]

Le Voyageur, at any rate, though performed for the first time on the 2nd May 1923, was written in 1912. In any case, Baty's main preoccupation appears to have been with the re-sources of décor, costume, and especially lighting, and the diverse types of play he presented were obviously chosen for the possi-bilities they offered to his virtuosity as a *metteur en scène*.

It is necessary at this stage to examine some of the work of authors with whom Baty is associated, not only in order to ascertain to what extent Baty influenced the post-1918 *Théâtre de l'Inexprimé*, but actually to help us to establish clearly what writers constitute this group. Bernard and Amiel must un-questionably be included on account of the theories which they published and endeavoured to put into practice. Other drama-tists, whose work had some affinities with that of Maeterlinck or Bernard, were often mistakenly included by contemporary critics. Many such dramatists were associated with the *Chimère*.

The plays of J.-V. Pellerin, for example, were often regarded as representative of the group, because he endeavoured to reveal on the stage the inner lives of human beings. His drama is, in my opinion, diametrically opposed to the ideas of the " silent " school. Pellerin's method is to " exteriorize " subconscious or half-realized thoughts and desires by human and scenic agencies. In *Intimité* [2] a man and his wife sit musing in the evening, ex-changing desultory remarks. From time to time, as they brood, their dreams and fancies appear materialized in the form of people with whom they converse aloud, each in turn, while the other is unaware that anything is going on. Again, in *Têtes de rechange* [3] we see a man, Ixe, with his uncle, Opéku. While the latter talks

---

[1] *Bulletin de la Chimère*, No. VIII, April 1923, p. 130, R. (see note on Collection Rondel in Bibliography, Section IV, p. 256).
[2] Written 1920-1, first performed 9th May 1922, *mise en scène* by Baty.
[3] Written 1924-5, first performed 15th Apr. 1926, *mise en scène* by Baty.

interminably about his affairs and his limited conception of life, the thoughts and fancies of Ixe appear in the form of characters and striking scenic effects. This is expressionism ; the processes are the contrary of those used by what we understand to be the *Théâtre de l'Inexprimé*, where the dramatists endeavour to convey the inner life of the character not by materializing it on the stage— an extension of the traditional method of " exteriorizing " it in words—but by the skilful use of silence and evocative dialogue. Expressionism found its place in the aesthetics of Gaston Baty because of the possibilities it offered in the realm of *mise en scène*.

Baty's predilection for the plays of Lenormand associates him in the minds of others with a " theatre of the subconscious ". Though Lenormand was not regarded as a member of the " silent " school, his work is an important manifestation of certain contemporary influences and, with a totally different treatment, his subject matter is, in an exaggerated form, akin to that of Bernard's " Freudian " plays. Strongly influenced by the theories of Freud, Lenormand exploits dramatically the mysteries of repressed unlawful desires, dreams, the hidden recesses of morbid personalities. But his is hardly a drama of the Unexpressed as we have defined it. The characters are conscious of their moral malaise and, as for example in *Les Ratés*,[1] torment them- selves by brooding over it and putting it into words. *Le Mangeur de rêves*,[2] one of the most " Freudian " of his pieces, although concerned with bringing to the surface a repressed memory of childhood, darkly indicated by dreams, is full of conscious analysis : self-analysis on the part of the main character, and analysis of each other by the remaining actors. In *Simoun*[3] Laurency is perfectly aware of his incestuous feelings towards his daughter and of his attempts at rationalization by identifying her with his dead wife, and he conveys this very clearly to his friend.[4]

We must not overlook the effective final scene of *Simoun*,

[1] First performed 22nd May 1920 ; performed season 1936-7, with *mise en scène* by Baty. [2] First performance in Paris 1st Feb. 1922.
[3] First performance in Paris 21st Dec. 1920, *mise en scène* by Baty.
[4] 12th tableau.

where Laurency, left alone with the body of his daughter, murdered by his half-caste mistress, gazes at her in complete silence. His expression changes from dull stupefaction to a kind of animal relief—" la détente physique de la bête poursuivie qui se sent hors d'atteinte. Et cela se traduit par trois larges aspirations involontaires qui soulèvent profondément tout son buste." Although more superficial in nature than the types of silence we shall examine later on, the theatrical effectiveness of this unspoken scene may well be imagined. The silence, moreover, allows the audience to perceive that the noise of the simoon, which has been a background to the play and has symbolized the turmoil within Laurency, has died down. Lenormand studies, in addition to the fatality which man carries within him, the external forces of nature, which not only have a symbolical significance but also directly affect the behaviour and temperament of his characters. The depressive effects of the misty marches of Holland in *Le Temps est un songe*,[1] the degenerating influence of the tropical climate in *Simoun*, have this double function. It might be said with truth that many of Lenormand's plays carry invisible non-speaking " characters "—those strange forces of nature which the Greeks embodied in the shape of gods speaking like men. It is this invisible character that Baty seized upon. He, and Pitoëff, who also produced plays by Lenormand, endeavoured by their *mise en scène* to liberate from the text the underlying theme, to " release the atmosphere into the décor ".

Cyclone[2] by Simon Gantillon, another play which shows in a striking manner the silent mysterious power of elemental forces, offered great opportunities to the *metteur en scène*. The scene is a sailing-ship, becalmed in a tropical sea. The overpowering heat, rising to its climax before transforming itself into the violence of the cyclone, weighs down on the crew, exhausts, stupefies and hallucinates. In this unnatural atmosphere strange primitive fears rise to the surface, and invisible powers of evil

[1] First performed 2nd Dec. 1919.
[2] First performed 29th May 1923, *mise en scène* by Baty.

seem to have a presence. A Russian has fallen overboard, his possessions are seized and shared, and in his box are discovered a woman's tresses. In the ship's cook, a negro, they evoke ancestral memories, and he relives the tale of the capture of a white woman by a black chief. To Aguistace, lying delirious after being struck by a pulley from the very mast from which the Russian has fallen, those sinuous tresses conjure up the phantom of a siren, and he goes, as in a trance, to join his comrade in the sea. The tropical heat, the cyclone, the strangeness of nature, working upon man, conjure up forces which normally remain submerged ; they create inexplicable terror in the young boy who feels that there must be some mysterious connection between the accident of the Russian and that of Aguistace ; they stir up the primitive recollections in the negro, and evoke the strange presence sensed by Aguistace. There is a hint of the invisible fatalities of Maeterlinck.

Another play of " atmosphere " produced by Gaston Baty is *Césaire* [1] by Jean Schlumberger. Césaire, a fisherman, whose physical weakness is compensated by over-developed powers of the mind, has come to revenge himself on Benoît, who has taken away his sweetheart, by subjecting him to a kind of mental torture. He succeeds in making the man believe that, impotent though he is, it is he, Césaire, who has really possessed Rose Marie, since, unlike Benoît, he has all his memories of her clearly engraved in his mind. Césaire diabolically exerts himself to destroy what memories the other man retains of the girl, and in the end Benoît is almost convinced that it was Césaire, not himself, who was with her at their last meeting. Half-crazed with mental torment, Benoît rushes out after Césaire and strikes him down. The play is punctuated with silences which stress the hypnotic influence of Césaire, allow his words to take full effect on Benoît, and create an atmosphere of terror and foreboding. But the dialogue itself is clear and Césaire expresses lucidly his consciousness of his powers.

[1] Written 1908, first performed in 1922 *mise en scène* by Baty.

Such plays of " atmosphere " and " exoticism " turn our thoughts to Shakespeare; we think of *The Tempest* and *King Lear* where the elements figure, and *Hamlet* and *Macbeth* where the mind creates an " ambiance " of fear. But whereas in Shakespeare these aspects are in due proportion, the play centring round the passions and destinies of man, in the modern plays the authors strive to attain special effects by isolating and stressing the powers of natural forces to which the human being becomes subordinate. This much they have in common with Maeterlinck. I shall not, however, on that account class them in the *Théâtre de l' Inex-primé*, since they lack the distinctive qualities of dialogue which give the authentic group its special character.

Let us note in passing that what is common to the diverse types of play favoured by Baty—plays of the subconscious, plays of atmosphere and exoticism, Theatre of the Unexpressed—is that " fuite à l'intérieur ", that " goût de l'évasion ", characteristic of post-1918 writers. Baty expresses his conception of the theatre as an escape from everyday life. " Nous souhaiterions que le spectateur pût, en passant notre seuil, déposer ses soucis et ses angoisses, se dépouiller de ses idées, ne plus penser qu'il est un homme d'aujourd'hui. Nous nous efforçons de lui faire vivre une autre vie, de l'emmener vers d'autres pays, d'autres temps, d'autres âmes." [1]

We see then that Gaston Baty, while promoting among other types of drama the *Théâtre de l'Inexprimé* of Bernard and Amiel, did not directly inspire it. His hostility to " Sire le Mot " sprang from a broad conception of the theatre, and silence was to play its part with the numerous other elements that go to make a work of dramatic art—colour, line, form, music, text. In so far as his *mise en scène* was intended to convey to the audience more than the content of the words spoken by the actors, it could be said that he worked with the Unexpressed. But he tended to dominate with his *mise en scène*, to burst asunder the confines of the drama and emulate the cinema. He could alter a text if it

---

[1] Quoted by Paul Blanchart, *op. cit.* p. 61.

suited him, and was fond of staging novels, for example *Crime and Punishment* and *Madame Bovary*, with the emphasis laid on scenic effect ; this in a new manner tended to restore to the stage the " tranche de vie ", flattening down the exciting curve of authentic dramatic action, and diluting the dramatic interest with the interest of the spectacle. His conception of the drama was, as one critic pointed out, dangerously near that of a mere scenario, to form a basis for artistry in light, colour and music. When the *mise en scène* is over-emphasized, the inspiration of the work of art is dispersed among several creators, and the form degenerates.

In the best examples of the *Théâtre de l'Inexprimé* the Un-expressed is closely interwoven with the text. I have expressed the view that the drama is and, at its greatest, always will remain, essentially literary, although not necessarily " de la littérature " in Verlaine's sense. The essence of the drama is change and crisis, and this must in the end be achieved by a concentration and selection of words, and if necessary silences, upon which the attention of the audience will be focused, the *mise en scène* being of necessity on a secondary plane. The best dramatists of the group in which we are interested, by employing silence and the Unexpressed, do in fact enhance the literary value of their works.

It is accordingly with dialogue that we must primarily con-cern ourselves in our efforts to place the dramatists of the post-1918 *Théâtre de l'Inexprimé*, and here another problem presents itself. The reaction against pre-1914 superficiality and verbal exaltation was fairly general. Many plays were being written in a more subdued style on quieter and more intimate themes ; the tendency to probe below the surface was spreading ; the rêverie and nostalgia of Bernard were contagious ; and moreover, the new plays were being interpreted with discretion and restraint and due concern for the value of the pause. Such characteristics were manifested in varying degrees ; when concentrated intensively in a single work, they might give the impression of a Theatre of the Unexpressed. By what standards could one determine which of these plays, whether any, or all, should be classed in this group ?

We must of course discount the effects of silence proceeding purely from the efforts of the producer, or from the stage directions given to facilitate the producer's task, rather than from the nature of the text itself. As I indicated in the first chapter, the fact that dramatists in the past gave relatively few stage directions does not imply that they attached no importance to them. Their value in relation to the work may perhaps be compared to that of the improvised cadenza in a concerto, where a certain liberty of inspiration is accorded to the virtuoso, provided he retains the spirit of the musical context ; whereas the effects of silence and the Unexpressed with which we are concerned are more in the nature of those diminuendos, rallentandos, rests and other musical indications which cannot be isolated from the notes as they are written on the score, and which cannot be left entirely to the discretion of the performer. The same applies when we consider the modern cinema-inspired devices of slowing down the pace of the acting or inserting pauses at certain stages in order to emphasize certain effects. To be sure, the nature and quality of any worth-while production flow inevitably out of the subject matter and dialogue. But it is by the text that value of a dramatic work stands or falls.

The name of Jean Sarment has been mentioned by some critics in connection with the *Théâtre de l'Inexprimé*, on account of the subtle nuances and suggestive power of his dialogue, and the frequency of the pause. In *Le Pêcheur d'ombres* [1] we find a passage which might have been written by Bernard. Through jealousy and frustrated love, Jean has fallen into a gentle, amiable madness. In response to his mother's pleading, Nelly, the girl who had spurned him, agrees to stay in the house, in the hope that her presence may eventually effect a cure. It is then that she

[1] First performance 15th Apr. 1921, a year before that of Jean-Jacques Bernard's *Martine*.

begins to love him. In the second act Jean and Nelly discuss why they could not understand one another before :

> JEAN. Oh ! Cela doit tenir à ce que je m'en tenais aux paroles ! . . . Je prenais les mots " au mot ". Maintenant non.
> NELLY. Vous me posez encore des questions.
> JEAN. Oui ! . . . Mais la réponse n'est pas dans les mots. Elle est . . . dans un clin d'œil . . . dans un mouvement de la lèvre . . . un geste de la main . . . une façon de jouer avec les plis de votre robe, ou les cerises de votre ceinture. . . . Les mots ! c'est une contenance qu'on se donne. . . . Vous m'avez répondu depuis longtemps. Vous avez répondu à des questions que je ne vous ai jamais posées. (. . .) Je vous connais mieux, parce que je ne fais pas attention à ce que vous dites." [1]

The implication is that since his reason has become clouded by loss of memory, Jean has attained a better and more intuitive understanding of people. He entrusts himself to the emotion of love and allows it free play. Emotion draws human beings close together. Language, which is bound up with the intellect, creates a barrier between them. This is one of the fundamental ideas behind Bernard's dramatic theories.

Jean gradually begins to regain his faculties, and at this stage his brother, who is also in love with Nelly, pretends that she is another girl sent to represent the one who had caused Jean's unhappiness, with a view to restoring him to health. The spell is broken. Jean cannot love this girl if she is not Nelly. Identity of emotion and its object are necessary to him. And with his returning reason he makes fateful comparisons. The real Nelly, whom he remembered so cruelly indifferent, would not have loved and pitied him. It cannot be the same person. The barrier is raised, and although memory and sanity have been returning, he chooses once more to escape from reality, this time with the aid of a pistol.

The little this play has in common with the work of Bernard is due to this idea of direct communication based on the uninhibited emotion of a hero whose reason is for the time being unbalanced. But in the main, with all its delicacy and poetry, Sarment's theatre is of the expressed, and this because of the rôle which reason normally has in it. Sarment's best plays (I omit those he wrote for the " Boulevard ") show an uneasy twentieth-century awareness superimposed on a kind of nineteenth-century romanticism. The heroes, all variants of the author, discontented with the pitiful realities of human nature, yearn towards an ideal, and remember with regret the lost purity of childhood. At the same time, retaining their critical faculties, they take a certain pleasure in ironically noting the disharmony between their dreams and reality, the contrast between the idealism of the spirit and the feeble accomplishments of the body. This irony and perspicacity, manifesting itself in a clearly expressed dialogue, had a basis of intellectualism and self-consciousness, which is at variance with the Theatre of the Unexpressed. The disparity between dreams and reality forms the subject of *L'Invitation au voyage*, one of the most typical examples of the " silent " school. Here, however, the comparison between Philippe and Olivier and the subsequent identification of the ideal with a commonplace individual take place in the realm of the subconscious, and are unexpressed because the heroine is unaware of what has been going on in the depths of her mind. Sarment's hero is generally a romantic introspective, whose scepticism and irony arise from his awareness of the situation, and his discernment of incongruities. These are conscious intellectual activities which must be conveyed to the audience by the spoken word. The main theme which runs through Sarment's work is not emotion, which, as I have already indicated, is the basis of the *Théâtre de l'Inexprimé*, but the perception of a relationship between human behaviour and an ideal.

We must remember that the expression *Théâtre du Silence* which was coming into use in the early 1920's did not and could not at that period have the rigidity of a scientific term. It served as a convenient description for a type of intimate drama produced by certain theorists, and its use in connection with other plays producing a similar general impression was natural enough with contemporary critics, who, living in the turmoil of all this dramatic production, were concerned not, primarily, with literary classifications, but with examining and savouring the individual merits of each freshly created work as it presented itself, new and exciting, to the public.   In an article on Vildrac's *Madame Béliard*,[1] Benjamin Crémieux speaks of the " théâtre intimiste qu'on nomme souvent à tort le théâtre du silence ", and names as its representatives Charles Vildrac, Paul Géraldy, Jean-Jacques Bernard and Denys Amiel in his capacity of author of *La Souriante Madame Beudet*.   Surveying the scene from a suitable distance, we are in a more favourable position for distinguishing the different tendencies in the post-1918 French drama.   I think we can discern among the plays written in a more subdued key a type of work in which, by a special handling of the dialogue as well as by the use of pause, the essential thoughts or emotions which give the work its own peculiar quality and value are conveyed to the audience without actually being expressed in precise words.   The post-1918 *Théâtre de l'Inexprimé* is usually a *Théâtre Intimiste*, but not all plays of the *Théâtre Intimiste* could be justly claimed as representative of the *Théâtre de l'Inexprimé*.

Does Paul Géraldy's work come within the scope of our subject ? His most characteristic plays, *Aimer*, *Robert et Marianne* and *Christine*, express in dramatic form the intricacies of a sentimental relationship between husband and wife, which in his collection of poems *Toi et moi* delighted and still delights a vast and mainly female public.   John Palmer in his *Studies in the Contemporary Theatre* says that he continues the tradition of Porto-Riche, and this is true in so far as he takes for his subject not the striving, not the chase, but love itself, attained and stabilized in marriage.   Without the suggestion of morbidness and sensuality which runs through the plays of Porto-Riche, there is a similar analysis of the substance of married love, its develop-

---

[1] *La Nouvelle Revue Française*, 1st Dec. 1925, R.

ment and its variations as it clashes with character and personality. No considerations of a material nature intervene in the purely psychological action. The characters are rich, the women are idle, have no children and nothing to occupy their thoughts but their own sentimental problems. As with Porto - Riche, the characters of Géraldy are intelligent, lucid, fully aware of every nuance of emotion within them, and are capable of expressing it all with delicate subtlety. There is a hint of *marivaudage* in the dialogue, with this important difference : the characters of Marivaux employ their delicate art in elaborating intricate reasons to justify and reconcile with their amour-propre movements and passions of whose real nature they are often scarcely conscious, whereas Géraldy's introspectives probe into their hearts, lucidly examine and re-assess the quality of their love in an anxious desire to ascertain whether years and familiarity have not caused it to deteriorate. In Marivaux the essential is, as a rule, undiscovered and unexpressed until the last moment. All the piquancy, as well as the human truth in the delicate word-play, derives from the emotions which it masks. Géraldy's efforts are directed to the task of seizing the emotion itself and fixing it in words. Nothing is left unsaid, every grain of sentiment is weighed and assessed, and it is this that places his three most important plays outside the range of the " silent " group.

One play, however, merits our attention on account of its subject matter and a certain aspect of its technique. *Les Grands Garçons* [1] develops a theme which had been touched upon in *Les Noces d'argent*,[2] the shyness and reserve which makes it difficult for parent and child to confide in one another. Jacques Pélissier and his father love and admire each other. They each try to communicate their feelings, but always choose the wrong moments, and their tactlessness and irritation invariably result in a quarrel. Consequently neither realizes the other's affection.

---

[1] First performed 18th Nov. 1922, but written five years previously, according to a contemporary critic, Maurice Bex—cutting dated 12th Nov. 1922, dossier of Paul Géraldy, R.

[2] First performance 5th May 1917.

The author contrives that both in turn unburden themselves to Dureux, Jacques' friend. Dureux's advice takes effect. They decide to make another attempt at a rapprochement but it results in the usual misunderstanding and outburst of temper, and Jacques' slamming the door. We witness the emotion of the father, left alone. But Jacques returns, makes a supreme effort, awkwardly shows his father his sweetheart's letter, and the two are soon affectionately embracing one another.

Although the play is based on that natural reserve which raises a psychological barrier between two people, it is hardly in the true sense a play of the Unexpressed, since the two main characters express themselves at some length to the confidant. The reserve which the father shows in the presence of his own son is absent when he is with another boy of the same age, although the disparity in years should have imposed it with equal force. The whole of this scene is unrealistic, embarrassing and distasteful. The presence of the confidant would not necessarily remove the play from the class of the Unexpressed. The essence of the matter lies, however, in the nature of the reserve which forms the theme of the play. In the case of Martine or Arvers in Bernard's plays, reticence is a quality of the soul, a reverent quietude of the spirit in the presence of love, as a man stands awed in a cathedral. Speech to the uncomprehending would violate its purity and diminish their own natures. Reticence is with them a positive quality. In this play it is negative, a matter of nerves, a kind of psychological paralysis arising mainly from fear and shame. In the father's long speech to Dureux the author (unintentionally, it would appear) allows Monsieur Pélissier to reveal the chief reason for the unsatisfactory relationship—his own selfishness. He has made little effort to win over the difficult, turbulent small boy, the lanky, indolent " bachelier ", the somnolent youth on military service, always short of money. But the sight of his son, now in the flower of manhood, having sloughed off the less attractive qualities, startles him into the realization that here is a rich source of affection, comradeship and sympathy.

And this shock of discovery is complicated by a suggestion of admiration, fear and dismay, for his son whom he had trained in boxing has recently shown himself physically superior. To Jacques, on the other hand, his father has never ceased to be a distant, intimidating person. Hero-worship is combined with the persistence of the initial defensive attitude. Even more fundamental with the son is that paralysing sense of shame at the thought of displaying intimate feelings to a near blood relation which in many people is as compelling as the sex taboo within the family, if indeed the two are not somehow connected. This is indicated by the tremendous effort Jacques has to make at the very end, in order, we cannot help feeling, that the play may have the dénouement the audience would welcome.

What silence there is in this play does not emanate from a deeply felt emotion left unexpressed through a choice made with all the strength of a quiet nature, which is the case with Bernard when the emotion is consciously experienced, but is a nervous reflex, due to a psychological maladjustment in which fear and shame play an important part. In *Martine* the silence of the heroine, never to be broken, is full of beauty and pathos, and satisfying in itself. Here the audience is caught by the contagion of irritation and distress, and fervently longs for the embarrassing situation to come to an end. One critic points out the symbolism in the scene where father and son try to approach one another and each from his side pulls at the door with no result. The action is slightly ridiculous, but certainly does, in a way, indicate the futile expenditure of nervous energy which is the principal impression left by the piece. Its length (it consists of one act) and the arbitrary conclusion which the author imposes on it both add to the feeling that Géraldy has scarcely succeeded in drawing authentic dramatic material from this kind of silence. Since, apart from this play, Géraldy's talents lie rather in the direction of subtle exactitude of expression, his work must remain outside the limits of our study.

It is comparatively easy to establish the fact that an author does not belong to the *Théâtre de l'Inexprimé* when, as in the case of Sarment or Géraldy, he shows recognizable characteristics of the Theatre of the Expressed. Much more difficult is the problem of the " subdued " plays where no such characteristics clearly appear. How is one to draw, as it were, a line of demarcation in order to determine whether the spirit of quietude and the suggestive power of the dialogue, varying in each, are used in sufficient strength to justify consideration as examples of this group ? In many cases the elements contributing to create the impression of " silence " are vague, intangible, incapable of analysis. It is tempting to facilitate our task by leaving out all writers who did not consciously experiment with the Unexpressed, and in whose work accordingly the Unexpressed does not show clearly as a deliberately chosen means of expression. Yet it seems that an examination of this " borderline " theatre is of considerable value in enabling us not only to situate the *Théâtre de l'Inexprimé* in the contemporary French theatre, but also to enrich our understanding of the school by considering its use of silence and the Unexpressed. We shall therefore turn our attention to Charles Vildrac, mentioned by Crémieux as being one of the " intimiste " dramatists, and by other contemporary critics as a member of the " silent " school. Certain of his plays show in a particularly concentrated form much of the quiet beauty and spiritual conception of everyday life which radiate from the work of Maeterlinck and Bernard, while his dialogue is often rich in overtones and pregnant pauses. If he does not fit so tidily into the group as the formalist would wish, a study of certain aspects of the Unexpressed in his work is a useful preliminary to our examination of Amiel and Bernard, the more orthodox representatives of the post-1918 movement.

CHAPTER VI

CHARLES VILDRAC

IT is impossible to consider Charles Vildrac without first speaking of the Abbaye de Créteil which he helped to found in 1906.[1] Though of short duration, it left a rich spiritual legacy to its members, and lived on in their finest work, much of which was produced after the First World War.

The Abbaye was an act of faith, a gesture against the materialism of the age, the sordid struggle for existence and the worship of the Golden Calf mordantly described by Romain Rolland in *La Foire sur la place*.[2] Here, like the Thelemites of Rabelais, a community of thinking men were to live and work fraternally together. The lease of an old house with an overgrown park was signed by René Arcos, Georges Duhamel, Albert Gleizes, Henri Martin and Charles Vildrac, and on the front door were inscribed the verses of Rabelais :

> Cy entrez, vous, et bien soyez venuz . . .
>
> . . . . .
>
> Ceans aurez un refuge et bastille
> Contre l'hostile erreur, qui tant postille
> Par son faulx stile empoizonner le monde ;
> Entrez, qu'on fonde icy la foy profonde . . .
>
> . . . . .
>
> Cy n'entrez pas, hypocrites, bigotz,
> Vieulx matagotz, marmiteux borsouflez.

Printing was to help to supply the material wants of the members. The printer Linard taught them his trade and with

[1] The idea of the Abbaye originated with Vildrac. *Vide* C. Sénéchal, *L'Abbaye de Créteil* (1930), pp. 18-19.
[2] Cf. C. Sénéchal, *op. cit.* p. 14.

I

their own press they produced twenty volumes. The young Jules Romains, still at the École Normale, brought them the manuscript of *La Vie unanime*. The experiment lasted fourteen months ; its failure, says René Arcos,[1] was due to youth, lack of discipline and difference of aims.

René Arcos declares that there was never any question of a literary " school " with a common doctrine. Individualism, freedom to develop in a congenial atmosphere stimulated by fraternal affection and untrammelled by considerations of a material nature, were the guiding inspiration of the Abbaye. It was not, as some people imagined, a chapel for the philosophy of unanimism. " Nous admirions les poèmes de Romains sans les discuter," said Albert Gleizes, " car si quelques points généraux nous rapprochaient, nous étions si foncièrement individualistes que le désir de liberté nous liait encore plus dans l'œuvre abba-tiale même." [2]

While noting that the Abbaye was not a literary school, M.-L. Bidal in her book *Les Écrivains de l'Abbaye* [3] detects a spiritual " atmosphere " and a similarity of ideas. For M.-L. Bidal the Abbaye marks a phase of assimilation and synthesis in French literary history. Contemporary writers, she points out, were reacting against the vagueness and remoteness of symbolism and the abstract nature of its analogies, and exerted every effort to come to grips with life, to savour directly its harsh but ex-hilarating qualities. The crude mechanical approach of the Naturalists did not satisfy them, but from naturalism they in-herited a taste for accurate observation and objective truth, while symbolism bequeathed them its preoccupation with the secret life of the soul, and also the instrument of sensation with which they endeavoured to reach the heart of things.

An affinity is noted between the ideas of the Abbaye and those of Maeterlinck expressed in *Le Trésor des humbles*. The mystery and beauty of everyday life and humble creatures, the attempt to

---

[1] Note forming an appendix to the *Histoire de la littérature française contemporaine* (1925), by René Lalou.   [2] Quoted by C. Sénéchal, *op. cit.* p. 66.   [3] 1938.

penetrate its hidden truths in " le silence efficace et la contemplation créatrice ",[1] the silent understanding of souls in the mysterious regions beyond physical realities, all find an echo in the work of the various members of the Abbaye.

Whitman, with his exuberant love of life, his reaching out to his fellow men, his lyrical apotheosis of friendship, is said to have had a considerable influence on the writers of the Abbaye, but the seeds of love and friendship were already there. " Une influence ", says Benjamin Crémieux, " n'est, en somme, que la cristallisation d'un besoin latent au contact d'un agent extérieur." [2] This affirmation of life, this religious exaltation of living it to the full, were related in some ways to the philosophy of Nietzsche, in others to the ideas of William James. Bergson's philosophy was, as M.-L. Bidal points out, at the basis of their ideas of " perception immédiate ", their desire to grasp reality from within by living it, instead of surveying it intellectually in the traditional style, and their linking of souls with each other and with the universe.

Before we proceed to examine Vildrac's plays, a glance at two of the unanimistic plays of Jules Romains would be useful. Although Jules Romains has not been classed among the dramatists of the Unexpressed, his use of the pause in his two great dramatic poems *L'Armée dans la ville* [3] and *Cromedeyre-le-Vieil* [4] is not without interest to our study.

The philosophy of Unanimism, which suffuses these plays, is based on the Bergsonian conception of a continuous psychic

---

[1] Title of a chapter of Duhamel in *Les Poètes et la poésie*, quoted by M.-L. Bidal, *op. cit.* p. 109.

[2] *Inquiétude et reconstruction* (1931), p. 207. M.-L. Bidal emphasizes the influence of Whitman on the writers of the Abbaye (*op. cit.* pp. 54-66). We must, however, take into consideration an article, " Talks with French Poets in 1913-14 " (*French Studies*, July 1948), by P. Mansell Jones, who recalls interviews he was given when collecting material for a study of Whitman's influence on modern French poets. He states that Vildrac resented the word " influence " and preferred *rapprochement* or *concordance*. His *Livre d'amour* was written before he had read Bazalgette's translation [which appeared in 1909], and none of the poets Vildrac knew could read Whitman in the original. Romains' *Vie unanime* was published before the translations appeared. But Vildrac admitted it possible that Whitman had had some effect on his *Découvertes*.

[3] First performed 4th Mar. 1911.   [4] Written 1911-18, performed 1920.

stream ; Romains imagines that individual souls, far from being separate and, as it were, hermetically closed, are a dynamic part of this stream. From it they may, by a conscious effort, enrich themselves and draw fresh energy, and through it they may not only communicate with each other, but prolong themselves over space and time. The formation of the group creates something new, different and more intense than each of its separate components. The spirit of the stable group, such as the town or the military camp, is richer and deeper than that of casual shifting encounters, and the group souls—Romains calls them Gods—take their place in the hierarchy of unanimism according to the degree of self-awareness they succeed in attaining.

On this philosophy of unanimism Romains builds a new theory of the drama. In his preface to *L'Armée dans la ville* he maintains that all dramatic work animates groups. " Au cours d'une pièce, ce qu'on appelle une scène, qu'est-ce d'autre que la vie d'un groupe précaire et ardente ? Un acte est une filiation de groupes. Le spectateur les voit qui se succèdent, se combattent, se pénètrent, s'engendrent." So far, says Romains, the couple has been the only group which the theatre has seized in its original unity and true nature. The dramatist must go farther than this and represent the crowd in action.

In *L'Armée dans la ville* [1] the town is occupied by the soldiers whom the people loathe. The townswomen concert and threaten to give themselves to the soldiers if the men do not band together and kill them. So powerful is the spirit of the town and the army that their individual components have no clear identity and no proper names. As with the strokes of a brush, line by line their talk builds up the picture of the group to which they belong. The brooding pauses of the townsfolk talking in the inn not only allow the audience to savour the solemn beauty of the dialogue, but in a sense bind together the members of the group. They

---

[1] Émile Verhaeren's " collective " drama *Les Aubes* is interesting as a precursor to *L'Armée dans la ville*, but I do not find in it the type of silence used by Romains and intimately bound up with his group philosophy.

speak for the most part dreamily, even lyrically ; the silences allow the spoken word to penetrate deeply to the others and reinforce the spirit of solidarity which already exists. *Cromedeyre-le-Vieil*, a rocky, ancient, savage village, lacks women. Its men descend to the gentle Laussonne, carry off fifteen girls and win them over to the Cromedeyre spirit. This drama is written in majestic verse, and again the frequent pauses, natural to these slow-thinking villagers, complement the august dignity of the poetry and harden into granite the sense of unity among the inhabitants of Cromedeyre.

In neither case, however, do the silences express a new development in action or a psychological transformation. These plays are based not on emotion but on instinct, the herd instinct, a direct elemental tendency to action which in Jules Romains is unrepressed, uncomplicated by conflicts. The fact that the mayor's wife loves the general does not for a moment deflect her from her course. Soldiers, quarrelling among themselves, cease, join forces, re-form the group, in order that they may humiliate a party of civilians just arrived. Strong natural forces are coming into play, but they are as simple as winds and tides, and their silences have only the beauty of an echo. The authentic Theatre of the Unexpressed is based on emotion, which disturbs and, as it were, modulates the human psyche, and often gives rise to unconscious conflicts—rich sources of dramatic interest. Again, the striking effects in the Unexpressed obtained by Maeterlinck and Bernard are connected with a negative attitude towards reality, an endeavour to escape from it or to ward off forces of evil. With Romains the attitude is positive—exaltation of life, plunging into the heart of it, living it to the full and sharing experiences with joy. Moreover, with Romains the instinct of solidarity is conscious. As I pointed out, conscious creative effort is an important aspect of his philosophy. " Si tu doutes de l'unanime, crée-le." [1] Accordingly his characters are self-conscious and repeatedly put their awareness of unity into words.

---

[1] *Manuel de déification*, p. 62, quoted by M.-L. Bidal, *op. cit.* p. 188.

Qu'on ferme la porte !
Rien de notre âme ne doit se perdre. . . .[1]

Laissez-vous saisir par notre joie.
Cromedeyre entre en vous longuement.
Ouvrez vos songes,
        Ouvrez vos veines,
Qu'y passe le feu des anciens jours ![2]

In spite of the interesting use of the pause these two dramas are, as we can see, essentially of the Theatre of the Expressed.

Let us now examine the work of Vildrac. The first productions of this writer (born in 1882) were in verse : *Poèmes*, 1905 ; *Images et mirages*, 1907, a collection of poems including *L'Abbaye*, printed on the Abbaye's own press, and republished in 1925 with some additions under the title *Poèmes de l'Abbaye* ; *Livre d'amour*, 1910, augmented in 1914; and *Chants du désespéré*, inspired by the First World War, in 1920. Vildrac's poetry is imbued with the ideals of the Abbaye—a deep love of his fellow men, especially of the humble artisans amongst whom he was brought up in Paris and in whose rough sincerity he detects the true accents of unsophisticated humanity. In his *Livre d'amour* love in its most universal sense is for him the solution to life's problems and the goal of the true artist.

Et nous essaierons d'ouvrir tous les yeux,
Et de greffer l'amour au cœur des hommes.[3]

Les Conquérants of whom he sings are those who conquer men's hearts through fraternal love. A quiet note of optimism, of faith in the regeneration of humanity by love, pervades his poetry. The disaster of 1914 with its brutal destruction of the fabric of human love brings a temporary feeling of despair.

Je voudrais avoir été
Le premier soldat tombé
Le premier jour de la guerre.[4]

---

[1] *L'Armée dans la ville* (1911), p. 12.   [2] *Cromedeyre-le-Vieil*, Act V, sc. 5.
[3] *Images et mirages* : " L'Abbaye, I ".
[4] *Chants du désespéré* : " Chant d'un fantassin ".

But throughout there is never any bitterness against the enemy, and his faith in the power of love persists. For Europe there will be one day

> . . . un seul destin, un amour, un arbre ! [1]

With this deep love of his fellow men is joined a desire for life which forms the theme of his play *Le Pèlerin*. He is weary of gazing inwards.

> Quels purs poètes sommes-nous :
> Au chaud musée de notre chambre. . . .
> Il y a là-bas des mers folles
> Et des cieux fous et des voiles folles,
> Il y a là-bas de fous bateaux.[2]

Découvertes,[3] except for a short one-act play, is a series of prose essays and anecdotes with the rhythm and music of poetry, its main inspiration being that of the *Livre d'amour*—the invisible bonds which link man to man, and man's affinity with nature. In some of the anecdotes, for example *La Récréation*, where the friendly horseplay of workmen attracts a crowd of onlookers and the euphoria created by sympathetic laughter not only links these complete strangers but leavens their souls and influences the acts of their day, we are reminded of the ideas of Jules Romains.

The quiet style and the content of Vildrac's poetry both in verse and prose, with its tendency to a kind of restrained sentimentality, have a certain affinity with Bernard's works, and it is not difficult to see in the anecdotal works a stage of development where, perhaps subconsciously, the author is beginning to grope towards an " intimiste " theatre. *En revenant* is a potential one-act play. A man and a woman meet, and each senses the other's interest, although only banal phrases have been exchanged. " Mais je le sens, je le sais ", says the woman on returning.

> Sûrement, entre nous deux,
> Quelque chose est commencé !

---

[1] *Chants du désespéré*: "Europe".
[2] *Livre d'amour* : " Commentaire ". [3] 1912.

> Sûrement, c'est aujourd'hui,
> — Car me voici trop contente —
> C'est aujourd'hui ce départ
> Que j'attendais, que j'attendais !

Let them only meet again and establish a real communication. But when they do meet

> Des gens s'amassèrent entre eux
> Comme un bois entre deux chaumières,
> Les empêchant de se rejoindre
> Fût-ce avec leurs yeux. . . . [1]

The stress of the outside world has been too great for this incipient love based on instinctive attraction.

Another poem *Visite* [2] actually forms the basis of *L'Indigent*, an early one-act play, contained in *Découvertes*. A man sitting cosily by his lamp as the snow falls outside suddenly remembers his repeated promise to visit a humble couple.

> Mais un ordre intérieur
> Le fit tressaillir soudain.

He goes through the snow to visit them

> Après les premières paroles,
> Lorsqu'il fut assis dans la lumière
> Entre cet homme et sa compagne
> Tous deux surpris et empressés,
> Il s'aperçut qu'on lui ménageait
> Ces silences qui interrogent
> Et font comme du blanc qu'on laisse
> A dessein parmi l'écriture.

Suddenly he understands their uneasiness. They cannot believe that he has come just for them; what service is he going to ask? Thus he is spiritually separated from them until it is time for him to leave.

> Alors ils osèrent comprendre ;
> Il n'était venu que pour eux !

---

[1] *Livre d'amour* (1914 edition).   [2] *Ibid.* (1910 edition).

Their joy overflows into rapid speech, and they try to make up for lost time. He promises to return but finds himself imprinting in his mind the image of the couple, the room and everything in it

> Tant il craignait au fond de lui
> De ne plus jamais revenir.

Although this poem with its speaking silences and its pre-occupation with the instinctive reaching out of one soul towards another appears to be a " silent " play in embryo, *L'Indigent* itself is from the point of view of technique scarcely representative of the *Théâtre de l'Inexprimé*. It shows the weaknesses of one who has not yet learned the métier of the dramatist ; the transition from poetry is not quite successfully effected. The interest is focused in this version of the story upon the friendless Toussaint, and the first part of the play is virtually a monologue, the wife acting as a colourless confidante, and the servant an obvious piece of machinery for getting Thibaut out of the room while the couple can hurriedly speculate on the possible reasons for his coming. Toussaint is an introspective. ". . . je n'ai jamais osé être assez familier." ". . . je ne me donne pas assez. Mon cœur se crispe trop sur ce qu'il contient. . . ." There is a kind of spoken rêverie, reminiscent of the drama of Chekhov with its similar pauses, but confined to one character and lacking the poetic, psychological cross-currents of the Russian author. Thibaut, the visitor, is round-faced, jovial, lively and full of kindness, superficial in comparison with the unnamed man in *Visite*. It is because his character is not drawn with the same depth and loving pity as that of Toussaint that *L'Indigent* fails to qualify as a work of the " silent " school. The characteristic silent communication we find in the works of Bernard cannot in the same way be established between two creatures on different psychological levels.

Le Paquebot Tenacity [1] is Vildrac's most striking contribution to the Theatre of the Unexpressed. The scene of the play is set

---

[1] Written 1919, first performed 6th Mar. 1920.

in a small workmen's restaurant in a seaport. "Au fond, les vitrines et la porte d'entrée ouverte, avec une vue sur un bassin encombré de navires. . . ." One is reminded of the symbolic door or window recurring in Maeterlinck. Two young workmen have arrived from Paris, intending to embark next morning on the steamer *Tenacity*, bound for Canada, where a new life of pioneer farming awaits them. It is Bastien, strong-willed, confident and enterprising, who, tired of conditions in a war weary Paris, has persuaded his dreamy, hesitant friend to take the bold step. Owing to a fault in her engines the *Tenacity*, however, must remain another fortnight in port. During their enforced stay at the inn, each of the friends is attracted to Thérèse, the pretty servant. While drawn to the timid poetic Ségard, Thérèse is unable to resist the bolder advances of Bastien, who, although at first intending the incident to be a casual adventure, soon finds himself captivated. And as Thérèse will not go to Canada, the two secretly go off when the time comes for the *Tenacity* to depart, ironically leaving Ségard, the dreamy, nostalgic one, to embark alone for the conquest of the new world.

Vildrac makes liberal use of the pause in this play. As in *Cromedeyre-le-Vieil*, it has the obvious effect of rendering with a kind of poetic realism slow-thinking workmen and sailors meditating between bouts of talk and drinking. In addition it emphasizes character by enabling actors and spectators to muse upon a revealing phrase, and, placed as they are at significant points, these silences serve to mark a new turning-point in events, a new stage in the psychological action. In the first act, Bastien has informed all present in the inn of the departure for Canada, emphasizing his own will-power and initiative in launching the project. The crowd muses for a short spell. When the English sailor has announced that the *Tenacity* will not, after all, be sailing on the appointed day, there is another pause to mark the new situation, and the question it asks. A chord has been struck and awaits to be resolved. A minor dramatic tension is achieved. Bastien, attracted physically to Thérèse, confidentially asks his friend if he has not made any advances to the girl, and Ségard, without looking at Bastien, makes a gesture signifying no. The slight silence following emphasizes Ségard's timidity, his habitual hesitation, his feeling of powerlessness in the presence of a stronger will; it marks a contrast between the spontaneous dreams he has dreamed aloud to Thérèse and his reserve in the presence of one who, although nominally a friend, has really nothing in common with him. It also points forward to Bastien's attempt to win over Thérèse. In Act II, scene 5, there is the silent tension as Thérèse puts away the glasses and tidies up before closing the inn, and an eloquent moment of silence at the end of the scene when she is on the point of yielding to Bastien but is still thinking of Ségard.

Even more interesting is the use of these pauses to render the psychological interaction between two characters : the transference of idea or suggestion from one to another, and the leaven working in the mind of the second, ready at that particular stage to receive it. In Act II, scene 3, Hidoux, the drunken philosopher, maintains to Bastien that Canada does not really mean freedom. Have not Bastien and Ségard contracted themselves to the Société Agricole which has lent them money and towards which they will have obligations ? . . . " Et tes récoltes, et tes troupeaux, tu verras à qui tu les vendras, à qui tu seras forcé de les vendre ! Comme par hasard le bateau qui les amènera ici sera toujours le Tenacity. . . ." He slowly empties his glass and Bastien sits pensive, his elbows on the table. In that moment operates the psychological change to which his desire for Thérèse has made him receptive. Hidoux's arguments are stored up and repeated to Thérèse by a man now exercised in justifying his actions to himself.[1] Similarly, for all his hesitancy, Ségard's sensitive poetic nature has left its mark on Thérèse, and even under the sway of her passion for Bastien, it is to Ségard that her thoughts keep recurring, when she is about to yield. After the short silence which I mentioned above she says : " Alors, il faut me promettre

[1] Act III, sc. 1.

de ne pas le dire.   De ne pas le dire à Ségard. . . . C'est à cause de Ségard que j'ai de l'inquiétude."

This receptivity of one soul to the message of another is a theme which runs through Vildrac's poetry and recurs in his one-act play *Le Pèlerin*. There is, as we have already indicated, some affinity with the unanimistic ideas of Jules Romains. *Donogoo*, for example, another play of Romains, is a striking study of mass suggestion through which a purely illusionary city becomes a reality. Here the individual, uniting himself with a group, desires to accept the group illusion, and believes because he wants to believe. There is a kind of wordless communication between the individuals as there is unity among the cells of a single organism. Jules Romains, however, proceeds from a pre-conceived group philosophy of which his work is a demonstra-tion, whereas Vildrac, like Bernard, approaches sympathetically the human being himself and thinks in terms of the individual. For him every man possesses a reserve of love and goodness which forms common ground between him and his fellow man, and enables him to respond when another reaches out to him, however hesitantly. This stage is not far removed from that of the " communication directe " of Maeterlinck and Bernard.

Vildrac does not go so far as Bernard in endeavouring to suggest by the Unexpressed the workings of hidden subconsious desires in conflict with the conscious life. Bastien and Ségard are, for the most part, lucid enough and analyse their own natures, Ségard even with a degree of subtlety and in a literary style uncommon in a working-class man :

> Moi, comprenez-vous, je m'accroche toujours au présent, voilà mon malheur.   C'est comme si une corde me filait dans les mains, tirée par une grande force. Je la serre, je retiens, quitte à me faire peler les mains.   Ce n'est pas moi qui la guide, la corde, c'est elle qui me bouscule et me secoue.
> Bastien est plus fort que moi. Il peut décider sa vie.
> Il a décidé pour moi, et j'aime mieux ça. Je vois clair dans les projets d'un autre, je sais s'ils sont bons ou mauvais. Mais

je ne sais adopter aucuns des miens. D'abord, je ne fais pas de projets, moi, je fais des espèces de rêves.[1]

This self-consciousness is not, however, like that of the group components in *L'Armée dans la ville* or *Cromedeyre-le-Vieil*. These are keenly aware of a vital world principle, evident and unquestioned, enfolding them from without, submerging their identity, responding at the same time to something already existing within, but simple and elemental, whereas Ségard, describing with accuracy the workings of his nature, still contrives to give an impression of the mystery of human personality. Characteristically Ségard is most voluble when speaking of the past, and Bastien when speaking of the future. Hidoux too possesses a marked degree of lucidity and analyses and explains the position with a certain finesse of expression.

The irony of the situation at the end has great dramatic force. Bastien's very boldness and self-confidence give him the courage to make the less adventurous choice, while Ségard's timidity and " peur de vivre " involve him in greater hazards. In both cases events are stronger than human beings, and it seems that Vildrac would have us believe that free choice is illusory. At the beginning of the play he quotes this sentence from Rabelais : " Les destinées mènent celuy qui consent, tirent celuy qui refuse ". A degree of determinism is implicit in the Theatre of the Unexpressed. We have seen this in the static drama of Maeterlinck, and we shall discuss it from another angle when dealing with the work of Bernard. In *Le Paquebot Tenacity*, the most characteristic example of Vildrac's " silent " plays, the fatality lies mainly in the nature of the individual ; at the same time, the author appears to echo Maeterlinck's idea of an invisible force silently influencing human beings. Hidoux in his cups expresses a deterministic philosophy. " Comme par hasard le bateau qui les amènera ici sera toujours le Tenacity."[2] "Et puis souvent, tu sais, quand on décide, on ne fait qu'obéir à la force des choses et alors on n'exécute qu'à la dernière extrémité, car le cours des

---

[1] Act II, sc. 1.　　　　　　[2] Act II, sc. 3.

événements peut des fois changer. . . ." [1] But he leaves room for an effort of will. " Oui. Il arrive que tu puisses choisir, si tu l'oses! Sinon, le courant choisit pour toi. . . ." [2] Apart from this play, there is no background of determinism to Vildrac's work. He has the faith of the Abbaye in the regeneration of mankind by love, a faith which implies a measure of free will, and even in his most pessimistic play L'Air du temps this faint possibility of regeneration is always present. This more energetic approach to human problems explains why his drama shades off into that of the Expressed.

Timidity, " peur de vivre ", a desire to escape from hard reality into a world of dreams, are manifest in Le Paquebot Tenacity as in the most characteristic plays of Bernard. Everyday life must continually impinge upon these escapist dreams and break the spell of the silence. Thérèse is captivated by Ségard's day-dreams. " Je vois une petite maison au soleil, quelque chose comme une maison de garde-barrière ; pas au Canada ", he adds, betraying himself ; an attraction is growing up without direct expression. But Madame Cordier the innkeeper recalls her to her duties. When Ségard leaves the inn to embark on the Tenacity, Madame Cordier stands silently on the threshold, and watches his departure. But life goes on ; new customers come in, and soon she is bustling round them.

It is unnecessary to dwell on Michel Auclair,[3] which has faults of technique and has little in common with the group we are studying, except that it deals with Vildrac's favourite theme of the influence for good of one human being on others. The hero talks too much, and the author himself later admits this defect.[4]

Le Pèlerin [5] expresses that yearning to live life to the full which we have already noted in Vildrac's poetry. Madame Dentin and her eldest daughter, narrow-minded " dévotes ",

[1] Act III, sc. 3. [2] Ibid.
[3] Written in 1919, first performed 21st Dec. 1922.
[4] C. H. Bissell, introduction to his edition of Michel Auclair (1941).
[5] First performed 14th Dec. 1923.

are " des êtres qui ne vivent pas et qui n'aiment pas la vie. Ils attendent la mort derrière leur fenêtre fermée en disant du mal de leurs voisins. Ils sont incapables de véritable joie, de véritable amour. . . ." Desavesnes, Madame Dentin's brother, one who loves life and has lived it to the full, makes a last pilgrimage to his home before leaving the country, in order to recapture memories of his childhood and especially of his adored mother, whose vitality and imagination he has inherited. He is met by Denise, the younger girl, who, as he sees, takes after his mother and resembles himself in character, and in her he kindles a love of real life, suggesting ways and means for her to contrive a visit to Paris in order to enrich her experience. When Madame Dentin and Henriette return, the reunion is soured by sisterly reproaches and delvings into the past. After the brother has left, Madame Dentin and Henriette begin to discuss Church affairs. Denise lets fall a question about her cousin in Paris, and daydreams, leaning with her elbows on the table. The seeds which her uncle has sown in her mind are germinating, and a horizon of new hope is suggested to us. In her silent rêverie we see once more the working of her uncle's personality. A loving gift of life and hope has been made from one human being to another. Employing the expressive device of recalling the past, the uncle to his niece, the brother and sister to each other, the author works up to the silent climax which is the effect of that past and of the uncle's personality on Denise, who in the final scene dreamily orientates herself to the new life.

Perhaps the most striking character in the play is one who does not appear at all, Desavesnes' late mother, whose joyous ardour and sprightly imagination rise vividly from the loving reminiscences of her son. The unseen character is not confined to the *École du Silence*. One thinks of the personality of Napoleon brooding over Rostand's *L'Aiglon*. But it is by nature in harmony with the style and content of the *Théâtre de l'Inexprimé*. Maeterlinck by the unseen queen of *La Mort de Tintagiles* symbolizes the horror and dread of death. Bernard uses the unseen actor to precipitate a crisis in human relationships [1] or a psychological conflict within one individual.[2] Here the memory of Madame Desavesnes, who lives again in her son, creates a silent change in the heart of Denise. Madame Desavesnes symbolizes joy in life, and by her influence we see that the bonds which link humanity extend not only over space through the present moment but also from the past over to the present.

In *Madame Béliard* [3] Robert Saulnier, the engineer and manager of a dyeing establishment, loves Pauline Béliard, the widowed proprietor, with all the force of a passionate nature. She, valuing his friendship, and grateful for his devoted services after the death of her husband, can give in return only calm affection. Incapable of seeing him suffer, loath to lose his friendship and perhaps with the unconfessed desire to retain his valuable services, she yields to him and becomes his mistress. " Dès que je vois souffrir, pleurer quelqu'un, je suis perdue . . . ," she says in a later act ; pusillanimity surely never went farther, and the strain imposed on our credulity and sympathy considerably weakens the effectiveness of this play.

Saulnier is silently adored by Madame Béliard's niece, Madeleine, who misinterprets emotion he has shown with Madame Béliard in mind and jumps to the conclusion that he loves her. She confides in her aunt who, powerless before another's suffering, does not enlighten her, nor does she discourage her. It is through a mutual friend that Saulnier learns of Madeleine's devotion. Amazed, shocked and cruelly grieved when Madame Béliard's attitude at last becomes clear, he can no longer deceive himself as to the true nature of her sentiments or the fundamental falsity of their relationship, and he leaves her with sorrow and dignity. Madeleine, who has learned out of devotion to serve him, is to take his place as manager and her love will find a narrow outlet in the fervent continuance of his work.

Fortunat Strowski, after calling the play a modern *Bérénice*

---

[1] *Le Feu qui reprend mal.*   [2] *L'Invitation au voyage.*
[3] Written 1924, first performed 9th Oct. 1925.

(the comparison is somewhat strained), sums up as follows :
" C'est le drame de deux êtres qui se chérissent, mais à des étages
différents ; ils s'unissent, mais ne s'accordent pas. L'un ' aime '.
L'autre ' aime beaucoup '. Ils s'en aperçoivent sous la brusque
illumination d'un troisième amour, d'une qualité supérieure.
Alors ils se quittent, malgré eux, comme on quitte la vie." [1]

Like other plays of the *Théâtre de l'Inexprimé*, *Madame
Béliard* is a tragedy of misunderstanding, of the impossibility of
communion between beings isolated by their own natures. As in
Bernard's *Nationale 6*, but more movingly here, the characters,
absorbed in their own dreams of happiness, seize upon words and
phrases and interpret them in accordance with their secret heartfelt
desire. The " silent " effects, less striking than in *Le Paquebot
Tenacity* and *Le Pèlerin*, are, so to speak, of a negative type.

Saulnier, for example, is a lyrical character. When he is
roused to passionate declaration or bitter reproach, his words
illustrate the " lyrisme exact " of Bataille. At the same time,
however, the author contrives to indicate moments of deep mental
strife and uneasiness, not by the dialogue, but by the reaction
to the pressing necessities of everyday life. When Madeleine
casually mentions that the piece Madame Béliard is playing was
the favourite of her late uncle, Saulnier's uneasiness betrays itself,
after a moment of silence, in a torrent of voluble instructions
to an employee over the telephone. His shock and dismay on
hearing of Madeleine's love for him finds its outlet in a burst of
annoyance when an employee brings in calculations on which
Madeleine has devotedly spent the whole evening. " De quoi se
mêle-t-elle. . . . Voilà un travail aux trois quarts inutile."
Silently agitated when left alone, as soon as Madeleine appears he
seizes his pen, begins to write and meets her tentative questions
with taciturnity. And after his final explanation with Madame
Béliard, when an old busybody of a work-woman comes in to
make trouble with the staff, his reactions are first absent-minded-
ness and then excessive exasperation.

[1] *Paris-Midi*, quoted by *La Petite Illustration* of 21st Nov. 1925.

The " silence " of Madame Béliard from which the action rises is neither admirable nor tragic. From facile pity and moral cowardice springs a vague self-deception which enables her, with the best intentions in the world, temporarily to cheat Saulnier and give false encouragement to Madeleine. The self-deception is superficial ; her uneasy glances at the door in the midst of Saulnier's passionate love-making speak for themselves. Weakness of character and lack of deep feeling, added to a morbid consideration for others, amount in effect to a kind of absent-minded selfishness. With a lamentable lack of foresight she creates, by her failure to speak frankly, a tragic situation which is dramatically unsatisfactory, since, at the fall of the curtain, the uneasy spectator is confronted with the new problem of what will henceforth be the life of these two women, left together after all that has passed between them.

Madeleine is the " silent ", intense type who will suffer inwardly. In the final scene she takes up a file of letters. " C'est le courrier. . . . Il m'a demandé d'y jeter un coup d'œil. . . ." These last revealing words on which the curtain falls point forward to a life of fervent toil in the factory which Saulnier has built up, the only way in which her reserved and passionate devotion can henceforth express itself.

In *Poucette*[1] Maurice, the foreman at a factory, falls in love with Yvonne, a work-girl. Through the malicious gossip of his landlady, who happens to find him alone in Yvonne's house, he discovers that before coming to the factory Yvonne had been a prostitute. Seeing the two together when she returns, Yvonne is terrified. She had frequently tried in the past to confess the truth about her previous existence, but could not bring herself to do so. Now, once more, she makes the painful effort. Full of pity and love, Maurice will not let her go on. " En tout cas, et quoi qu'il ait pu arriver, il est clair que, depuis qu'ils sont au monde, ces yeux-là n'ont jamais changé."

This short play, built on the refusal of a fine character to allow

[1] First performed 20th Feb. 1936, but dated 1924.

an ugly fact to be put into painful words, also puts a strain on the powers of belief. Yvonne is presented as a timid ingénue ; her eyes and mouth betray no signs of deterioration resulting from a dissolute life with the soldiers. It is difficult to believe that thoughts of such a lurid past will not return to haunt Maurice and trouble the purity of his love. But the piece is a moving expression of the faith of Vildrac in the regeneration of humanity through pity and love, and his belief in the essential purity of the soul, unsullied by acts of the body, is reminiscent of Maeterlinck. The play, based upon the conscious reticence of characters with a recognized secret between them, is of the type favoured by Denys Amiel in his doctrinaire play *Le Voyageur*. It is dramatically effective up to a point, but the fact that the secret is known and so near to the surface offers little opportunity for development and the possibilities of such material in both cases do not extend beyond one act. The development in Bernard's *Martine* is possible only because one of the characters, Julien, remains throughout the whole play in ignorance of Martine's secret. The Unexpressed is rich only when it remains at the level of the unconscious.

L'Air du temps[1] seems to shade off from the school of " silence " to the school of the Expressed. In an " avant-première " quoted by *La Petite Illustration*[2] the author describes his aims : " L'inconséquence, la faiblesse ou le laisser-faire, la trop grande facilité des mœurs, l'absence ou la fragilité du sens moral, une certaine inconscience dans la trahison, tous les traits qui marquent notre époque chaotique, et d'autre part le cynisme plus ou moins affecté, ce détachement, ce repli sur soi-même et peut-être ce désespoir que montrent certains jeunes gens, voilà ce que j'ai voulu peindre ".

Capellan, a sculptor of genius, embittered by his wife's infidelity, returns against his will to the corrupt atmosphere of Paris, only to discover later that he is being systematically cheated by his wife, to whom he had become reconciled, his business

[1] Written 1935, first performed 23rd Feb. 1938.   [2] 16th Apr. 1938.

agent and his own son. Out of the greatness of his heart he pardons, and with sad realism decides to continue the comedy.

More pessimistic and bitter than Vildrac's other works, the play nevertheless contains the idea of regeneration. In spite of the degradation of the characters, the shadow of a scruple, the faintest potentiality for good, is suggested.[1] Restrained in style, it has some of the features of the " silent " school. There is reserve and a certain sympathetic intuition. Paulette, for all her moral abasement, is sensitive to the good in Robert, her stepson, and detects sincere repentance veiled in the cynicisms of his letter to his father. The pause is used for realistic effect. In Act I, scene 2, the silences which punctuate the dialogue between Capellan and Devilder, the agent, who is trying to persuade him to return to Paris and be reconciled with his wife, effectively allow us to watch the doubts and the emotional conflict in the sculptor's mind. In Act III, scenes 2 and 4, Robert's preoccupation before making the decision to clear the memory of Capellan's friend, who has been unjustly suspected, is evident. But in general the silences are similar to those used in the conventional drama for simple effects of realism, and it would be a mistake to overstress their significance.

The other available plays by Vildrac are of the Expressed. We are not concerned with Le Jardinier de Samos,[2] which is a witty political satire. La Brouille [3] and Trois Mois de prison [4] do, however, contribute to our understanding of the dramatist. In the first we find the old Abbaye theme of virile friendship. This excellent comedy is particularly interesting as it illustrates in a work of the " silent " group a technique directly the converse of that of the Théâtre de l'Inexprimé : the gradual verbal elucidation of a complex psychological situation, classic in tradition, instead of the working up to a crisis of recognition or choice which takes place in silence, or is to be inferred from indirect

[1] Cf. J.-R. Bloch, quoted in La Petite Illustration, 16th Apr. 1938.
[2] Written 1930.
[3] Written 1930, first performed 1st Dec. 1930.
[4] Written 1938, first performed 23rd Feb. 1942.

language. The temporary estrangement based on wounded pride and repressed jealousy, not at all inconsistent with a fundamental and unshakable affection, forms the subject of discussion for each of the leading characters as well as for the others who, in their anxiety to reconcile the friends without loss of amour-propre on either side, analyse every aspect of the situation with considerable delicacy and subtlety and not a little *marivaudage*. Thus gradually, with expressive words, the subconscious hostility and the real and imaginary injuries are brought to the surface. The only point of similarity to the *Théâtre de l'Inexprimé* is the author's preoccupation with hidden and confused motives.

In *Trois Mois de prison* the author is concerned with simple, working-class people, hemmed in by a mean environment, and longing to escape into beauty. After a hard life, a young couple at last find this beauty when the husband is given the chance of taking over a barge on the Seine. This play of escape does not come into the *Théâtre de l'Inexprimé* mainly because, instead of the " fuite à l'intérieur ", the author envisages escape into another, more beautiful reality. The characters are simple, ordinary people, extroverts, if we may use the term, urged on by a sane desire for a practical life of modest beauty, the same desire which, years before, inspired the idea of the Abbaye. The notion of a practical goal—the barge travelling sleepily past the poplar trees, a little post-office, a farmer's life in Canada—keeps Vildrac's characters in closer touch with reality.

Maeterlinck, Bernard and Amiel have all in essay, article or introduction to plays defined a dramatic art based on the use of the Unexpressed, taking as a starting-point, in the case of Maeterlinck a philosophy of mysticism, in the case of Bernard a desire for truth and realism, in the case of Amiel an endeavour to detect passion beneath banal conversation. No pronouncements by Vildrac on the dramatic technique of the Unexpressed are available, and it seems as if he has been concerned with subject matter rather than form. His subdued theatre evolves naturally out of the quiet intimate verse which was his first form of expression and flowers out of his own fine character, enriched by the atmosphere of the Abbaye. *La Petite Illustration* [1] quotes the biographical note figuring on the programme of the Comédie des Champs-Élysées :

> Un visage presque sévère, quelque chose de fruste dans la voix et le geste, l'expression d'une nature rude, voilà ce que donne souvent Vildrac au premier abord, puis le ton de ses paroles et son regard vous gagnent par une sorte de douceur inflexible ; son silence est insistance sympathique.
>
> Cette double expression de gravité et de tendresse est le signe même de son âme et de son œuvre.

Vildrac's belief in the salvation of humanity through love, his notion of men and women united by bonds of love and pity, his constant preoccupation with friendship rather than sexual love, lead him often to explore the quieter and subtler aspects of human nature rather than work up to the traditional climax of lyricism. It is the quietude of his theatre which forms the main subject of contemporary criticisms. Speaking of the second act of *Madame Béliard*, in *Figaro*,[2] Robert de Flers says that Vildrac's truth is too minute to be dramatic truth; the author deliberately neglects "les déformations que le théâtre exige". I shall discuss in a later chapter the points raised by this observation. In the meantime, let us note that Vildrac's dramas have a classic tendency. The dialogue is simple and the sentiments have universality but at the same time are convincingly real. Although his plays are based on emotion—love, friendship, pity—the dramatic force of his silences is more limited than with Bernard, because the emotions with which he is concerned are less complicated and not in the same way repressed. In accordance with the philosophy of the Abbaye, these emotions are in the main altruistic, universal and tending to flow freely outwards, whereas those of Jean-Jacques Bernard are self-regarding, individual and directed inwards by some obstacle or controlling force. Vildrac's men

[1] 21st Nov. 1925.   [2] 19th Oct. 1925, R.

and women do not generally seek to escape from reality, unless it be into another healthier reality, and they remain closely linked to their fellow men. The sane humanism of the Abbaye is reflected in his drama. He avoids the shadowiness of Maeterlinck, the case histories of Bernard and the arbitrary situations of Amiel. It is this very humanism which brings a large part of his theatre into line with the Expressed.

Vildrac's use of the Unexpressed is, however, dramatically interesting. The silences create something new, mark fresh stages of development in the action, and show the interaction of characters upon one another. Moreover, they call our attention to the beauty of the dialogue. Although he does not aspire to effects of "langage indirect" where, by the arrangement of words, subconscious desire or motive is revealed, yet his dialogue is often more than what it actually means. Vildrac at his best can use words in such a way that even though their meaning corresponds closely with what is in the mind of the character, and even though conflicting subconscious motives may be absent, there emanates a suggestion of the mystery of life and human personality. This faculty for evocative language is by no means a prerogative of the *Théâtre de l'Inexprimé*. No dramatist can be really great without it in some measure. It is, however, a dramatic characteristic on which Maeterlinck and Bernard lay great stress, and its noticeable presence in the work of Vildrac, together with his use of the pause, establish a certain kinship with the " silent " group.

CHAPTER VII

DENYS AMIEL

EFORE we proceed to our study of Jean-Jacques Bernard, the *chef d'école*, we shall consider the work of Denys Amiel, the other theorist of the Unexpressed in the drama. Amiel, whose name is linked with that of Bernard, is essentially a dramatist of the " Boulevard ", and I cannot see that his plays have any abiding qualities. His theories, however, received publicity in print and helped to stimulate interest in the dramatic use of the Unexpressed. It is more than probable that these theories were directly inspired by the ideas of Henry Bataille, to whom he was for some years secretary, and on whom he wrote an essay.[1] In the first chapter I noted the ideas on " langage indirect ", elaborated in the preface to *La Marche nuptiale*, and observed that, on account of his lyrical temperament, Bataille had never succeeded in putting them into practice in his plays. Amiel, for other reasons, is not constitutionally the man to express himself through the medium of the unexpressed. This in a way makes his doctrinaire plays interesting to study.

Bataille certainly influenced his drama. In an interview with Simonne Ratel,[2] Amiel tells of his affection for Bataille. As an adolescent he had thought in the same way as the master, but for twelve years, he maintains, he had had nothing in common with him. This is hardly the case. While lacking that touch of genius which one must concede to Bataille, he has enough of his bad taste and obsession with sex to produce a recognizable family

---

[1] *Henry Bataille : Le Règne intérieur, pensées sélectionnées et précédées d'une introduction par Denys Amiel*, s.d. In this introduction Amiel stresses the author's preoccupation with " l'inexprimé " and " la vérité intérieure ", and quotes the passage from *Le Masque*, referred to in Chapter I.

[2] *Comœdia*, 25th Aug. 1928, " Les Grands Courants de la pensée contemporaine ", R.

likeness. Two youthful unpublished efforts of 1911, *Près de lui* [1]
and *Le Clair-Obscur*,[2] have a strong flavour of Bataille, and even
in later plays, where Amiel develops a style of his own, the
material is generally the same—the casual sex relationships of
individuals living in a continual state of physical excitement. In
the *Revue Hebdomadaire* of 16th December 1922,[3] he acknowledges a debt to Porto-Riche, especially to the play *Le Vieil
Homme*. From this author he says he learned " que le détail doit
être rattaché à la ligne centrale comme la plus fragile arborescence
des neurones est directement tributaire de la colonne vertébrale ".
But it is impossible not to believe that, in addition to this point of
technique, he was also impressed by that which Porto-Riche had
in common with Bataille, an exclusive preoccupation with physical
love ; although again, in Amiel, we fail to discover those subtle,
if rather morbid, powers of psychological analysis which lend a
certain distinction to the work of Porto-Riche.

Amiel's material is that of the " Boulevard " : the relationship
of husband, wife and lover, and sex problems such as whether a
wife is " justified " in taking a lover once she has been deceived
by her husband ; and it would seem, from what we have seen of
the *Théâtre de l'Inexprimé*, very difficult to reconcile such material
with the use of the unexpressed in drama. With regard to style,
he states in the article already quoted from the *Revue Hebdomadaire* that he learned much from the economy of Jules Renard.
" Monsieur Lepic est une divinité de silence qui aurait ingurgité
la vie, et l'ayant digérée, la régurgiterait à petits coups." Else-
where [4] he says that Renard purged him of the verbiage of
D' Annunzio. On the same occasion he makes it clear that he
had read nothing of Maeterlinck when writing *Le Voyageur* in
1912 at the age of twenty-three, having been brought up by
Jesuits and denied access to literature. Let us, however, first
examine his theories.

In the preface to his collected works written in January 1925,

[1] Calligraphic copy in Bibliothèque de l'Arsenal.
[2] Typescript in Bibliothèque de l'Arsenal.
Enquête sur la jeune littérature, R. [4] Interview with Simonne Ratel, *loc. cit.*

Amiel quotes the sentence which he had inscribed in 1912 at the head of *Le Voyageur*, a sentence in which, he states, " je me traçais à moi-même une esthétique que je crois avoir rigoureusement suivie ". It runs :

> Penchés sur un texte comme sur un aquarium, nous devons voir par transparence tout ce qui se meut en dessous, descend, zigzague, remonte à la surface de temps à autre . . . comme la promenade soumarine de nos sentiments. Les gestes doivent être des raccourcis appropriés et aussi éloquents que des vaticinations. Voilà, je crois, l'avenir de notre théâtre, si nous ne voulons pas continuer de bâtir nos monuments avec des pierres tumulaires. [He adds :] D'ailleurs, je faisais illustrer cet acte de foi de prosodie dramatique par un de mes personnages qui disait : "Ah ! L'admirable et la poignante chose que la vie ! . . . Les minutes les plus insignifiantes sont peut-être grosses de drame intérieur. . . . On voit des gens paisiblement assis qui causent avec calme, leurs gestes sont ceux de tous les autres gens polis et sociables et peut-être que dans leurs cœurs s'agitent en remous la convoitise . . . la haine . . . la passion de la bête ancestrale. . . ."

This speech from *Le Voyageur*, which Amiel frequently quotes in his writings, appears in the *Chimère*, No. VIII of April 1923, and he adds :

> Vous pouvez aisément imaginer par là les ressources que nous fournira le silence, enflé, pour ainsi dire, des tumultes entre lesquels il forme une oasis de calme faux et angoissant.
>
> A quoi cela nous amènera-t-il ? J'entrevois un *essai* de théâtre presque uniquement basé sur l'emploi du silence avec, de loin en loin, des mots comme des timbres résultants . . . sortes de centres synoptiques autour desquels l'action viendra se ranger docilement.

Let us now examine *Le Voyageur*, a play written to illustrate these theories.[1]

Paul, a musician in his thirties, has returned from a successful tour in America, where he had gone to forget a woman.

---

[1] " J'ai voulu à cette époque-là [1912] faire du *Voyageur* une sorte de démonstration systématique de ces convictions."—Preface to *Théâtre*, vol. 1, 1925. *Le Voyageur* was first performed 2nd May 1923.

Madeleine, who had treated his love as a passing experience, has not succeeded in forgetting him and tries to find tranquillity in his timid, sensitive young friend, Jacques. " C'est de son amour, un amour simple et bon, que je vis aujourd'hui." As the old affair is to be considered over, Madeleine invites Paul to her house in order that he may reassure Jacques, who dimly suspects that his friend has been, and still is, something to her. Paul is amazed and hurt to discover that the woman he still loves has taken from him his best friend, whose character he had lovingly tried to mould, but Madeleine pleads with him to say nothing of their bygone passion and contrives that he shall be left alone when Jacques comes. The meeting of the friends is a sombre one and they find themselves almost at once disagreeing about even the most trivial topics that crop up in their conversation. Paul's troubled state of mind is revealed in a kind of incoherent and inconsequential dialogue which disconcerts Jacques. Finally, there is ". . . un silence lourd d'ambiguïté . . . de doute . . . d'angoisse — fausse situation. Ils sont ainsi muets un moment. Madeleine rentre." . . .

> Madeleine entre, l'air dégagé et gai, d'une gaieté frivole et élégante, dont elle va s'efforcer de ne pas se départir durant toute la scène. Cette scène est jouée dans une atmosphère presque électrique, tant sont tendus les nerfs et contenues les pensées. Les paroles qu'expriment les trois êtres ne sont que des revêtements menteurs de pensées bien différentes. Il faudrait lire, à travers la transparence fardée des mots, jusque dans leur conscience en détresse.

There follows a tense nervous dialogue in which nearly every sentence has a double meaning. Paul has practically promised to be silent about the passion which had existed between Madeleine and himself. He keeps his promise to the letter, but a bitter vindictiveness betrays itself in the choice of every word. Jacques is tormented, but too pusillanimous and too intimidated to protest. Madeleine is agitated and embarrassed. At one stage her suppressed anguish is so great that she rushes out of the room and leaves the rivals in smouldering but unexpressed hostility. Paul's taunts become for Jacques more and more unbearable. Why has Jacques produced no literary works of late ? Life is full of inspiration. And he proceeds, in the passage already quoted, to discourse meaningly upon the invisible under-currents of everyday life. Trivial words and gestures of civilized men and women can conceal " la passion de la bête ancestrale . . .". " Mais c'est admirable, la duplicité des gestes. . . ." The strain is too much for Jacques, who takes his departure.

Paul now goes to the piano and improvises a melody " où semble être enfermée toute la fatalité douloureuse de la volupté subie ". Madeleine asks him again and again to leave, but he goes on playing without a word, and finally she is standing behind him, caressing him. " Et tandis que le rideau descend, le piano s'est arrêté et les mains de Paul, abandonnant le clavier, tombent le long de son corps dans un geste d'une grande lassitude devant l'inévitable."

Here are Amiel's own comments on the technique of *Le Voyageur* :

> J'ai voulu que l'action fût cette enveloppe provisoire, cette gaze gaufrée, lustrée et clinquante, sous laquelle se joue un drame sec et dur qui n'affleure à la surface que de loin en loin comme ces émanations délétères qui viennent, par petites bulles intermittentes, crever leur fièvre à la surface d'une eau calme, semée de romantiques nénuphars. . . . Ne vous est-il donc jamais arrivé de passer entre amis assemblés, une de ces soirées de malaise dont vous sortiez brisés, l'âme endolorie par une compression de deux heures, sans que toutefois, rien ait été dit d'explicitement et de concrètement pénible ? Mais prévenus d'un fait avant d'entrer, vous avez assisté à sa pro-menade sousmarine à travers l'urbanité de la conversation, vous en aviez suivi le cheminement sous les phrases et les rires, vous aviez regardé et écouté tous les gestes et tous les mots par l'envers, vous aviez éclairé l'insignifiance quotidienne des paroles à la lumière de votre connaissance anticipée de la situation latente.[1]

---

[1] Preface to *Théâtre*, vol. 1, 1925.

The action here is on two levels. On the surface is the exchange of urbane conversation on the part of three civilized human beings ; below, but very close to the surface, is the conflict of elemental passions. Beneath conventional phrases a friendship between two men is broken, an old love is reborn, a new love is destroyed and a woman chooses between two rivals.

As with Vildrac's *Poucette,* the characters are perfectly aware of the thoughts and emotions which are unexpressed. There are examples of this awareness in the plays of Bernard. In *Le Secret d'Arvers,* the poet's deliberate and conscious silence contrasts movingly with his friend's romantic lyricism and the charming prattle of Marie Nodier. And Bernard's most effective silent climaxes come at the moment of " recognition " ; the sudden realization of the truth flashes simultaneously upon the two characters, this again forming a striking contrast to the slow subconscious travail which has preceded it. But the self-consciousness of three people sustained throughout a long act without, as it were, a contrasting background of normality, is over-elaborate and strained. A certain interest, a certain tension, is produced by this deliberate and conscious dissimulation. But the dramatic intensity is diminished by the fact that not only must the veiled sentiments remain very close to the surface in order to appear clearly through the equivocal text, but unless they are finally allowed to break through in a traditional lyric outburst, they must remain, as it were, on the same level throughout. There is no real development, no gathering momentum. We have a static situation over which three people work themselves into a state of nerves. "Trois êtres sont là," says the author, " une vérité est entre eux qui les ronge et dont ils feignent, les uns vis-à-vis des autres, d'ignorer la gravité. D'abord ils jouent autour d'elle, puis ils se mettent à la manier avec une sorte de griserie farouche, chacun au fond de sa poche, pour ainsi dire, comme on tripote fébrilement une clef, jusqu'à ce que tout à coup l'un d'entre eux, harassé par le jeu, demande grâce. . . ." [1]

[1] Quoted in *La Petite Illustration* of 18th Aug. 1923.

Unconsciously Amiel himself betrays the play's weakness, its atmosphere of strain and artificiality. The characters are playing a game of pretence and evasion around the truth until the weakest gives in. A drawing-room game may be considered adequate material for serious drama if we can be made to feel that it is the one inevitable means of conveying that particular conflict of passions. But our impression is that silence here is not inevitable. It does not proceed inexorably from character and circumstance. There is no reason why, constituted as they are, such close friends as Paul and Jacques should not have attempted to " have it out " in Madeleine's absence. If Paul has kept the agreement to be silent to the letter, he has dishonestly broken it in the spirit, and Jacques' silence is due merely to moral cowardice. The author has arbitrarily imposed upon us a painful, embarrassing drawing-room situation, and made the most of it. An embarrassing situation may be interesting, but it cannot move us very deeply.

It especially fails to move us when we feel that it is neither necessary nor worth while. The characters concerned in it are second rate. Paul is cynical, aggressive and bad-mannered. Madeleine is sensual with a hint of perversity—the critic Nozière [1] sees in her appeal to Paul to reassure Jacques a subconscious desire to win Paul back, together with the coquettish and slightly sadistic idea of making comparisons between the two and weighing up their claims to her favours ; the text, however, really does not make this clear. Jacques is weak and completely intimidated by his " friend's " aggressiveness. It is his incredible feebleness of will that prevents him from speaking out and makes the drama possible. In an interview published in *La Rampe*,[2] Amiel recalls the fact that Bataille liked *Le Voyageur* of which he knew only the first act. A second act existed, continues the author, but it was so daring for the time that he could not show it even to him. The play as published consists of one long act, presumably the first of the original version, since the susceptibilities of the audience are not unduly offended. But even allowing for the

---

[1] Dossier of Amiel, cutting dated 6th May 1923, R.   [2] 15th Oct. 1932, R.

youthful desire to " épater le bourgeois ", the statement itself
sheds some light on Amiel's artistic outlook, which indeed
becomes obvious enough as we examine his subsequent plays.
He wishes to create sensations with daring and unusual situations
rather than move and interest an audience with genuine human
experience, and the " silent " technique which he imposes on
this second-rate material has something of the appearance of a
" stunt ".

At its most eloquent the Unexpressed does more than convey,
as in *Le Voyageur*, a single clear-cut issue; it hints at the mysterious unknowable, whether in human personality or in external
forces governing the universe, and in doing so it awakens strange
echoes in the minds of the spectators. Here the concealed drama,
well-defined, familiar, triangular, is too near the surface to produce any effect of awe or mystery and the elaborately contrived
double meanings and mathematical correspondence of movement
on each plane of action are unrealistic and shriek out what Pierre
Brisson calls " la préméditation et la volonté systématique ".[1]

As well as indirect language the significant pause is used.
The silence of the two friends stresses the unhappiness latent in
the first words of greeting and emphasizes the falseness of the
situation already foreshadowed in the preliminary dialogue between Madeleine and Paul. A crisis within Madeleine is indicated
by her silently staring in front of her in anguish, and then with
her eyes comparing the two men as they stand for a moment
side by side. The surrender to the old passion takes place without
a word of love being spoken. None of these pauses can compare
in dynamic force with those of Bernard, which derive their intensity, not only from the gathering momentum of the preceding
action, but also from the contrast with the unconstrained dialogue
of other characters.

In the plays of Bernard we shall observe the importance of
objects external to the text ; a fan, a book of poetry, a mirror, a
piece of music, all have a wordless significance or a symbolism

[1] *La Petite Illustration* of 18th Aug. 1923.

which enriches the character or underlines the action and economizes the text. In the concluding scenes of *Le Voyageur*, Amiel makes effective use of Paul's music, but its relation to dialogue and character is not so intimate as that of the Chopin nocturne in *L'Invitation au voyage*. What is extremely original is the elaborate use of lighting to emphasize the different stages of the conflict. Here are the author's minute stage directions :

> L'éclairage vient de trois sources ; à gauche, premier plan, une psyché ovale fait écran devant des lampes invisibles qui répandent sur tout l'arrière-plan gauche une nappe de clarté, le premier plan restant dans l'ombre. La porte qui donne accès du vestibule dans le salon est dans ce coin. C'est dans cette plage éclairée que les visiteurs se tiennent d'abord. S'ils font quelques pas, ils arrivent aux limites de ce champ lumineux et leur masque est déjà dans l'ombre. La seconde source lumineuse est un lustre voilé de violet et de vert accroché aux frises ; il ne sera allumé qu'à la scène IV et éclairera le moment décisif du conflit, projetant un cône de lumière sur le divan. Les deux hommes joueront ainsi tour à tour dans la lumière ou se replongeront dans l'ombre selon qu'ils gagneront ou perdront du terrain dans l'esprit de la femme qui est le centre de la lutte et de leurs convoitises.

The use of stage lighting for the purpose of focusing the attention of the audience on a specific character and the vivid symbolic contrast between light and shadow are reminiscent of cinema technique. We are reminded of the impressive cinematic scene in *La Puissance des morts* by Maeterlinck, where all the lighting is concentrated on the tragic clutching hand of the dying money-lender. Maeterlinck's play, however, was published in 1927 ; Amiel's play dates back to 1912. In an interview Amiel states : " J'ai écrit ' Le Voyageur ' en 1912. Onze ans déjà ; mais je n'y ai pas changé une virgule." [1] If we assume that he had in mind, as well as the dialogue, the stage directions and that these were not elaborated at a later date in harmony with the aesthetic theories of Gaston Baty, we observe a skilful use of

[1] *Figaro*, 3rd May 1923, R.

cinematic devices at a time when the cinema was in its crude infancy. The assumption is to be stated because, before the first performance of *Le Voyageur*, Gaston Baty produced in the season 1921–2 *Intimité* by J.-V. Pellerin and, as Paul Blanchart tells us, the problem of " materializing " the thoughts of the actors was resolved in part by manipulating light and shade with enchanting virtuosity.[1] Light and shadow abound in the idealist dramas of Maeterlinck, but their function is slightly different. The symbolism of the moonlight in *Pelléas et Mélisande* is less clear cut, but it goes deeper ; its poetry and meaning are closely knit with the text and, besides serving the immediate purposes of the drama, it is fraught with the mystery and beauty of the invisible forces at work behind the drama. The lighting in Amiel's play has no connection whatsoever with the text and is in no way essential to the action. It is a superimposed device of the *metteur en scène*, serving to draw our attention to the hidden conflict and, effective though it is, its use seems to indicate a consciousness on the part of the author of the inadequacy, or at least the vagueness of the text.

Café-Tabac[2] is generally ranked by critics as a play of the " silent school ". L. Dubech goes as far as to say that this piece " poussait à l'extrême les théories de l'école du silence, au point qu'elle devenait un jeu littéraire sans aucun intérêt pour le public ".[3] Its theories are certainly in sympathy with those of the *Théâtre de l'Inexprimé* ; it is an attempt to convey the inner lives of a group of human beings fortuitously gathered together in a small " débit ". Its technique, however, apart from affinities with the cinema play, does not make use of any of the devices with which Maeterlinck or Bernard produce their most telling effects.

" Dans *Café-Tabac*," says the author in the preface to his plays, " j'ai tâché d'exprimer l'hermétisme des êtres, rivés à leurs préoccupations personnelles, la vie bouchée par l'horizon professionnel, quoique égarés dans le simultanéisme de la vie. Je me

---

[1] Paul Blanchart, *Gaston Baty* (1939), p. 32.
[2] Written in 1922, produced in the season 1932-3.
[3] *La Crise du théâtre* (1928), p. 139.

représente jusqu'à l'obsession les êtres comme des entités presque étanches et qui roulent fermées jusqu'à la mort avec entre elles à peine un peu de capillarité. . . . Et ce tohu-bohu de sentiments 'cloisonnés', je me suis efforcé de l'organiser ici en quelque sorte symphoniquement."

The play is an impression of a small " débit " on a day of pouring rain, where the customers talk and reveal by snatches of conversation glimpses of a deeper life. In the ebb and flow of drenched humanity groups are distinguished, each with a hidden drama. The postmen from the Midi talk nostalgically about their homes and curse the drabness of their lives in Paris. In another corner, opposite her lover, sits a woman tortured by remorse and fear of her suspecting husband. Another table is the scene of a sentimental drama between three young people. André, " le sentimental timide ", introduces to his friend Robert, " le sûr de lui-même ", his new girl Renée, " la midinette co-quette ", and we see Robert gradually enticing the girl to himself. The telephone-box itself affords snatches of drama. Its door does not shut properly, and as it opens one-sided conversations can be heard from a business man or from a young man pleading with an implacable mistress.

A certain unity and coherence is effected through the dialogue between a " violoniste de brasserie " and a " littérateur ". The latter is telling his friend the plot of his new play, a palpitating drama in the style of Henry Bataille. His friend listens absent-mindedly, is scarcely impressed by the artificial intrigue and suggests that the dramatist should write about the life surrounding him.

> Je ne sais pas, tout est intéressant . . . la vie . . . la vie . . . c'est partout, comprends-tu, il suffit d'écouter, de re-garder n'importe quoi. Je ne sais pas . . . ici, ces gens, avec leurs préoccupations microscopiques et quotidiennes. . . .

The dramatist asks for writing-paper and feverishly starts taking notes of what is going on around him. And gradually the room empties.

Le panneau lentement, lentement, se ferme comme un obturateur et quand il est complètement fermé on peut voir écrit au centre " Café-Tabac " et au-dessous trois billes de billard en triangle.

This play is unique among Amiel's available works in that here, instead of confining himself to a small number of individuals, he attempts to integrate diverse groups. As with many of the plays of " l'école du silence ", the action is on two planes. Superficially there is the bustling life of a café with the perpetual coming and going of crowds, the clink of glasses, the uncorking of bottles, the hum of conversation, the sounds emanating from the back room. For these effects Amiel depends greatly upon the skill of the *metteur en scène* and his stage directions are in the nature of a rough scenario. We may assume that those groups which are not for the moment in the dramatic foreground are either silent or engaged in inaudible conversation. Reporting the play in *L'Avenir*,[1] Madeleine Lindauer says, presumably of members of these groups : " Il y en a qui se taisent et ce sont parfois les plus éloquents ". These, however, are " producer's silences ", and we scarcely need to dwell on them. Then the inner lives of the diverse groups which constitute this heterogeneous whole are revealed in snatches. Our attention is focused upon the different groups in turn, as with the cinema " shot ", and for a moment unfinished dramas surge up to the surface.

In Madeleine Lindauer's report [2] the play is described as a " tranche de vie ". At the rise of the curtain we see the actors fixed in absolute immobility. The picture comes to life. At the end of the act it is once more immobilized. The author is attempting what Chekhov achieves in his plays—to give a sample of the texture of life. Amiel, however, does not go very deep ; no profound philosophy of life emanates from the piece to give it meaning and pathos. Apart from the touch of poetry in the group of Méridionaux, the unedifying glimpses of the commonplace afforded to us are lacking in mystery or beauty. It is the

---

[1] 10th Nov. 1932, R.   [2] *Loc. cit.*

usual " drama ", clearly expressed, of the more sensational press, or the novelette—a woman betraying her husband and afraid of being found out, a man stealing his friend's girl—without the poetry or universality characteristic of true tragedy. The inner life of the café is revealed to us at a given moment as a cluster of sensational " Boulevard " situations.

La Souriante Madame Beudet,[1] written in collaboration with André Obey, impressed contemporary critics as being typical of the " silent " group. Madeleine Beudet, sensitive and refined, is the wife of a worthy, good-hearted but coarse Philistine ; she bears in silence, and even with a gentle smile, his total incomprehension of her nature, his low humour, his swearing and his meannesses. Beudet's idea of a joke is repeatedly to scare his guests by threatening to commit suicide with the unloaded revolver he keeps in his desk. One day, goaded to extremity, she loads the revolver in order that he may perish in an apparent accident. The next day, panic-stricken and repentant, she attempts to retrieve it, but is interrupted. When Beudet does eventually draw forth the weapon, instead of pointing it as usual to his own head, he aims in the direction of his wife. It goes off, but misses Madeleine. Beudet jumps to the conclusion that Madeleine had intended to kill herself and only then does he realize the measure of her suffering, while his awkward and pathetic emotion brings home to Madeleine the depths and sincerity of his love for her. Impulsively she falls on her knees. " Ah ! pardon, Paul, pardon ! . . . tu es bon . . . tu es bon . . . je ne savais pas que tu étais si bon." The attempted crime will remain for ever a secret, and what is meant to be a perpetual reconciliation is built on the basis of a lie.

The play does not satisfy us as being an adequate expression of the theories of silence. It lacks the coherence of mood which is imposed by the inwardness of the " silent " characters in the best plays of the Unexpressed, and the final choice resolves the problem in emotional disorder instead of tragic calm. With

[1] First performed 16th Apr. 1921.

regard to technique, there is no " langage indirect ", no subtle hint of unrealized emotions submerged in the subconscious, nor even the thinly veiled allusions characteristic of *Le Voyageur*. Madeleine is fully aware of her unhappiness and defines it clearly to a confidante.

The climax of the play, however contrary to the traditions of the French drama, is realized for the most part in expressive mime. Because she will not accompany the theatre party, Beudet mortifies his wife before their guests and departs with them, after vindictively locking the piano, which is her sole joy and consolation. Alone, Madeleine retires to her corner of the room, takes a handglass and with anguish examines her face for signs of age. When the pretty, fresh maid comes in, she makes her talk about her sailor sweetheart in order that she may vicariously enjoy a little happiness, and then falls to weeping. Alone once more, she approaches the piano. " On sent que la musique sera l'épanchement naturel, obligé, d'un bouillonnement de sensations et de désirs. Le piano est fermé. Rage. Elle se jette sur le portrait de Beudet qui vit au mur, lui montre le poing : ' Brute ! oh, brute! ' "

But Amiel finds it necessary to express the essential part of the crisis in monologue. " Cet homme . . . oh ! cet homme-là. . . . Je le hais ! Mais qu'il s'en aille (. . .) Un accident . . . ce sera un accident . . . oui . . . un accident (*très calme*) terrible. . . . (*Silence. S'exaltant soudain.*) Et ma vie à moi, à moi, ma vie, est-ce qu'elle n'est pas une catastrophe . . . pis que ça . . . (*amère*) une bêtise (. . .). Moi, vous comprenez, je veux vivre, je veux vivre. . . ." The words which escape Madeleine in the stress of the moment are certainly an inadequate indication of the turmoil within—anguish at the sterile passing of the years, yearning for love and beauty, violent frustration, rage and hatred, the resolution to murder and the bitter determination to grasp the fleeting joys of life. The comparative self-restraint of the author and his avoidance of the traditional purple passage offered by the emotional situation no doubt contributed at the time

towards the impression that the work was essentially of the Unexpressed. There is in addition the self-imposed silence of Madeleine at the end of the play. As in other works of Amiel, the
heroine is condemned to live a lie in order to preserve the forms
of domestic accord.

Setting could be said to play a part in conveying meaning
without the intermediary of words. For motives of bourgeois
as well as dramatic economy, one room has to serve both as
office for Beudet and as drawing-room for his wife. On the left
is the desk with its crude green light ; on the right, a soft pink
lamp and the piano. Our attention is drawn to the characteristic
gestures of Beudet, who, every time he enters, meticulously
arranges the cushions in order of size, thrusts the artistically
arranged flowers deep into the vase and replaces on the piano
the horror of a statue which Madeleine keeps removing to the
desk.

The value of the partially silent crisis, and indeed of the work
as a whole, is greatly reduced by obvious weaknesses of plot and
character : Madeleine's panic and repentance through a belated
realization of her husband's kindness, for which nothing in the
previous scenes has prepared us, the reconciliation and apparent
change of heart brought about through an emotional shock, the
utter unlikelihood that incompatibility should cease to trouble
the marriage, the failure to foreshadow the psychological torments
which are bound to ensue in Madeleine on account of that continued incompatibility, now complicated by the suppression of a
horrible secret. The total effect is not improved by the unleavened
mixture of satire, broad comedy, pathos and melodrama.

Of the total of Amiel's available plays only four, in addition
to the three discussed above, have any connection with the
Théâtre de l'Inexprimé. With very few exceptions, the moral
climate and style of treatment of the rest of his theatre, " silent "
or otherwise, is reminiscent of Bataille, Bernstein and Porto-
Riche. The subject is invariably physical love, although the
characters occasionally talk unconvincingly of its spiritual aspect.

The plays are either studies of the behaviour of people in love or attempts to state and solve problems concerning the relations of men and women. In every case the characters, few in number, are drawn from a milieu—they are rich bourgeois, business men or successful artistes—in which the struggle for existence, the preoccupations of everyday life, or hidden reserves of intellectual or spiritual resources do not appear to exist in order to trouble their single-minded absorption in these relationships. And in every case the absence of that sexual morality upon which the larger part of society bases its behaviour is an accepted convention ; the unconvincing " spiritual " or " intellectual " needs of which certain characters talk never really complicate the insouciant and unquestioned gratification of physical desires. For example, in *L'Engrenage* Francine helps the advancement of her husband, a talented architect whom she " loves ", by becoming, unknown to him, the mistress first of an elderly " Inspecteur des Arts ", and then of the rich young man who commissions a château which is to be his masterpiece. And *L'Homme* shows us a woman who, in order to ensure her husband's mental and emotional equilibrium, encourages him to take a mistress, provided it is with her knowledge and consent. The impossible situation thus created ends with the suicide of her young rival, and the " moral " of the story appears to be that one should never tell one's wife when one proposes to take a mistress.

Except for a few subtle allusions in *Ma Liberté* to the heroine's father fixation and part of the first act of *L'Homme*, where the husband betrays by his manner an awakening love for the other woman, most of Amiel's " Boulevard " plays are outside the range of the *Théâtre de l'Inexprimé*. But *Monsieur et Madame Un Tel*, *Le Couple*, *La Femme en fleur* and *Mon Ami* undoubtedly possess some of its characteristics, and they are similar in subject matter and treatment.

In *Monsieur et Madame Un Tel*[1] Suzanne, the young wife of a middle-aged industrialist, " bon bourgeois ", is physically

[1] Written Oct. 1923–Jan. 1924, first performance 24th Sept. 1925.

attracted by Robert, the " type sportif ", and finally departs with him to the Midi. Almost fifteen months later, Georges, the husband, alone in his mistress's house, is surprised by a visit from his wife. After trying pluckily to carry off her position, she finally confesses that Robert had left her after three months, and that she has been supporting herself ever since as an assistant to a fashionable dressmaker. A poem from Géraldy's *Toi et moi*, heard on the wireless, switched on by chance—" Tu ne peux pas partir par ce temps, allons, reste ! . . . " draws the couple together again. Georges takes out a piece of paper which he consults surreptitiously while talking. It has notes for an excursion, headed " Pour quand Suzanne reviendra . . .". They go home together, Suzanne his own wife again, fussing over his cold and his muffler in true domestic style.

The progressive stages of Suzanne's infatuation and Georges' awakening suspicions are indicated in mime. Robert starts a stimulating discussion on bodily fitness and the physical attractions of female ski-ers at Chamonix, where he is shortly going. " Suzanne a écouté tout cela, d'abord avec nostalgie, puis tout à coup, avec une espèce de rage nerveuse, elle s'est mise à déchirer un beau catalogue qu'elle feuilletait." Robert proceeds to demonstrate physical exercises to the unmuscular Georges " pendant que Suzanne, à l'écart, regarde les deux hommes avec une curiosité bizarre et très significative ". She allows Robert to kiss her when Georges is out and shows increasing exasperation when Georges, returning clad in pyjamas, begins to burlesque Robert's gymnastics. Robert leaves hastily, and Georges' features betray a sudden " divination télépathique ". Left alone, he expresses in mime growing suspicions, casts them away with a shrug of the shoulders, sees suddenly that a small statue of a naked woman, which for Robert's edification he had compared with his wife's figure, has changed its position, " et déjà une sorte d'angoisse passe sur son visage ".

The triviality of the plot—the physical attraction of a muscular man for a silly woman—against the background of superficial modernity and the general impression of bad taste are scarcely worthy of comment. It is obvious that miming scenes in such a context, with so little to express, have a minimum of artistic interest.

The same applies to *Le Couple* and *Mon Ami*. *Le Couple* [1] is a " problem " play. Is the deceived wife justified in deceiving in her turn, and should she be judged by moral standards different from those generally applied in matters of sex to men ? Henry and Claude, the " happily married couple ", leave Paris to escape the atmosphere of promiscuity and piquant gossip which troubles them in a perverse way. With incredible naïveté, however, they take with them two choice samples of the very types they are fleeing—Robert, a sort of Parisian Don Juan, and his wife, the far from chaste Suzanne. " Peut-être," says the author in his programme analysis, " y a-t-il chez les deux époux une arrière-pensée secrète et inconsciente, quelque chose comme une réserve de sensualité . . . une nostalgie d'aventure inachevée ; car rares sont les êtres qui peuvent retourner leur âme comme une doublure de poche et dire franchement : ' il n'y a plus rien ! ' " " Peut-être. . . ." The author, if anyone, should know.

Inevitably, Henry makes Suzanne his mistress and Claude, discovering this, announces, to her husband's bewildered fury, that she now considers herself free to act likewise in her own good time. When she eventually takes Robert as a lover, Henry, guessing the truth, has a voluble " crise de nerfs " in the true tradition of Henry Bataille. He tries to persuade himself that in love the heart alone matters, but wounded pride and crude physical jealousy reduce him first to hysterics and then to nervous prostration. "On parle, on se croit très fort, on n'est pas mûr pour les idées que l'on se fait, et le corps ne suit pas l'esprit, on n'est pas mûr ! " Claude, learning of her husband's anguish, resolves, with Robert's agreement and co-operation, to lie. Robert, who, as we are now expected to believe, has begun to fall in love with Claude, nobly drowns his " sufferings " by strumming popular

[1] First performed 20th Nov. 1923.

songs on the piano ("sa figure angoissée contraste avec la musique") and takes his departure with Suzanne under the cover of deceptively gay horseplay.

At the beginning of the published play the author quotes the well-worn paragraph, already mentioned, from the text of *Le Voyageur* : "Ah ! L'admirable et la poignante chose que la vie ! . . . Les minutes les plus insignifiantes sont peut-être grosses de drame intérieur. . . ." He apparently considers the work to be in the same tradition as *Le Voyageur*. This does not seem to be wholly the case. Apart from the fact that it lacks the technical ingenuity of *Le Voyageur* where, from the entry of Jacques, the author has contrived that every banal expression should have a corresponding hidden significance, there is even less here of " la passion de la bête ancestrale ". Throughout the play there is never any question of Henry and Claude ceasing to " love " one another ; the author is clearly concerned with the " problem " of the casual indulgence of extraneous desires perversely stimulated by bad company and spicy tittle-tattle, and unpleasant passages could be quoted in evidence of this. With such second-rate material little can be expected in the way of moving effects and the few examples of the Unexpressed have a comparatively small artistic value. The majority of spectators will be completely indifferent to the " anguish " of a frivolous man-about-town such as Robert, while he strums on the piano in the traditional style of the broken-hearted clown. The scene in Act I, scene 19, where Henry praises Robert while thinking of Suzanne, and Claude praises Suzanne while thinking of Robert and "ils se regardent bizarrement comme si réciproquement ils devinaient leurs arrière-pensées ", would be more impressive if it masked the awakening of genuine passion instead of sophisticated sensual interest. The scene where Henry, warned by Suzanne that Claude knows all, bursts into a flow of guilty nervous chatter which contrasts with his wife's calm self-possession and enigmatic silence is realistic enough and effective as far as it goes. It increases the tension up to the point of

Henry's realization of how Claude proposes to have her "re-vanche", and the fact that the revelation is not actually put into words serves to emphasize the climax.

> HENRY (*plantant son regard dans le sien*). Regarde-moi, toi ! (*On sent les adversaires.*)
> CLAUDE (*un temps*). Tu as compris ? (*Henry serre Claude si rageusement que celle-ci pousse un cri.*) Ah ! brute que tu es. . . . (*Elle s'arrache à son étreinte et se frotte le bras.*) Eh bien, je suis fixée, tu as compris. . . . Ah ! Tu y as mis le temps, mais enfin tu as compris.
> HENRY. Claude, si tu me trompes, je ne te le pardonnerai jamais. . . ."

But, again, it is a silence which is not necessary in the sense that the silences of Bernard or Maeterlinck are necessary, and a few explanatory words on the part of Claude, while perhaps lessening the dramatic tension, would not materially alter the nature of the play.

A similar atmosphere of decadent sentimentality is present in *Mon Ami*.[1] The involved plot is even more trivial than that of *Le Couple*. The author endeavours to interest us in a sensual woman whose promiscuity is to be excused by her beauty and charm, whose senses are so demanding and whose morals are so lax that, without any feeling of strain, she can live ten years of deceit with innumerable lovers by the side of a husband whom at the same time she is supposed to "love". The husband for his part is fully aware of his wife's polyandrous tendencies, but maintains a discreet silence throughout because he loves his wife and desires at all costs to continue to own her legally. (He even finds a post for the current lover whom Mona wishes to prevent from leaving Paris.) Not her husband's generosity but the stress of an impending scandal effects a transformation of character, which takes place in silence.

> Mona, la face tournée maintenant vers le public, réfléchit, et on sent une femme complètement nouvelle, comme si une

---

[1] Written 1936, but not produced till 10th Feb. 1943.

> série de voiles tombait. Son accent est large, profond, et
> jusqu'à la fin de cette scène il y a un ton de vérité indubitable.

This sudden statuesque reform, unmotivated, after ten years of free-and-easy existence, taxes our credulity to the utmost.

Mona's chief concern now is to discover by an artful ruse whether André suspects anything of her past debauchery, and when he deliberately plays the rôle of the trustful husband, she is silently " transformée . . . détendue, délivrée ". Her love, she conveys to André, is not just a matter of the senses ; she is his for ever.

> Alors André empoigne les mains de Mona et les étreint
> avec un tel élan et une telle fougue que toute phrase serait
> inutile.

The whole of this last grotesque scene is typical of Amiel's " unexpressed ". It is superficial in nature, is based on duplicity and deceit, and resolves itself into a protracted and unpleasant lie.

La Femme en fleur [1] merits more attention, representing as it does an attempt to express emotions which, for a time at any rate, are in the realm of the unconscious. Pierre Vignal, a sensitive, artistic type, on meeting his fiancée's young mother for the first time, immediately falls victim to her grace and charm, and gradually this attraction develops into love, which, unconsciously at first, is reciprocated by Valentine, starved of affection by her cold-hearted husband. This state of affairs is soon appreciated by Huguette, the fiancée, brusque, direct and keen in perception (she is one of Amiel's " modern girls "). She breaks off the engagement and announces her intention of marrying a " modern young man ". Still unconscious of the real nature of her sentiments, Valentine, through her excessive disappointment at the family's loss of Pierre, exasperates Huguette into speaking out. In a rather daring scene, skilfully handled, not only does she enlighten her mother on the true state of the latter's emotions, but she also signifies her filial approval, and even hints at a continuance of the relationship after her own intended departure.

---

[1] First performed 10th Dec. 1935.

Eventually, when Huguette marries, Pierre asks for his release from employment with Valentine's husband, declares himself to Valentine and asks her to come to his house to start life anew.

The unconscious growth of Valentine's love is adroitly suggested. In Act I, scene 8, she is smiling to herself and confesses to her daughter that she is thinking of whether she would like to have Pierre as a son-in-law. " Eh bien, je me disais qu'il me plairait."

> HUGUETTE (*en pirouette, plaisante et rageuse à la fois*). Eh bien, épouse-le.

But Valentine does not take her seriously. In Act II, scene 1, we see Valentine's intense anxiety in anticipation of Pierre's unhappiness when Huguette is about to break the engagement, and in Act II, scene 3, her deeply felt disappointment when Huguette announces that all is over between her and Pierre :

> VALENTINE. . . . Vous venez de briser notre bonheur.
> HUGUETTE.   Pardon, le nôtre, si tu veux bien.
> VALENTINE. . . . votre bonheur, notre bonheur, c'est la même chose (. . .) c'est à pleurer de désespoir.

She expatiates with enthusiasm on Pierre's qualities :

> Quelqu'un enfin sur qui pouvoir compter, quelqu'un à qui parler, quelqu'un que l'on voudrait choyer, gâter, soigner s'il lui arrivait du mal, quelqu'un à qui penser, quelqu'un dont l'arrivée était l'enchantement dans ce sinistre appartement (*expression tristement ironique d'Huguette*). Mais moi, tu sais, je n'ai jamais eu ça (. . .) Non, tu ne l'as, au fond, jamais aimé !
> HUGUETTE (*sous l'invective commence à se durcir*). Ah ! en tout cas, je ne l'aimais pas tant que toi, je m'aperçois !
> VALENTINE. Mais oui, mais oui, je l'adorais, moi, ce garçon, je l'adorais !

At this point, the exasperated Huguette tells Valentine that she is in love with Pierre and that Pierre is, perhaps without realizing it, in love with her. At first Valentine is shocked, then " un silence, pendant lequel se fait dans l'esprit de Valentine un lent travail de construction qui ne s'arrêtera plus. Le coup a porté ; elle va se défendre avec moins de violence d'abord, puis avec mollesse ; elle dira des répliques conventionnelles ; mais sur son visage, plein d'attention, on doit voir cheminer la révélation, dont peut-être elle fera son profit." Valentine protests, but as Huguette elaborates, " un imperceptible sourire, en tout cas, une très grande curiosité attendrie, se dessine sur le visage de Valentine ", and as Huguette goes on speaking, she only half listens, following her own train of thought. Huguette hints that there is no reason why Valentine should not continue to see Pierre when she is away, but breaks off with sudden reserve, and the false situation is glossed over with artificial conversation and laughter.

As we see, the actual truth has been put into precise words by Huguette, but silence is used to enable the full realization of it to develop within Valentine.

The theme of the play invites comparison with that of Bernard's *Le Printemps des autres*, and the differences in treatment are apparent. Bernard's play is " moral ", in the sense that a controlling ethical law in matters of love is recognized and accepted. Clarisse's love for her son-in-law, acknowledged by her as guilty, or at least impossible (for she is not really a " moral " woman), has been deliberately thrust below the level of consciousness. In the silent realization which comes upon Clarisse, as the moral law still applies, the necessity for making a choice arises. In the conflict between instinct and duty she opts for duty. Without at this stage examining further the nature of Clarisse's action, it is clear that her choice could never have been made had not at least the existence, if not the rightness, of the moral law been acknowledged by her. In addition to this conflict, there is also the growing antagonism between mother and daughter which reaches its climax when the full truth flashes simultaneously upon the two women without the utterance of a word. Amiel's play, on the contrary, is amoral in the sense that, in conformity with his other dramas, no controlling law, at least where love is concerned, is recognized and accordingly no conflict ensues. Valentine's love, unconscious at first, is not deliberately repressed, but germinates and flowers naturally. Her husband has starved her affections and betrayed her, her instincts demand happiness, and without compunction she follows her instincts. And the daughter's will being in harmony with the mother's, the action flows smoothly to its natural issue. That Bernard's version, firm within its moral framework, is infinitely more dramatic, will scarcely be questioned.

The difference between the masterful economy of Bernard and the diffuseness of Amiel is apparent in Act II, scene 2, the scene of the parting of Pierre and Huguette. Pierre's love for Valentine is conveyed without direct expression by a series of evasive circumlocutions. Pierre says he no longer loves Huguette. She is too young for him. Their little differences would in time become unbearable divergences. " Et puis (. . .) tu ne ressembles pas assez à la femme que je souhaite, que je cherche idéalement ! Mais cette femme-là . . . n'existe pas ! (. . .) Je traverse une crise, une crise effroyable, dont je ne puis absolument pas te parler. (*Aveu peut-être imprudent.*) Tu es la dernière à laquelle je pourrais en parler." Huguette tells him she has understood, and here the scene is allowed to peter out.

The avoidance of direct expression is necessitated no doubt by the demands of realism, for the truth is too crude under the circumstances to be put into words, but little else is gained except that the audience is kept on tenterhooks, wondering how far Amiel's daring will go.

Similar circumlocutions are employed in the final scene, where Pierre declares his love to Valentine. He invents a story with circumstances similar to those of reality, to the growing emotion of Valentine, who at last says, trembling : " Comme c'est curieux et émouvant ! On marche un certain temps à travers des phrases à double et triple sens . . . comme on irait à travers un souterrain . . . et tout à coup on arrive au grand jour . . . on est là, tous les deux, en pleine vérité ! "

At this stage she sees clearly and expresses what has gone on in her heart. At first she did not realize what had happened. In her happiness to have him as a son-in-law, she was identifying herself with Huguette. " Huguette était comme un prolongement physique de moi-même qui se nourrissait de votre amour." Only after the broken engagement, when she saw he would never come back, did the full realization of the truth dawn on her.

Thus, instead of leading to a silent climax, the scene in " langage indirect " is allowed to develop into a perfectly explicit unmasking.

In the " avant-première " to this play mentioned in *La Petite Illustration* of 11th April 1936 the author states : " Cette pièce demeure rigoureusement dans la tradition de tout mon théâtre et dans la formule même que j'inscrivais en tête de ma première pièce ", and once more he quotes his other cherished dictum : " Penchés sur un texte comme sur un aquarium, nous devons voir par transparence tout ce qui se meut en dessous . . .". Having made a minute study of his plays, I cannot accept the idea that the whole of Amiel's drama conforms to the theories of the Unexpressed. As far as we can judge from information available, he discarded the theories roughly between 1924 and 1934 (*L'Homme d'un soir, La Carcasse, L'Image, Décalage, L'Age du fer, Trois et une, L'Homme*), returned to them with *La Femme en fleur* (10th December 1935) and discarded them again with *Ma Liberté, La Maison Monestier* and *Famille*.

What is the contribution of Amiel to the development of the technique of the Unexpressed in the theatre ? The very word Unexpressed implies that there is something to express—something of value which the dramatist deliberately elects to convey by means other than its direct and clear translation into speech. Thus in Maeterlinck the audience is immediately aware of unseen forces at work—not only fate, death and love from without, but also the mysterious stirrings of the individual's instinct from within. And in the case of Bernard, though he lacks that vast background of mystic philosophy which lends universality to the drama of his predecessor, yet, in the best of his works, we respond deeply to the studies of the human heart with the glimpses of unconscious motive and impulse in conflict with everyday life. What is it that Amiel has to convey through the medium of pauses, mime, allusive language and external symbolism ?

As we have seen, he generally works within an exceedingly narrow framework, confining himself mostly to the study of love, or rather, physical attraction. The women (Amiel is a specialist in women's " problems ") are in the main idle, egotistical, sentimental, sensual and deceitful. And for Amiel, woman is the "modern" woman, the "girl" of 1931, or whatever year he may be writing in, although he occasionally varies this with a study of her mature counterpart, the " femme de quarante ans ". (He is a little more generous than Balzac in the matter of a woman's age.) The subject, characters and period are thus extremely limited in range. He does attempt, in theory, to lend some kind of universality to his themes—" Ma préoccupation en matière dramatique a toujours été de confronter le transitoire avec le permanent, de me pencher sur les variations autour d'un thème éternel et de noter leur rattachement à l'immuable épine dorsale des lois de l'espèce et de la vie " [1]—but one scarcely has the impression that he succeeds. For not only is the invisible background of external forces or the submerged obscurity of a subconscious world completely absent, but even a framework of elementary ethical standards is lacking. Without any exterior controlling force, the promiscuous physical desires of his characters never attain the intensity of genuine passion, accompanied by the pathos of conflict, but remain shallow, trivial and ephemeral. The eternally human which we seek and are entitled to expect in serious drama simply is not there. All we have is elementary physical attraction thinly veiled by the banalities of everyday conversation imposed by the conventions of modern society.

Apart from the absence of sexual morality, there is in so much of Amiel's work a lack of even the most elementary standards of honesty. In *La Souriante Madame Beudet*, *Le Couple* and *Mon*

---

[1] " Avant-première " to *Ma Liberté* in *Figaro*, quoted in *La Petite Illustration* of 13th Feb. 1937.

Ami, the heroines base their future life on a lie. The whole of the hidden action of *Le Voyageur* is founded on what amounts to a piece of cheating. And yet, if we are to take Amiel seriously, from human hypocrisy great dramatic developments are possible. " Nous devenons de plus en plus subtils. Nous comprenons à demi-mot ; un jour viendra où nous aurons appris si parfaitement la rouerie et l'hypocrisie faciale que le visage suffira à exprimer tout ce que l'on voudra avec le minimum de l'action. Car nous tendons vers une télépathie supérieure." [1] Even allowing for journalistic exaggeration, we see in this passage an attitude and a state of mind totally opposed to those of Maeterlinck and Bernard. For them silence is a medium for direct communication of fundamental truths which become distorted by the spoken word. Here, however, there is an implication that silence will be used not for truth but for lying. For Jean-Jacques Bernard's unfortunate people who unconsciously delude themselves as to their true motives, we experience a sense of pity, and in addition we have the interest of what Crémieux calls the " tragique de connaissance ", which forms the climax of the play. But what can we say of individuals who deliberately practise systematic hypocrisy ? Without passing moral judgments, we find it difficult even to work up an interest in these characters. They are small, they are common, they are nothing. There is no love, there is no passion, there are just " affaires". The material for an effective Theatre of the Unexpressed does not exist.

Weakness of plot and character also detract from the value of the Unexpressed in Amiel. Beudet's strange habits with his revolver in *La Souriante Madame Beudet*, the melodramatic affair of the emerald brooch in *Mon Ami*, are singularly unconvincing, yet on these circumstances the whole drama is made to hinge. Each is closely connected with a silent inner transformation on the part of the heroine, completely unmotivated, brought about through panic and strain, and totally lacking in verisimilitude. And we have the feeling that the eloquent pause, instead

[1] *Chimère*, No. VIII, Apr. 1923, R.

of being the inevitable climax of a closely knit set of circumstances and deriving its intensity from the dynamics of the preceding action, is often an arbitrary interpolation of the author.

Besides, we have seen in our studies of Maeterlinck and Vildrac, and we shall see with Bernard, that much of the value of the silence depends not only on the significance but also on the intrinsic beauty of the text to which it is juxtaposed. With his cult of the contemporary, Amiel's text lacks beauty or depth ; it is full of ephemeral slang and often in questionable taste. And let us in passing note the heavy responsibility which the author places upon the *metteur en scène* and especially on the actress. The elaborate stage directions, the minute indications of all the subtleties the heroine is expected to convey by facial expression, frequently do not seem to flow naturally out of the text, and without them the text is nothing.

For these reasons I find that the use of the Unexpressed which Amiel emphasizes in theory never, in practice, gets farther than being an ingenious " tour de force ", as in *Le Voyageur*, or, as one critic points out, a skilful device to throw into relief occasional explosive scenes, as in *La Femme en fleur*. Within very narrow limits, however, the author has succeeded by means of the technique of the Unexpressed in increasing realism, and has lent a certain piquancy of interest to scenes of drawing-room life.

CHAPTER VIII

JEAN-JACQUES BERNARD : I

JEAN-JACQUES BERNARD frequently put into print his theories on the use of the Unexpressed in drama during the period when his most characteristic plays were being performed.

In his essay *De la valeur du silence dans les arts du spectacle* [1] he states that he prefers the term *Théâtre de l'Inexprimé*, which he had used from the beginning, to the misleading phrase *Théâtre du Silence* employed by the critics. There must be no confusion, he says, between " silence " and " silences ". Silences are the intervals between the replies ; their value is felt only in exceptional cases and they must be used with the greatest discretion. Silence, broadly speaking, is " tout ce que les personnages ne veulent ou ne peuvent dire, c'est toute la série des pensées ou des désirs qui échappent aux mots, qui ne peuvent s'échanger que par allusion indirecte, voire par le regard ou par l'attitude, c'est toute la gamme des sentiments inexprimés, inavoués ou inconscients ".

The unexpressed is for Bernard one of the fundamental elements of dramatic art :

> Seulement, il faut élargir le sens du mot jusqu'à y englober tout ce qui relève de l'inconscient. Si les hommes n'expriment pas toujours leurs sentiments profonds, ce n'est pas uniquement parce qu'ils les cachent, par honte, par pudeur ou par hypocrisie. C'est encore plus souvent parce qu'ils n'en ont pas conscience ou parce que ces sentiments arrivent à la conscience claire sous une forme tellement méconnaissable que les mobiles réels n'en sont plus perceptibles. [2]

[1] Printed in *Témoignages* (1933) ; originally a lecture given at the Théâtre Montparnasse, 22nd Nov. 1930, a version of which was published in *Les Nouvelles littéraires*, 25th Apr. 1931 and 9th May 1931.   [2] *Ibid.*

The author's ideas on dialogue are expressed in the *Bulletin de la Chimère*, No. V of May 1922, in connection with *Martine* :

> Le théâtre est avant tout l'art de l'inexprimé. C'est moins par les répliques même que par le choc des répliques que doivent se révéler les sentiments les plus profonds. Il y a sous le dialogue entendu comme un dialogue sous-jacent qu'il s'agit de rendre sensible.
> Aussi le théâtre n'a pas de pire ennemi que la littérature. Elle exprime et dilue ce qu'il ne devrait que suggérer. . . .
> Un sentiment commenté perd de sa force. La logique du théâtre n'admet pas les sentiments que la situation n'impose pas. Et si la situation les impose, il n'est pas besoin de les exprimer. . . .

Bernard's conception of a " dialogue sous-jacent " is strikingly similar to that expressed by Maeterlinck in the passage from *Le Trésor des humbles* which we quoted in Chapter III,[1] although Maeterlinck was protesting against the drama of violent action and Bernard against unrealistic rhetoric in the theatre. How far did Maeterlinck's theories influence those of Bernard? Critics were quick to link the names of the two dramatists. " Ne parlait-on pas en 1922 à propos de *Martine* de M. J.-J. Bernard du Théâtre du Silence comme genre établi ? " says Dorothy Knowles in connection with Maeterlinck.[2] In *De la valeur du silence dans les arts du spectacle* Bernard declares that Maeterlinck was indeed the first to realize what Paul Blanchart calls " la valeur pathétique du silence et la densité de l'inexprimé ", but he continues :

> . . . il se servit des choses qu'on ne dit pas au point d'en faire un système. C'est pourquoi certaines scènes de Maeterlinck, quand on les relit maintenant, paraissent un peu appuyées. Le langage allusif, au lieu d'éclairer pour le spectateur les sentiments des personnages, semble les lui cacher. Ou parfois on a l'impression qu'il n'y a rien derrière, et que le langage allusif n'est employé que pour lui-même. Ce qui montre l'inconvénient de considérer comme un but ce qui doit rester un simple moyen.

---

[1] *Le Trésor des humbles*, pp. 173-4.
[2] *La Réaction idéaliste au théâtre depuis 1890*, p. 294.

Des moyens, des instruments de travail, voilà ce que doivent être le langage indirect et le silence, et l'attitude et la mimique. S'engager dans la voie indiquée par Maeterlinck et quelques autres serait une erreur aussi grave que celle que commettent les auteurs beaucoup plus nombreux, ceux-là qui n'emploient pas le mot comme instrument, ce qu'il doit être et rester, mais l'emploient pour lui-même, et se grisent de verbiage.

The criticism that Maeterlinck's Unexpressed does not reveal the sentiments of the characters proceeds from the assumption that psychological realism is the purpose of the drama. I have endeavoured to show that although Maeterlinck achieves a limited degree of psychological realism, that is not his main concern. He desires to represent dramatically " le chant mystérieux de l'infini, le silence menaçant des âmes ou des Dieux, l'éternité qui gronde à l'horizon, la destinée ou la fatalité qu'on aperçoit intérieurement . . .".[1] Maeterlinck is preoccupied with the reactions of the human soul to the ideas of Fate and Death ; Bernard with the complex human personality. Bernard's Unexpressed is a means of revealing some of the hidden springs and motives which determine conduct. Maeterlinck's Unexpressed very clearly conveys a notion of invisible menacing influences, though it certainly throws no light on the psychology of the individual.

The two writers arrive at the notion of " le dialogue sousjacent " from different starting-points. Maeterlinck writes as a mystic philosopher. For him, as we have seen, silence is the element in which the soul really lives. A man withdrawing into silence allows to operate freely that mysterious spiritual force which flows through him, as it flows through the universe, and which is the most vital part of his being. Maeterlinck's psychology, according to modern standards, is elementary : " plus on descend dans la conscience de l'homme, moins on y trouve de conflits ".[2]

Bernard writes as an observant psychologist. For him silence, the Unexpressed, embraces all that relates to the subconscious ; it may proceed, not only from conscious reserve or shame, but

---

[1] *Le Trésor des humbles*, p. 162.   [2] *Le Double Jardin*, p. 122.

also from motives and desires unrealized and perhaps reaching the level of consciousness in a transformed and unrecognizable state. Moreover, these desires may have been submerged in the subconscious as a result of what we may, for the present, term an act of will. A Freudian conception of the subconscious is implicit in his theatre, although it is likely that most of his effects were realized intuitively and not from the study of the psychological text-book. In a reply to an *Enquête sur la jeune littérature* [1] speaking of the " recherche de l'inconscient " as being one of the tendencies of contemporary dramatic authors, he points out that young writers did not wait for the propagation of Freud's theories. But he indicates the importance of those theories and the controversies they aroused. " Certes il y aurait imprudence à les surfaire et à s'abandonner à des exagérations de doctrine. Mais on ne peut nier que la psychanalyse représente un instrument de travail neuf et puissant." He also mentions Freud in an article in *Comœdia* [2] in connection with *Le Printemps des autres*. And, in any case, it would have been difficult for anyone closely connected with *La Chimère* to avoid breathing an atmosphere permeated with Freud's theories. The drama of Lenormand, a fellow member of the reading committee of *La Chimère*, was steeped in them, and Lenormand had written some interesting pages on the subject in the *Bulletin de la Chimère*,[3] to which journal Bernard was also a contributor.

Bernard, who accuses Maeterlinck of " system ", has to defend himself against similar accusations from contemporary critics. In the preface to the first volume of his plays, published in 1925,[4] he quotes the theories on dialogue which he had written for the *Chimère* of May 1922, and says with regard to the " théorie du silence " :

En réalité, il ne s'agit pas de silence et il n'y a là aucune

[1] *Revue Hebdomadaire*, 16th Dec. 1922.
[2] *Quelques Précisions après deux récentes expériences*, 7th Apr. 1924, R.
[3] *Bulletin de la Chimère*, No. V, May 1922, " L'Inconscient dans la littérature dramatique ", R.   [4] *Théâtre*, vol. i, p. 6.

théorie. J'ai été frappé de la valeur dramatique des sentiments inexprimés et, loin de présenter cela comme une nouveauté, j'ai puisé un exemple dans Marivaux, comme j'aurais pu aussi facilement le trouver dans Racine. Je pense qu'un théâtre sobre et dépouillé pourra faire une place de plus en plus grande aux passions inavouées ou inconscientes.

The plays in the first volume [1] form " un moment de mon travail. Mais, pas plus que ceux qui suivront, ils n'en sauraient être l'expression arrêtée . . . il n'y a en définitive qu'une formule viable : celle du renouvellement perpétuel."

Bernard's total work by no means fits into the neat classifications of the critics. Of the twenty plays available to date, excluding unimportant sketches, twelve might be included in the *Théâtre de l'Inexprimé*, and some of these are " borderline cases ". There is accordingly justification in his protest, repeated in the preface to Volume II of his dramatic works : " C'est ainsi que l'auteur de ces lignes, alors qu'il tente de dégager, sous l'apparence quotidienne, la vie secrète ou mystérieuse des êtres, alors qu'il cherche, d'ouvrage en ouvrage, à élargir son univers, voit trop souvent ses efforts ramenés à ce qu'il y a de plus superficiel dans cette ' théorie du silence ' qui n'a jamais été dans ses préoccupations qu'un accessoire ou un moyen." Unlike Maeterlinck, whose drama proceeds from an *a priori* mysticism, Bernard attempts a series of experimental portraits proceeding from a poetic insight into the human heart, and in doing so he gropes his way towards a general philosophy. Between 1922 and 1935 this purpose is achieved mainly through the Unexpressed, the most fitting medium for the dramatist's message at that stage of his development. But the author reserves for himself the right to use other methods should he think fit.

In the volumes of his complete dramatic works Bernard omits three early plays, *Le Voyage à deux*, *La Joie du sacrifice* and *La Maison épargnée*. *Le Voyage à deux* [2] is a humorous

---

[1] *Le Feu qui reprend mal* ; *Martine* ; *Le Printemps des autres* ; *L'Invitation au voyage*.

[2] First performed 22nd Mar. 1909 by the Société de l'Inédit at a literary and artistic club in the rue Volney.

trifle somewhat in the manner of his father, the famous Tristan Bernard. The situation is the "Boulevard" favourite of husband and wife and the lover who is also the husband's best friend; it is treated light-heartedly and ends with the wife's going off with another while the men console each other with two-handed bridge. *La Joie du sacrifice* [1] is a rather arbitrary and symmetrical study of two couples : Robert, married to Céline who is older than himself, and Adrien, married to Françoise who is younger. Adrien and Céline, convinced that the younger people are in love, make up their minds to simulate love on their own account and depart together. But the young people are not in love. They decide to let the other two enjoy their sacrifice, and depart, each to a separate destination. The piece is not wanting in gentle irony and psychological insight, but its machinery creaks a good deal. These two youthful efforts [2] lack maturity and are not worth dwelling upon.

In January 1914 had appeared *L'Épicier*, containing three *nouvelles*, in which were manifest that sensitivity and penetration into the inner life of human beings so characteristic of all his later dramas. *L'Épicier* is a tragedy of unconscious jealousy which lies beneath the monotony of everyday existence and leads in the end to a crime which seems inexplicable to all, including the pitiful criminal. The action is the outcome of childhood miseries, and Paul Blanchart points out [3] how the story appears to be based on the psychological theories of Freud at a time when Freud had no influence on French literature. The same critic shows how another tale in this book, *Le Meuble*, is really a first sketch for *Martine*, only the principal character here is a man who, after awkwardly trying to express his love, adores in silence the niece of his employer. Like Martine, he has to witness the betrothal and married happiness of the one he loves.

The First World War, in which Bernard saw active service, created a lasting impression on him, deepening the sensitivity

---

First performed 8th Mar. 1912.   [2] Jean-Jacques Bernard was born in 1888.
[3] *Jean-Jacques Bernard* (1928), pp. 30-1.

already manifest in *L'Épicier* and determining the trend of his subsequent work. *Les Enfants jouent*, appearing in 1919, is a volume of war stories, or rather impressions, full of troubled melancholy and delicate feeling. The same characteristics were to appear in a later volume of tales, *Les Tendresses menacées*, published in 1924. Bernard wrote numerous *contes* and *essais* ; it is perhaps not irrelevant to mention here two recent non-dramatic works, *Le Camp de la mort lente* [1] and *Le Pain rouge*.[2] The first tells with dignity and restraint of his experiences in a concentration camp for Jews at Compiègne ; the second comprises three *nouvelles* based on the sufferings of child victims of the Second World War. One of these stories, quietly told and painful to read, is about a little French boy, forced to wear a star because of his Jewish blood.

Can Bernard's extreme, almost morbid sensitivity be attributed in part to race ? The special position of Jews, until recently a minority in every country in the world, has over centuries, with other factors, produced in them noticeable psychological effects. Even those whose associations with the country of adoption are long and rich are sooner or later made to feel conscious of being in a false position. A deep-rooted sense of uneasiness and insecurity has frequently resulted either in hypersensitiveness or in cultivated callousness, and at present we do not often find in Jewish writers the serenity and balance of people secure in their unquestioned rights. The problem of double loyalties is imposed by the attitude of non-Jews, and Bernard, like every Jew, has to face it. He considers himself first and foremost a Frenchman. " Il est bien entendu que, si je devais périr dans cette aventure, je serais mort pour la France ; je ne veux pas être revendiqué comme victime par le judaïsme ", he says to two fellow captives at Compiègne,[3] and he writes movingly of a Jew's love for France in *L'Intouchable*, the second story in *Le Pain rouge*. Whatever the choice made, however,

---

[1] Published 1944.   [2] Published 1947.
[3] *Le Camp de la mort lente*, p. 69.

the duality usually persists, if not in the conscious mind, still in subconscious racial memory, and this, together with neurotic tendencies sown by persecutions and humiliations recurring over a period of two thousand years, is apt to colour the temperament of a Jewish writer.

The 5th November 1919 saw the first performance of *La Maison épargnée*, the third play which Bernard decided not to include in his complete works, but which has merit and shows some of the characteristics of the *Théâtre de l'Inexprimé*.

During the First World War, Fabien, the mayor of a little French village, without collaborating with the Germans, has done his best to make life as easy as possible for the villagers during the occupation. One day the Germans depart after burning every house in the village except that of Fabien. Although he continues to live honourably and to render services to the community, gradually he is shunned, and unexpressed suspicion begins to show on every face. Unable to bear it any longer, he leaves with his wife and daughter. But on the cross-roads, seeing his house standing " comme un grand point d'inter-rogation ironique ", he returns and sets it on fire.

A morbid sensitivity of character gives rise here to unbearable anguish and an irrational sense of guilt. " Je n'ai rien fait de mal pourtant ! Et j'éprouve comme des remords." Reason and the conviction of innocence have nothing to do with this over-whelming sensation which has its roots in the subconscious. Fabien has a lack of confidence, a " peur de vivre " which renders existence impossible once he has lost the respect of his fellow men. Imagination, stronger than intelligence, creates its own overpowering realities : " Après tout, que valent mon innocence et mon honnêteté, si ma maison me condamne aux yeux du monde ? Est-ce qu'après mon départ elle ne continuera pas à parler de moi ? . . . Ma maison et mon nom sont liés." The suggestibility of a normal rational man, the compelling hypnotic power of the House, that material symbol of other men's accusing thoughts, hint at unfathomable mysteries of human personality.

The suspicions of the villagers are never clearly expressed and are sometimes made evident by awkward pauses or attitudes of distrust. Fabien's anguish is expressed in silence. By mute looks he tries to reach the hearts of those whom he loves and who trust him no longer. As he fixes his eyes upon the house, the compulsion of its presence is made evident. In the last scene the workmen from the factory instinctively stop talking as they pass him ; an old man mutters something to the little boy by his side and the child looks round. Fabien, after gazing at the village in silence, makes his decision ; he burns down the house. These are the first examples of Bernard's use of silence for realistic effects. Silence is of course the natural reaction of suspicious people towards a man they distrust, and the silent fascination of a symbolic object is a common manifestation of a compulsion neurosis. At this stage, however, silence has no positive function in the dramatic structure.

The first of the plays included in Bernard's complete dramatic works, *Le Feu qui reprend mal*,[1] does not employ the technique of the Unexpressed. In one respect, however, it is similar to *La Maison épargnée* ; it shows, as Léon Lemonnier points out, the same " divorce entre l'intelligence et le subconscient ".[2] Maurice Coindreau detects in this play an echo of Maeterlinck. " Ce titre même : *Le Feu qui reprend mal* ne semble-t-il pas né de la phrase de Golaud : ' Vois-tu, là-bas, ces pauvres qui essaient d'allumer un petit feu dans la forêt ? Il a plu.' "[3]

André Mérin, a prisoner of war, is joyfully reunited to his wife Blanche, and then discovers that she has had an American officer billeted on her during his absence. Doubt and jealousy grow within him ; he is positive that Blanche has been this man's mistress. Blanche has indeed been attracted to the American, but has remained faithful to André, whom she loves. André cannot believe her, his suspicions gradually poison their existence until,

---

[1] First performed 9th June 1921.

[2] Léon Lemonnier, " Le Théâtre de Jean-Jacques Bernard " ; extract from the *Revue Mondiale*, with illegible date ; dossier of Jean-Jacques Bernard, R.

[3] *La Farce est jouée* (1942), p. 216.

goaded beyond endurance, she is on the point of joining the American. But André's father comes in; his wistful words about old age and lost happiness move Blanche to pity ; she looks round ; everything in the room reminds her of old times, and she cannot find it in her heart to leave.

Writing of the " reprise " of this play,[1] Henry Bidou points out the two truths upon which it is founded : the impossibility of reading into the most limpid soul, and the fact that even the most faithful heart conceals at least the shadow of a secret, enough to poison love. This is the stuff of the Theatre of the Unexpressed, the spiritual isolation which may be felt by two beings physically near one another, the frustration of Golaud in *Pelléas et Mélisande*, and his anguish at the impossibility of ever knowing the truth, the hidden secrets of the subconscious, the tremendous power of the imagination over reason. " Un doute infernal, par instants, m'obscurcit la raison. C'est comme une fièvre qui vous prend et contre laquelle on ne lutte pas." [2] The technique of the Unexpressed, however, is not employed here ; the characters put their thoughts and doubts into words, sometimes even dreaming aloud in the Chekhovian manner. André is fully aware of his irrational jealousy, and defines and analyses it quite subtly. Blanche is perfectly lucid on the subject of her mixed feelings for the American, and communicates them clearly to a confidante. The play in substance contains the germs of Jean-Jacques Bernard's later drama. There are affinities especially with *L'Invitation au voyage*; in both plays a decisive character—here the American officer—does not appear on the stage ; in both cases it is in reality not the character himself, but the imagination of another working upon him, that is the all-important factor. In both cases, too, the ending is unsatisfactory. We have the feeling that distrust and suspicion will grow up again between André and Blanche ; that Marie-Louise of *L'Invitation au voyage* will start dreaming again.

The theories of Bernard quoted at the beginning of this

[1] Feuilleton of the *Journal des Débats*, 21st Oct. 1929, R.   [2] Act II.

chapter indicate a certain variety in the Unexpressed which manifests itself in his drama and enables us, in a way, to group his " silent " plays.   Broadly speaking, they divide into plays concerned with unexpressed emotions of which the character is aware, and plays dealing with sentiments and desires submerged in the subconscious, and unrealized by the person in whom they are at work.

Two plays in the first group, *Martine* and *Le Secret d'Arvers*, deal with characters who consciously suffer in silence.   The subject in both cases is unrequited love, and for the first time it is the very silence of the principals on this essential point, illuminated and set off by the dialogue of the others, which is the highlight of the play.   In both cases the silence upon which the audience's attention is riveted is a telling indication of character, for it alone can convey the delicacy and timid reserve which is the essential beauty of the person's nature.

In *Martine* [1] we see a peasant girl resting beneath an apple tree one hot summer's day.   On the highway appears a young man making his way towards the village of Grandchin.   Returning from foreign service, he is going to visit his beloved grandmother and to renew friendship with a charming girl whom he knew in childhood days.   He asks Martine the way, sits down beside her and starts an innocent flirtation.   Martine falls in love with him ; it is the passion of her life.   But Julien is ignorant of the depths of feeling he has aroused.   In Jeanne, the friend of his childhood, now a woman of culture and refinement, he finds his life's companion.   Martine is fated to witness in painful silence the happiness of the young couple, and even to be the recipient of Jeanne's confidences.

After their departure to Paris, Martine takes refuge with the old grandmother, in whom she finds something of Julien.   The grandmother, moved by the girl's silent suffering, advises her to marry Alfred, an honest though uncouth peasant who has always loved her, and with the indifference of despair she agrees.   Much later,

when Julien and Jeanne return to the village after the grandmother's death and visit Martine, they find her transformed into
a peasant's wife, her lovely fair hair screwed back, her face
expressionless. Finding himself for a moment alone with her,
Julien speaks tenderly of the past, thus renewing involuntarily
the torments she had managed to repress. Sadly he departs with
Jeanne. They will return on All Saints' Day, a date Martine will
live for. But on All Saints' Day the grandmother's house will
be sold. Nothing will remain of Martine's love but Madame
Mervan's grave, and there she will go to tend the flowers ; this
act of devotion, religiously repeated, will be the rite by which
her deep, hidden emotion will find its sole means of expression.

The subject of the play—love arising out of a misunderstanding and its torments suffered in silence—is by no means new.
Most of the contemporary critics are reminded of Rosette in
Musset's *On ne badine pas avec l'amour*. In both cases a simple,
innocent peasant girl is made to suffer by two intelligent, subtle
and rather selfish people. In Musset's play, however, the interest
is centred on the dialogue of Perdican and Camille ; in Bernard's
on the silences of Martine. Rosette's unhappiness, her fainting
on hearing from concealment proof of Perdican's faithlessness,
her death in the oratoire, are stages in a cruel game of two self-
centred lovers. Her death forms a climax to her sufferings and
resolves the situation between Perdican and Camille ; her pain is
over and, as far as she is concerned, the spectator experiences a
sense of " détente " ; pity for her past sufferings is mingled with
calm relief at the thought that they are now at an end. In the
case of Martine our feelings are more painful ; those who unintentionally caused her unhappiness fade out of the picture, and
we have the conviction that the sufferings transmitted to us
through her eloquent silences will last as long as she lives.

In a passage previously quoted,[1] Bernard says that he had
taken an example for a play from Marivaux. He does not specify

---

[1] Preface to *Théâtre*, vol. i, p. 6.

the example or the play. There is in *Martine* a reminiscence of the case of Marton in *Les Fausses Confidences* and the resemblance in names, possibly fortuitous, is striking. Marton's love, the result of a misunderstanding, is again subordinate to the main interest ; although not lacking in pathos, she is not the " silent " type, and her case has not the tragic intensity of that of Martine. Angélique in *L'Épreuve* loves silently and suffers cruelly in the gratuitous test to which her selfish lover subjects her. There are of course many passages in Marivaux's dialogue which could have suggested the idea of *Martine* :

> Il y a des manières qui valent des paroles ; on dit, je vous aime, avec un regard ; et on le dit bien.[1]

> Regardez-la quand elle aime, et qu'elle ne veut pas le dire, morbleu ! nos tendresses les plus babillardes approchent-elles de l'amour qui passe à travers son silence ? [2]

The silences of Martine arise in the first place from the author's attempts at impersonal realism. Instead of trying to put himself inside the character of Martine, he reveals her from the outside. Emotions are conveyed not by the spoken word but by behaviour, just as a sudden ripple on the surface of a lake indicates that there is something moving beneath. The beginnings of love show in little instinctive movements and hesitations ; dismay at its hopelessness, agitation at the sight of her cultured rival, anguish at the torments thoughtlessly inflicted on her by the one she loves—all appear in attitude, gesture and expression. Stage directions are part of the structure of the play and are as important as the text.

In *Martine* the dramatic function of silence has not yet reached full capacity, but it has advanced far beyond *La Maison épargnée*, and its nature is so different from that of the theatre of Maeterlinck that *Martine* is hailed as a " classic " of the new school of silence and is still considered as the typical " silent "

---

[1] *Les Serments indiscrets*, Act II, sc. 10.   [2] *La Surprise de l'amour*, Act I, sc. 2.

play. It is true that Régis Gignoux, in connection with *Martine*, speaks of Maeterlinck and his " petites princesses qui gardaient leur grand secret et ne parlaient qu'avec des voix étouffées ".[1] In Martine, however, silence is a positive quality of a normal character and she has little in common with the vague Maleine or Mélisande. Bernard uses silence to convey realistically a deeply felt emotion. We have mentioned certain realistic silences in Maeterlinck in connection with love and fear, but, generally speaking, love with him finds its ultimate expression in a subdued lyricism, and fear is uttered in stammering phrases. The essential that is left unsaid is the idea of Fate and Death, inferred by the spectator from the representation of the emotion, or from a symbolic dialogue such as we find in *Les Aveugles*. The Unexpressed is usually linked by Maeterlinck, not with character, but with intangible influences and radiates, so to speak, over the whole play. In *Martine* we have silence intimately associated with one individual. It is a logical outcome of the girl's character, it is indeed the supreme expression of her character ; she is the " silent " type. Natural reticence combined with deep, controlled emotion produces a painful intensity of passion which would become diffuse in a romantic torrent of words. This intense and dramatic passion concentrates our whole attention on the individual and we are concerned, not with the mysteries of the universe, but with a human being who is suffering.

That silence which is the most vital part of Martine's character develops and moves with the events with which it comes into conflict. We are not yet at the point where silence is used to mark stages in the dramatic action : conflict, peripeteia, recognition. *Martine* is a character study, episodic in construction. Five tableaux replace the customary acts. The intensity of emotion increases with almost every silence. At the end, when Martine and Alfred are alone in the lamplight and nothing is heard but the ticking of the clock, we feel that the subterranean tide of emotion will flow on, never ceasing.

Quoted in *La Petite Illustration* of 22nd July 1922.

N

The significance of the important dramatic silences has to be brought out by the dialogue preceding them. Martine's hopeless love must be recognized and made the subject of comment by others. Even in this task the author employs a discretion and sobriety which scarcely allow him to touch on direct expression. Julien is talking to his grandmother : " Ce qui fait le fond de ma vie, je l'aime sans manifester ; et à côté de cela, je m'extasierai sur une fleur passagère ".[1] " Pauvre Martine ! " says Madame Mervan, as if to herself ; and that is all. Even in lucid conversation the essential is not spoken and the course of the tragedy is hastened. What does her grandson want of Martine, Madame Mervan goes on to ask. " Julien, je suis liée avec les parents de cette petite. Les Gévin sont de braves gens. Qu'arriverait-il si . . . ? "[2] Julien replies : " Grand'mère . . . que te dire ? Ne me connais-tu pas ? . . . Ne m'avez-vous pas légué un fonds d'honnêteté . . . qui m'a déjà privé de bien des joies, hélas ! . . ." and it stops at that. Julien will not understand that, although incapable of common seduction, he is responsible for a much deeper tragedy. That the grandmother does not try to make him understand is the fundamental weakness of the play.

Very moving is the conversation at the end of the fourth tableau between Madame Mervan and Martine ; it is practically a monologue, for Martine says hardly a word. The old lady is persuading her to marry Alfred and grasp the happiness which is within her reach ; neither mentions Julien's name, although each is aware that the other is thinking of him, and Martine knows that her secret is shared and understood. Martine accepts with the faint murmur : " Ça m'est égal ". Only once, after Martine has rushed out of the room in anguish, is the situation actually put into words. " Pourquoi ne pas parler franchement ? " says Jeanne to Julien. " Je vois clair à présent. Nous ne saurons jamais ce qu'un flirt de quelques jours, qui n'a eu aucune importance pour toi, a pu laisser dans cette âme simple."[3]

The situation preceding this last speech is that of the silent

[1] Tableau II.　　[2] *Ibid.*　　[3] Tableau IV.

character placed beside speaking actors, examples of which we mentioned in Aeschylus. Here it is used with special effect. Martine is in the room with Jeanne when Julien returns from Paris. The young married people begin to talk awkwardly. They obviously desire to be alone. But Martine is incapable of tearing herself away from the one she loves with the tenacity of a true peasant. " Pendant qu'ils parlaient, Martine les regardait fixement, sans bouger. Elle avait bien conscience de sa situation fausse, mais partir était au-dessus de ses forces. . . . Quand Julien se tait, elle essaye de parler, mais vainement. Et tout à coup, sans un mot, elle sort." Every word spoken by the happy couple increases her mute torment, but instead of allowing it to culminate in speech, she rushes out of the room. The intensity of her suffering reaches its height here and is very painful.

A dialogue which is to explain dramatic silences necessitates a certain intelligence, perspicacity and facility in self-expression on the part of at least one of the " non-silent " characters. Julien and Jeanne are intelligent people who are capable of analysing a situation, and even their own characters, up to a certain limit. Their analysis is subtle and exact as far as it goes, but reason, the instrument of analysis, is inadequate for dealing with the problem, since certain factors are not taken into consideration, things which they do not know, or do not wish to know. The dramatic situation is produced by an effective antithesis of types. We have the inarticulate young girl filled with a simple, direct emotion of which she is fully conscious, and two subtle people, capable of expressing themselves, but influenced by complicated motives of which they are not fully aware.

The most civilized and lucid character is Jeanne, the only one who goes the length of putting the situation into words. It is her sensitive culture and her subtle instinct, contrasting so vividly with the simplicity of the peasant girl, which attract Julien to her. She is fundamentally kind, honest and straightforward, yet her attitude towards Martine is complicated by a certain cruelty of which she is uneasily aware and which she tries to analyse.

Although she senses that Martine is suffering, she has taken her as her confidante :

> JEANNE. . . . Naturellement, ce qui m'attire, ce n'est pas de faire souffrir ; c'est de sentir en cette petite l'inconscient désir de se raccrocher à cela. . . . Je suis tout ce qui lui reste de toi.
> JULIEN. Si tu le sens, comment ne réagis-tu pas ?
> JEANNE. J'essaye . . . Et c'est plus fort que moi. Car, comprends : moi aussi, je te retrouve en elle. (. . .) Mais le plus cruel, c'est qu'aussitôt que tu reviens, elle n'existe plus pour moi. Pour un peu sa présence m'agacerait. . . ." [1]

She realizes that there is a subtle perversity in her conduct towards Martine and attempts to justify herself by attributing it to praiseworthy motives—pity and sympathy for the little peasant girl who clings to her as a symbol of Julien, love of her husband whom she sees in Martine. These motives are there, but obviously the fundamental cause is her unconscious jealousy.

Julien is capable of analysing his own character, as indeed he does in the words to Madame Mervan which we previously quoted, but he cannot see the implications of these words with regard to Martine. For an educated and intelligent man his total incomprehension of the state of affairs he has brought about is disquieting. It is indeed an outstanding weakness in the play. Martine has ceased to be important to him now that he is married, and he is convinced that Jeanne is exaggerating when she tries to make things clear. It is difficult, too, to excuse his apparent lack of feeling in the closing stages of the play. Troubled by the change he finds in Martine, now a typical peasant's wife, he begins to dwell sentimentally on the past. Is she happy ? Is there no moment in her life which she remembers sometimes with tenderness ? ". . . dites-moi que vous gardez un coin dans votre cœur pour le beau mois de juillet où nous nous sommes rencontrés sur la route. . . . Moi, je n'y penserai jamais sans émotion." Every word he pronounces makes the young woman suffer more and

[1] Tableau IV.

more, until a cry of despair and reproach is torn from her. But immediately, terrified by what she has said, she begins to stammer and is silent, clinging to the table and unable to hold back her tears. " Qu'est-ce qui m'a pris ? . . . Qu'est-ce que j'ai dit là ? " he mutters. He is a well-meaning young man but, as with Jeanne, there is a suggestion of moral sadism, this time unconscious, combined with a certain emotional dilettantism and the thoughtlessness of the self-centred.

There is in this play a development of the dramatist's conception of the subconscious. In *La Maison épargnée* and *Le Feu qui reprend mal* the principal characters are overwhelmed by an obsession with which their intellect cannot cope. Fabien's sense of guilt, André's jealousy, obviously have their roots in the subconscious. The author does not dwell on this aspect, but the morbidness and irrationality of the obsession point to it. There is no attempt at Freudian analysis such as we have in Lenormand's *Mangeur de rêves*, although it is quite possible that such cases have their origin in some forgotten and submerged incident. We feel, at any rate, that the obsession is bound up with the mystery of a hypersensitive personality, either bruised by some external influence like André's experiences as a prisoner of war, or morbid through some inborn hereditary tendency, a general " peur de vivre ", as no doubt is the case with Fabien. The emotion of these characters is symptomatic of some deep, inner cause which the author here does not attempt to explain. There is the same sense of bafflement and frustration as a doctor might experience when confronted by a physical lesion whose cause cannot be fathomed.

In *Martine* we can detect the beginnings of a tendency towards Freudian analysis which is to reach full expression in *Le Printemps des autres* and *L'Invitation au voyage*. In the two previously mentioned plays Bernard is primarily concerned with the passion or obsession itself, fully realized by the character. This is indeed in the tradition of Racine. In the case of Julien and Jeanne, however, he is dealing not with the essential passion but with behaviour and attitude ; the emotion which is their fundamental cause—Jeanne's jealousy, Julien's cruelty—is sunk below the level of consciousness and is scarcely even hinted at. The play, of course, centres round Martine's conscious reticence ; the rôle of the subconscious in Julien and Jeanne is subordinate. Bernard has not yet reached the stage of analysing behaviour dramatically through the Unexpressed, which he does when unconscious emotion is the main problem under consideration. The subconscious emotions of Julien and Jeanne are merely inferred in a vague fashion by the spectator from the sum total of the dramatic content. What analysis there is, for example, in the lines of Jeanne already quoted is concerned with conscious feeling. But there are seeds here of later experiments. The idea, for example, of the conflicting feelings experienced, as by Jeanne, towards an object of affection is developed in *Le Printemps des autres* and *Le Jardinier d'Ispahan.*

Also to be found in *Martine* are two characteristics of the *Théâtre de L'Inexprimé*, apparently contradictory, but in fact expressing two different aspects of the one reality. They are the sense of isolation of human souls and the idea of the communion of souls without words. (The first was movingly expressed in *La Maison épargnée* and in *Le Feu qui reprend mal*.) Martine will never be understood by Julien whom she loves, and she will always remain spiritually separated from Alfred who loves her. Yet at the same time, reaching out desperately after some reminder, some symbol of Julien, she communes wordlessly with Jeanne, with the old grandmother. Between Julien and Jeanne there is the same direct spiritual communication. Julien tries to define it to Jeanne : " Je parlais une langue étrangère et je retrouve un parler familier, une façon directe de comprendre les choses . . . sans explications. Le langage de ce qui ne s'exprime pas. . . . Et il y a tant de choses qui ne s'expriment pas et qu'il faut comprendre . . . comme ça . . . n'est-ce pas ? " [1] In the case of Maeterlinck, both the sense of isolation and the direct

[1] Tableau II.

communication accord with the degree to which the soul is attuned
to mystic truth. With Bernard it is a question of human love
experienced and fully shared. Maeterlinck's treatment is metaphysical; Bernard's emotional. In his monograph on Bernard,
Paul Blanchart [1] quotes a line of Julien's : " Vous êtes d'une
intelligence qui m'émeut " and maintains that Bernard's whole
art is " d'une intelligence qui émeut ". He goes on to say : " La
part du cœur et celle de l'esprit s'y équilibrent et s'y mêlent
harmonieusement. *Comprendre* y devient synonyme de *sentir*." [2]
With Martine the emotion giving rise to " communication
directe " is deep, pure and silent, but in the subtler characters
the emotion, diffused to a certain extent by the ideas and
associations which have formed round it, finds some expression in
hesitant words. " Il me semble que je retrouve une atmosphère
. . . un peu oubliée . . . et sympathique . . .", says Julien,
feeling the attraction to Jeanne growing. ". . . Certaines choses
ont un parfum d'autrefois qui monte à la tête. . . ." [3] Jeanne's
mind works in the same way as his ; she is moved by the same
things. The idea of the cornfield being shaped like a cornucopia
—which Martine laughs at uncomprehendingly—Jeanne finds
moving, and the lines by Chénier to which Martine listens
blankly Jeanne takes up and finishes, to Julien's delight.

In his article, *Le Silence au théâtre*,[4] Bernard declares that
Martine was not written in accordance with a formula. " Ce
n'est qu'après coup qu'une certaine formule a pu s'en dégager
pour moi." I have attempted to show how, in the earlier plays,
various characteristics of the *Théâtre de l'Inexprimé* begin to
emerge. With *Martine* the author becomes fully conscious of the
new instrument he has forged and begins his series of experiments
with the Unexpressed.

Le Secret d'Arvers, although first performed on the 6th June
1926, was, as Bernard tells us in the preface to the second volume

[1] *Op. cit.* p. 28.
[2] Paul Blanchart entitles an article in *Chantecler*, 28th Apr. 1928, " Jean-Jacques
Bernard ou l'intelligence de la sensibilité ", R.
[3] Tableau II.   [4] *Bulletin de la Chimère*, No. V, May 1922, R.

of his dramatic works, finished less than a year after *Martine*. It had been refused by the Théâtre Français because there was no anniversary of Arvers in sight. The subject matter closely resembles that of *Martine*, only this time the one who suffers is a poet, capable of expressing himself, but choosing to remain silent through reserve and timidity. It is February 1831 ; we see the salon of Charles Nodier at the Bibliothèque de l'Arsenal. Charming Marie Nodier, who has become Madame Ménessier, has come to stay for a short time at her father's place. There she finds two former admirers, Fontaney and Arvers. Gay, witty, insouciant, she prattles about her husband, whom she loves, about the literary gatherings of before her marriage, about anything and everything ; she is interested in the young men's plans, she plays the piano. . . . Arvers, who all this time has hardly said a word, writes in her album a sonnet which he had already composed. She reads it absently, continually interrupted. For Marie it is a charming little literary effort ; for Arvers it is a life's passion.

> Hélas ! j'aurai passé près d'elle inaperçu,
> Toujours à ses côtés et toujours solitaire,
> Et j'aurai jusqu'au bout fait mon temps sur la terre,
> N'osant rien demander, et n'ayant rien reçu. . . .

In this short one-act play there is no opportunity for development in silences, as in the case of *Martine*. It centres round one silence arising out of character and situation. By the Unexpressed the writer represents the state of mind at a time of crisis of a man hopelessly and silently in love ; he has staked all on the message of the sonnet and has lost. He will take his secret with him to the grave. His reserve is set off by Fontaney's romantic lyricism and his silence is contrasted with Marie's gay, thoughtless chatter. L. Dubech pertinently remarks : " Pour que le spectateur d'intelligence moyenne puisse comprendre la passion d'Arvers, M. Bernard est forcé d'en souligner les effets au point que le public ne comprend plus que Marie ne comprenne pas ".[1] There may of course be something in René

[1] *Action Française*, 20th June 1926, R.

Wisner's comment : " Elle est femme de lettres ; cela veut dire qu'elle n'est pas psychologue ".[1]   Nevertheless, we cannot but feel that, for a daughter of Charles Nodier, Marie is lacking in finesse and even in common courtesy. There is just a hint of " tour de force " in this play, yet even Dubech, wary and hostile to what he considers " système " in Bernard, admits that this is a " piécette ravissante ".

The comments of H. R. Lenormand on the final scene, coloured by his own Freudian theories, show in an interesting manner another aspect of Bernard's treatment of the subconscious. Marie has finished reading the poem after many interruptions. She remains for a long moment lost in rêverie, staring in front or her ; then she starts to arrange the flowers, humming to the tune of *Malbrough* the last words of the poem : " Et ne comprendra pas ".

> C'est à dire que si la divination du secret d'Arvers ne l'a même pas effleurée, sur le plan de la conscience claire, il a tout de même frayé son chemin, ce secret, jusqu'aux régions obscures de l'être. Il a atteint en Marie la personne cachée, l'hôtesse inconnue, qui ordonne les rêves et recueille les émanations de la force psychique. Charles Nodier paraît et lui demande ce qu'elle chante ; elle ne savait pas qu'elle chantait.[2]

We now come to plays in which the interest is shifted to the functioning of subconscious emotion. The first of these is *Le Printemps des autres*.[3] At a hotel in Stresa, Clarisse, a woman of some forty years, still beautiful, is approached by a timid young man who is anxious to make her acquaintance. Accustomed to receiving homage to her beauty, she thinks at first that this is a new admirer ; he has, moreover, appeared at a critical stage in her life : her lover has left her, and wounded pride and an aching heart are in need of consolation and rehabilitation. In order to give him confidence she speaks a little of her life and even confides something of her past sorrows. Maurice, however, had been trying to ask for the hand of her daughter Gilberte. When

---

[1] *Carnet*, 13th June 1926, R.   [2] *Chantecler*, 12th June 1926, R.
[3] First performed 19th Mar. 1924.

Gilberte appears, he retires awkwardly without saying anything. Impulsively the girl confesses their love to her mother, who listens in silence without ceasing to look at her face. " C'est vrai . . . c'est vrai que tu es belle ", is all that she says. And when Gilberte has gone out she takes her looking-glass and gazes at her reflection for a long time. In an eloquent silence comes the revelation that her youth is past. Her daughter is no longer a child ; she is beautiful and she is a rival.

The young couple marry and we see them a year later at Neuilly. Clarisse tries to make herself believe that she is their good and helpful companion, but, actuated by unconscious jealousy, she lets fall little reproaches, slight criticisms, which, although she is scarcely aware of it, are aimed at the destruction of the marriage. Her reproaches, often expressed in a light bantering tone, are addressed to Maurice. The author's psychology is penetrating here, for not only does Clarisse desire to separate the young people, but, loving Maurice unconsciously, she experiences the need to approach him in some way and this continual nagging does, paradoxically enough, constitute a kind of rapprochement. Racine has effective touches of this nature. When Phèdre, struggling with her unlawful love, starts to persecute Hippolyte, it is partly because she wants to be noticed by him. For a similar reason Ériphile derives a kind of pleasure from talking to Iphigénie of the cruelties of Achille. At a conscious level, Clarisse rationalizes her actions by attributing them to her love for Gilberte, although it is obvious from the first act that she has often hurt the girl by her cold indifference and her selfishness.

As a result of Clarisse's machinations, Maurice frequently finds himself in the company of Madame Desgrées, a dangerous woman whom Gilberte detests. One day Gilberte rushes in distress to her mother's house with the lamentable news that he has left her for this woman. Clarisse nearly betrays herself.

> GILBERTE. Tu t'y attendais ?
> CLARISSE (*rêveuse*). Malgré moi parfois, une pensée . . .
> une crainte fugitive m'effleurait : ' Elle me reviendra, et il

faudra que je lui donne tout '. Peut-être, sans m'en douter, vivais-je pour cet instant . . . (*vivement*) cet instant cruel. . . .[1]

Clarisse speaks to her tenderly ; they are going to resume their former life, to live like two sisters. She makes plans for the future. Suddenly Maurice telephones, and Clarisse tells him that Gilberte is not there. Gilberte, distracted, cannot understand why this chance of a reconciliation is destroyed. Violent words are exchanged before the final silent anagnorisis :

> GILBERTE. Tu le hais.
> CLARISSE. Ce n'est pas vrai.
> GILBERTE. Alors ? Alors ? Alors ? (*Elles se tiennent un instant, l'une devant l'autre, comme deux ennemies. Et soudain Clarisse recule, terrifiée*) Maman ?
> CLARISSE (*qui prend conscience pour la première fois de toute la réalité*). Tais-toi, tais-toi. . . . (*Brusquement*) Va-t'en.[2]

Maurice comes in to explain and Gilberte takes refuge in his arms. The logical dénouement is expressed in a final silence. Gilberte understands and pardons. Clarisse makes the right decision. She will go to Spain alone. " Très long regard muet, regard d'intelligence de femme à femme." They embrace and Clarisse is left alone. " Alors, d'un mouvement machinal, elle prend le sac de voyage, et s'y appuie des deux mains, brisée. . . ."

Le Printemps des autres is nearer to ancient tragedy than any of the other plays of Bernard. First we have something approaching a conflict between human and divine will—if we may regard as equivalent to the divine will the Freudian Censor—causing repression of the unlawful emotion. In *Martine* there was no real conflict, only suffering ; in La *Maison épargnée* and *Le Feu qui reprend mal* there is conflict in the cases of Fabien and André between two different aspects of their characters. But the dramatic use of a controlling moral law is new in Bernard. The conflict within Clarisse results in a course of action undertaken, which is presented here on two planes. Clarisse has fallen in love ; then comes the silent peripeteia, when the person she imagines about to confess love for her proves to be in love with her daughter, putting her in the position not of a beloved woman, but of one for whom life is finished. This is followed by the deliberate thrusting of the passion into the realm of the subconscious, from which source resentment, frustration and desire to be noticed give rise to acts of apparent hostility to one she loves, while jealousy inspires acts of apparent love to one she has really disliked. Finally, the silent anagnorisis, or realization of the true situation, brings the submerged emotions to the surface and results in a decision which rounds off the play. Thus the work is an imitation of psychological action which is complete, having, as we see, a beginning, a middle and an end. There is not, in the true sense, an analysis of character or of the passions, love and jealousy, themselves, but a realistic and impersonal representation of a selfish, frustrated human being's behaviour split into two layers.

From the résumé I have given, the dramatic function of the pure silences, that is, absence of dialogue, becomes clear. Instead of a tirade, it is silence that contains the whole of a crisis. Instead of the *scène à faire*, we have, as Edmond Sée puts it, the *scène à taire*. It is for action and dialogue to lead up to these silent crises and make them clear. In order to bring this about, Bernard contrived to have in *Martine* one character, Jeanne, who was capable of seeing clearly into the situation and putting it into words. He contrives the same effect in *L'Invitation au voyage* with the character of Jacqueline. In *Le Printemps des autres*, however, as such a situation could never be prolonged, were any of the actors aware of its significance, it is necessary for all three to remain in ignorance until the scene of " realization " ; Maurice indeed remains unenlightened throughout. Maurice and Gilberte analyse Clarisse's temperamental behaviour in an attempt to account for her fits of seeming inconsistency, but they remain ignorant of the essential hidden factor.

In order, therefore, to make the situation clear, the author employs various devices. There are Clarisse's mechanical gestures and reflex actions at certain points in the drama : looking into her mirror when she realizes that Gilberte is no longer a child but a rival ; taking out her lipstick when she is expecting Maurice ; movements of nervous irritation when, for example, the young people call her " maman " instead of treating her as a " bonne camarade ", as was agreed ; an involuntary cry when she sees the young couple embracing. There are displays of emotion inappropriate to the outward situation : her agitation when Gilberte comes in desperate (she thinks an accident has befallen Maurice) is followed by relative calm when she hears that Maurice has gone to Madame Desgrées, and we witness also her excessive happiness when making plans for herself and the disconsolate Gilberte. In addition, as in *Martine*, we have silence against a significant dialogue ; while the young couple talk and plan their ménage, her eyes are fixed on them and in that steady gaze is revealed her unconscious jealousy. Finally, there is " le langage indirect " ; by the subconscious choice and arrangement of words her true sentiments are betrayed. Her words to Gilberte in the last scene, already quoted, form only one of many examples.

The latter part of Act II contains a most effective example of "langage indirect" leading, in addition, to a significant peripeteia. Clarisse has summoned Maurice at Gilberte's request to dissuade him from going riding with Madame Desgrées. She starts to reproach him for being too attentive to that woman. Her own emotion surges up and on the pretext of Gilberte's distress at his thoughtlessness, she bursts forth : " Ah ! vous êtes un enfant, vous êtes un enfant. Vous ne savez pas quelles souffrances provoque un geste maladroit. Vous ne savez pas ce qu'un regard de vous mal dirigé peut blesser un cœur qui vous aime. Enfant, enfant, vous faites mal, vous faites mal. . . . Vous ne devez pas faire tant de mal. . . ." One thinks of Phèdre's speech to Hippolyte ; she, of course, ends by expressing her love, whereas Clarisse's emotion, of which she is not wholly conscious, remains muted and is never in any way communicated to Maurice. In distress Maurice suggests that he should not see Madame Desgrées again. " Je ne vous ai pas dit cela ", says Clarisse in a toneless voice. " Je ne sais pas, moi. . . . Je vous ai mis en garde. . . . Mais il ne faut rien . . . exagérer. . . ." She prevents him from rushing to reassure Gilberte, who, she untruthfully suggests, knows nothing of this interview, and finally, when Maurice announces his intention of going riding to distract his mind, the very thing Gilberte wanted to prevent, she cannot summon the power to stop him.

The Unexpressed is used, as I indicated, for purposes of external realism. The sentiments entertained by Clarisse are of a kind which cannot be discussed. Clarisse is not a naturally reticent type of woman. She has had the indelicacy to take a young man of twenty-six as a confidant concerning a recent irregular liaison. She is a woman of a certain culture and finesse and she is not inarticulate. The intense emotions of which she does not speak are unlawful emotions, deliberately shut out of her mind. They reveal themselves at the conscious level by inconsistent and disconcerting behaviour. Clarisse is, in fact, a mildly psychopathic case. Psychopathic tendencies are shown in Fabien and André. They, however, remain perfectly lucid throughout ; reason still operates, and indeed one of the causes of the weakness of the two early plays is that in each case the character is a prey to two forces of equal strength, reason on the one hand and an irrational emotion on the other, and the situation is a deadlock. Fabien does indeed try to solve his problem by removing himself from and eventually destroying the physical symbol of his irrational guilt, but we feel that he will still remain haunted by the image of the house. It is the same with André. The two forces within him remaining of equal strength, he finds it impossible to perform a decisive action and the author has to impose an arbitrary conclusion. Old Monsieur Mérin might never have come in when he did and we feel, in any case, that the barrier between him and Blanche will always remain. But in Le Printemps des autres the decisive action has been taken. The decision is contrary to that of the classical theatre. Instead of facing the issue and consciously choosing either to relinquish or to indulge in the passion, Clarisse, who desires both to maintain her self-respect and to cling to an agreeable emotion, makes a temporary escape from reality by deliberately making part of her mind a blank. The irony of the drama is in her temporary ignorance of her real personality ; the tragedy is in her sudden realization of it. Benjamin Crémieux detects an element of Pirandello in the Theatre of the Unexpressed ; he indicates that it is one of the manifestations of the " tragique de connaissance " introduced into the drama by Pirandello.[1]

Bernard's probing into the unconscious leads him more and more to " cases " rather than character, and this removes his plays from the highest ranks of tragedy. Phèdre is the tragic heroine, essentially noble and worthy of admiration, but with just that human frailty which Aristotle indicates as necessary in order that her downfall should inspire pity and terror. There is nothing noble in a " case ". Clarisse is displeasing, an egoistic, self-indulgent woman ; Marie-Louise of *L'Invitation au voyage* is of the vague Emma Bovary type ; Francine of *Nationale 6* appears to be an example of arrested mental development. With them we experience no tragic exaltation ; a sense of pity, perhaps, but mostly a kind of painful curiosity.

L'Invitation au voyage, although first performed on the 15th February 1924, that is a month before *Le Printemps des autres*, was written after it, according to the order in the first volume, which, as the author tells us in his preface to Volume II, is the order of their composition. In an article in *Le Journal*[2] Bernard tells how the idea of the play grew. Near Verdun, in 1914, he had imagined the wife of a French patriot becoming the mistress of a German spy. After successive refinements he dropped the idea of espionage, then adultery, then war, then passion, and finally it became, in his own words, " la cristallisation des aspirations secrètes d'une jeune femme heureuse autour de l'image d'un

---

[1] *Encyclopédie Française*, December 1935. Tome xvii, ch. 2, *Les Arts du temps*, iv, " Les Tendances actuelles du théâtre ".

[2] 23rd Feb. 1924, R.

indifférent parti pour un pays lointain ". Last of all, he thought of the poem by Baudelaire which gives the title to the play.

In *L'Invitation au voyage* we have a more marked case of " escapism ". Marie-Louise lives happily with her husband Olivier and her little boy Gérard, although from time to time she feels irked by the narrowness of her provincial life. Philippe, an acquaintance of Olivier's who had been staying with them, has just left for Argentina on business and, although she had found him uninteresting while he was with them, the magic word Argentina sets her dreaming. Argentina is irrealizable desire, adventure, freedom. Unconsciously she identifies Argentina with Philippe ; all that the longed-for country represents is embodied in a man transformed by her lively imagination. One day she learns that Philippe has returned unexpectedly to Épinal. She goes to join him. It is still the same mediocre Philippe. The shock of reality cures her ; we cannot help wondering whether the cure will last.

Paul Blanchart [1] suggests that Marie-Louise's annoyance with Philippe is perhaps the reflex of an inner agitation which cannot be confessed, that possibly the attraction to one whom she sees destined to become another business man like her husband has already begun. This, however, is inconsistent with the idea of " cristallisation " submitted by the author and makes the anagnorisis meaningless. Marie-Louise is really an example of " bovarisme ", of a special form of that malady—desire to escape from life, a desire which invades her whole personality and produces a slight psychic abnormality. Clarisse of *Le Printemps des autres* is a normal woman. The series of false and inconsistent actions on her part is the result of a genuine emotion, repressed for the time being in obedience to a recognized moral law. In *L'Invitation au voyage* the conscious feeling of love for Philippe is unreal. It is the outward manifestation of submerged longings which themselves arise from a fundamental weakness of character, an incapacity for dealing with life, the " peur de

[1] *Op. cit.* p. 13.

vivre " of the post-1918 generation. There is no repression.
The vague aspirations simply crystallize at the mention of
Argentina.   Philippe, with whom she associates Argentina,
becomes the symbol of her deep longings ; he gives them an
apparent reality and, by providing her with the kind of world ·
suited to her weak personality, momentarily restores her self-
confidence.

This false love is seen to rise from the subconscious to the
conscious level, and the emotion, unlike that of the previous play,
develops in silence, to culminate in lucid expression, when,
agitated by the news of Philippe's presence in Épinal, Marie-
Louise confides in her sister. Jacqueline, as we have already
indicated, is one of those perspicacious characters whom Bernard
often places beside his " case " in order to elucidate the unexpressed or subconscious emotion.

> JACQUELINE. Je t'assure que je comprends beaucoup mieux
> que tu ne crois. J'ai des yeux pour voir. Et je sais bien que
> l'Argentine t'a fait rêver. (. . .)
> MARIE-LOUISE. Peut-être le vrai bonheur manqué . . .
> et par ma faute. . . .
> JACQUELINE. Par ta faute ? . . . Quelle idée !
> MARIE-LOUISE. Pour un mot que je n'ai pas dit. . . . Lu
> répondre, simplement. . . . Et je n'ai pas osé. . . .
> JACQUELINE. Lui répondre ? . . . Mais il ne t'avait rien
> demandé.
> MARIE-LOUISE. Rien demandé.
> JACQUELINE. Quoi ?
> MARIE-LOUISE. En tout cas, c'est tout comme. Il y a des
> questions qui sont au bord des lèvres. Il ne dépendait que de
> moi de les faire naître. . . .[1]

The fabric constructed by her imagination is complete and
logical. If Philippe had been silently in love with her, why did
he not come to the house when he was in the district ? Because
he was waiting for her. Because he was testing her. Local
gossip would quickly inform her of his presence. She must prove

---

[1] Act III, Tableau I.

her love by taking the initiative. The rôle of the imagination, already important in *La Maison épargnée* and *Le Feu qui reprend mal*, reaches its height in this play. As in *Le Feu qui reprend mal*, Philippe, the character who sets the psychological action into movement, does not appear on the stage. The idea of the man is of greater significance than the man himself.

The silent development of Marie-Louise's unreal love up to its culmination in the scene with Jacqueline is indicated by dreamy silences, by " langage indirect " and by symbolism. She asks Olivier to embrace her. " Plus fort . . . comme si tu voulais me retenir et me protéger. . . ." [1] " Oh là, comme tu es lourd pour huit ans ! " she says, lifting her little boy, and betraying that she is living a year in the past. " Neuf ans, maman ", he corrects her.[2] The whole scene of the geography lesson when she muses over her son's map of Argentina is an example of " langage indirect ". The protracted symbolism is, however, a new development with Jean-Jacques Bernard. In *Martine*, people—first Jeanne and then Madame Mervan— symbolized for the peasant girl the love which was denied her. In *La Maison épargnée*, the inanimate house was a physical representation of Fabien's irrational guilt. In *Le Printemps des autres* the mirror of Clarisse is used symbolically. Here symbolism becomes almost a system. The vast unchanging forest of fir-trees, seen through the numerous windows of the semicircular bay, symbolizes the oppressive effect of provincial life. The fans and the book of Baudelaire, presents from Philippe, the chair where Philippe sat, represent the dreams of Marie-Louise and reappear in the drama like leitmotivs in Wagner. In a neat and tidy dénouement, having lost her illusions, she silently removes these objects in the presence of Olivier. The poem *Invitation au voyage* to the music of Duparc symbolizes her morbid desires, while the Chopin nocturne which she played at the beginning of the piece and which she takes up again at the end represents the real happiness and sane beauty of her life with Olivier. The inner

[1] Act I, Tableau II.   [2] *Ibid.*

transformation of Marie-Louise is indicated by the modification of her attitude towards those objects, and by the reflex actions to which those objects give rise. Some time after Philippe's departure they are discussing his photograph. Olivier and Jacqueline think it a good likeness. When alone Marie-Louise tears up the picture which no longer represents the person she has idealized. The chair he occupied must remain in exactly the same place, and Jacqueline is not allowed to sit on it.

The importance attached to objects and to the reactions of individuals confronted by those objects is reminiscent of the theories of Maeterlinck on " le tragique quotidien " ; it establishes in a way the essential harmony between the human being and the inanimate world surrounding him. It gives an effect of " passive " drama, similar to that of Maeterlinck, and is in keeping with the impression of automatism produced by characters with psychopathic tendencies. We are far from the traditional drama where it is a question of an act of conscious will, where the people are so energetic that the external surroundings count for nothing. The symbolism, therefore, although somewhat arbitrary, is bound up with the spirit of the play and is in harmony with its realism. There is, however, one case where it strikes one as being superimposed for the sake of effect. The transition from the first tableau of Act I where Philippe means nothing to Marie-Louise to the second where, six weeks later, the " cristallisation " is taking place is marked by Philippe's dazzling Marie-Louise with a mirror from off-stage. He wants her to come and play tennis and Marie-Louise refuses.

> MARIE-LOUISE. . . . Mais il m'aveugle, je ne vois rien.
> JACQUELINE. Tu n'as qu'à ne pas rester dans le rayon.
> MARIE-LOUISE (*sans l'écouter*). Vous aurez beau faire, je n'irai pas. (*Elle balance la tête de droite à gauche comme si elle jouait avec le rayon.*)
> JACQUELINE. Mais, voyons, écarte-toi. . . .[1]

—and the game goes on till the curtain falls.

[1] Act I, Tableau I.

As with *Le Printemps des autres*, the climax of the play is in the Pirandellian recognition of the true personality through the sudden shock of reality. Here the anagnorisis takes place off stage and therefore is not so effective dramatically as in *Le Printemps des autres*. But the crises and the turning-point in Marie-Louise's emotional relationship with Olivier are shown and are never put into precise words. Once more the dramatist makes use of absence of dialogue. Olivier comes in and finds his wife singing the *Invitation au voyage* to the melody of Duparc, and watches her day-dreaming. Her guilty start when he puts on the light and little Gérard's announcement that she has been revising with him the geography of South America, cause Olivier's vague misgivings to take a definite form. They look at each other in silence and he tries in vain to stammer out a few questions. The next stage is reached when Olivier discovers from a business letter that Philippe is at Épinal, where Marie-Louise has gone ; without verbal explanation his distress is passed on to his father-in-law, and his anguish grows in silence while Gérard chatters to his grandfather, until the little boy remarks that his father looks as if he were crying—a reminiscence of *Pelléas et Mélisande*. Finally, when Marie-Louise returns and makes it obvious that Philippe is " un homme mort ", the rapprochement takes place in silence ; Olivier watches Marie-Louise removing all the objects associated with Philippe and they embrace. Then she plays the Chopin nocturne, symbolic of their happy married life. " Oui, oui, ce *Nocturne* de Chopin . . . que tu aimais tant. . . . Merci. . . ."

Marie-Louise, although explicit to Jacqueline, is silent to her husband, because, as in the case of Clarisse, her emotion is illicit. Mainly because of his reserved nature, Olivier never puts his suspicions into words, although in the end he sees things as clearly as Jacqueline. He is trying to reach out to her, to communicate directly without words. " Ce que tu me donnes, un autre s'en contenterait ; fidèle, honnête, bonne ménagère. . . . Tout ce qu'il faut pour satisfaire un homme sans idéal. . . . Je ne peux pas t'expliquer, mais tu comprends bien. . . ." [1] A sense of isolation, of frustration torments him, as it did Golaud. ". . . Qu'y a-t-il là derrière?" he asks, touching her brow. "Je sens des tas de pensées . . . si profondes . . . si cachées. . . ." [2] In the end, as we have seen, the wordless communication is established when Marie-Louise's symbolic actions show that Philippe is forgotten—at least for the time being.

The most extreme of Bernard's psychopathic cases is contained in his play *L'Ame en peine*,[3] based on the platonic theory of twin souls. Marceline and Antoine suffer because they never meet. Created for one another, they are separated by destiny and it happens that during the whole play these two characters never exchange a word.

Marceline and Philippe, married for six months, are on their way to Spain. In obedience to an inexplicable caprice of Marceline's, the young couple decide to stop at Saint-Jean-de-Luz. During the evening Marceline falls victim to a strange feeling of agitation. A railway official has just entered the hotel lounge and is absently looking at some papers on a table. Marceline goes out slowly, brushing past him, but without looking at him. The stranger, troubled, stares in front of him for a while. . . .

Some years later Antoine, the former railway official, and Marceline find themselves in the Jardin des Tuileries. A little child nearly falls into the water. The man and woman dash forward at the same time to save him. They remain for a moment beside one another gazing in front of them and then, without addressing a word to each other, they separate, each slowly going a different way. . . .

More years pass. Marceline and Philippe are on the point of separating. Although admiring her husband, Marceline has never loved him. Always discontented, never knowing what was the matter with her, she has been leading a troubled life, a prey to strange caprices ; she has visited hospitals and prisons, taken lovers and even had recourse to opium. One evening she

---

[1] Act II.   [2] *Ibid.*   [3] First performed 12th Jan. 1926.

comes down from her room, ill, to have a long talk with her husband. Her agitation increases and she makes instinctive movements towards the door. At last she feels as if she is stifling, and begs her husband to open the door. The body of Antoine, dead of cold and hunger, sinks into the room, and Marceline loses her reason.

Bernard has a great affection for this piece, which he describes as " sortie de mon cœur, plus personnelle ainsi que d'autres ouvrages ".[1] All his plays are marked by his deep pity for the frailties of the human heart ; here he attempts to provide a philosophical explanation for the vague subconscious motives which determine the erratic behaviour of human beings.

In the preface to his English translation of Bernard's plays, J. Leslie Frith tells us that the writer, when questioned about the twin souls theory, replied, smiling, that it was not a thesis but a hypothesis. The presence of such a hypothesis in a play aroused strong reaction among the contemporary critics. Paul Blanchart suggests that the prestige of Freud might allow us to accept this symbol that the complete soul is both male and female.[2] But most critics question the validity of the theory. " Le grand défaut de cette philosophie, a déjà observé justement Voltaire, c'est de prendre des idées abstraites pour des choses réelles ", says Lucien Descaves.[3] " Pourquoi deux moitiés seulement ? Le théâtre et le roman modernes ont élargi la formule ; ils nous montrent à présent des tiers et des quarts d'âmes errant dans la vie et résignés aux petites satisfactions qu'ils trouvent dans le relatif de l'à peu près des rencontres." Jacques Boulenger [4] accuses Bernard of " fausse profondeur " and Louis Schneider [5] declares that the dramatist only states in a tortuous way that perfect happiness is difficult to attain. L. Dubech [6] quotes ironically the definition of Branchut du Tic in Le Chat maigre by Anatole France : " L'amour n'est absolu qu'entre deux êtres qui ne se sont jamais vus ".

[1] Preface to vol. ii of Théâtre, p. 6.   [2] Op. cit. p. 24.
[3] L'Intransigeant, 20th Mar. 1926, R.   [4] Nouveau Siècle, 19th Mar. 1926, R.
[5] Gaulois, 21st Mar. 1926, R.   [6] Action Française, 23rd Mar. 1926, R.

In this "pièce à hypothèse" the author abandons realism. So far, all his characters, even the psychopathic cases, have been truly and justly observed and the behaviour is within the bounds of probability. Here Bernard gives us an idealist, Symbolist theatre. However much one may believe in telepathic communication or even in the theory of twin souls, one cannot accept as realistic a situation which presents two people psychically disturbed by physical proximity, yet never speaking to one another, never even seeing each other. The play is a symbol of two souls, made for each other, lost in the welter of humanity. And it incurs the same reproach as the Symbolist dramas : it strays too far from the fundamentally human, which is the true province of the theatre. Not that Bernard's psychology is as elementary as that of the Symbolist theatre tends to be. Marceline and Antoine, two bewildered people, unable to account for their inability to adapt themselves to life, are convincing enough cases of neurosis. But he attempts to explain, that is, to intervene, as well as to describe ; accordingly, behaviour has to be fitted in to a rigid, preconceived plan and results in an unreal automatism. In his previous psychopathic cases there was at least the suggestion of a psychological norm from which the character temporarily deviated. The dramatic interest lay in the return to that norm. Here the characters recede farther and farther from normality and real life, until they finally escape from it altogether, he by death and she by madness. Hence the episodic structure rather than the traditional dramatic curve. In his previous plays the characters could, within a limited field, make a choice. Here we have the total sacrifice of two victims without apparent reason. We are nearer to the dramas of Maeterlinck, where innocent souls are pitilessly hounded down by a blind fatality, and as in Maeterlinck, the spectator has a sense of oppression instead of a feeling of exaltation which is in the true nature of dramatic appreciation.

Many critics—even those who had found pleasure in his previous works—were bound, with some justice, to accuse

Bernard of having attempted a piece of gratuitous theatrical virtuosity. Lucien Dubech says that he has " battu son propre record, si l'on ose s'exprimer ainsi ; il nous a fait voir au théâtre des Arts une pièce dont les deux personnages principaux étaient attirés l'un vers l'autre pendant trois actes par un penchant si irrésistible qu'ils vivaient et mouraient l'un pour l'autre, et cependant, ils réussissaient ce tour de force de ne pas s'adresser la parole. On a pu dire à M. Bernard qu'il avait atteint ce jour-là la limite de l'école du silence, et que, la fois suivante, à moins que les acteurs ne parlent pas du tout, il serait bien empêché de pousser plus loin le parti pris." [1] This failure to establish communication is, however, the very essence, the poetic truth of the work, and indeed the most effective means of conveying the poet's message. The utter isolation of the human soul is contained in those symbolic silences. Each time they chance to be near one another, Marceline and Antoine gaze troubled and silent ahead. As they are destined never to meet, there is no " communication directe " effected by the mute exchange of looks, so characteristic of Bernard's other plays ; only a vague intuitive foreboding of the other's presence exists to hasten the tragedy of each. There is no dramatic " recognition " ; its very absence constitutes the poignancy and irony of the play in which every scene works up to a climax of " non-recognition ".

With regard to the dialogue, we have, rather than " le langage indirect ", a bewildered self-searching, an attempt to analyse strange feelings whose cause is unaccountable. " J'ai souvent l'impression qu'il y a en moi quelque chose d'incomplet ", says Antoine to his friend Ida. " Mais quoi ? Une case qui me manque peut-être. . . . Comment te faire comprendre cela ? Tiens ! Tu n'as qu'à imaginer un homme qui serait né pour être un grand peintre, mais qui en même temps serait aveugle. . . ." [2] " Toi aussi, n'as-tu pas l'impression souvent, d'être mené par quelque chose de plus fort que toi ", says Marceline to Philippe in

[1] *Les Cahiers de la république des lettres, des sciences et des arts*, No. III, 15th July 1926, " Où va le théâtre ? ", p. 35.   [2] Act II.

agitation.[1] "Le langage indirect" is generally the result of a subconscious emotion centring on some definite and usually forbidden object : Clarisse's love for Maurice, for example, or, before it reaches conscious love, Marie-Louise's attraction to Philippe. In this case we have only a vague yearning towards something unknown, imposed from without, an indefinite emotion which can produce only confusion and bewilderment. Once more, for the elucidation of the silences, the perspicacious character is necessary. This is Robert, Marceline's brother, who, at the beginning of the play, attempts to analyse Marceline's character and behaviour. His theory is that Marceline has married Philippe *because* she does not love him. He reminds her that she has had several infatuations with men quite different from Philippe in nature and physique (Antoine's type, in fact) and that she has always been disillusioned. He goes on to quote from Maeterlinck's *L'Oiseau bleu* ; in the Kingdom of the Future two children love one another but Time parts them ruthlessly. "Monsieur le Temps, j'arriverai trop tard — Je ne serai plus là quand elle descendra — Je ne la verrai plus — Nous serons seuls au monde." And he mentions Plato's theory of twin souls. But Marceline does not take him seriously.

Bernard's stressing of intuitive knowledge and even telepathy is in keeping with the tradition of Maeterlinck. It harmonizes with his own personal outlook on life. In *Le Théâtre et l'esprit international* [2] he says :

> Les liens de peuple à peuple ne sont pas seulement des liens matériels. Il y a des forces qui nous dépassent, que nous subissons à notre insu. Il se produit des courants mystérieux qui marquent l'interdépendance où sont les âmes humaines, qui vont d'un homme à un autre, d'un peuple à un peuple à travers l'espace, qui relient sans qu'ils s'en doutent des hommes qui ne se connaissent pas, qui ne se verront peut-être jamais, que des montagnes ou des océans séparent.

[1] Act III.
[2] A speech made on the 24th March 1928 at the *Amitiés Internationales* and included in his book *Témoignages* (1933).

This, he says, is particularly true where individuals are concerned. He mentions, among other examples, Cesare Lodovici, whose work is akin to his own. At the time they were writing they did not know one another. When they did become acquainted they found that almost at the same period they had entertained the same aesthetic ideas and had been visited by the same kind of doubts. Neither had at the time read Chekhov, yet everyone saw his influence in their works.

L'Ame en peine brings to an end this series of probings into the subconscious. Dealing with the interaction of two different aspects of a personality on different planes, they form, as we have seen, dramatic enough material. But there is not the rich variety which is to be found in the Racinian analysis of the passion itself at a conscious level. In this type of art the submerged emotion or motive, in order to be clearly conveyed by the Unexpressed, must be simple and direct. In fact, it is not so much the passion as the varying degrees of consciousness in the individual which is the main interest. We saw the difference in the treatment of this in *Le Printemps des autres* and *L'Invitation au voyage*. But there are limits to what can be done dramatically with this aspect of human personality. In *L'Ame en peine* the author goes as far as is possible with the Unexpressed and with the subconscious. Not only do the characters fail to express what is submerged, but they never even reach the stage of becoming conscious of it. Bernard must now seek fresh fields. Abandoning his preoccupation with Freudian cases, he turns once more to normal men and women.

CHAPTER IX

JEAN-JACQUES BERNARD: II

MOST of the " silent " plays which follow *L'Ame en peine* show a falling-off in technique and a diminishing of the force and effectiveness of the Unexpressed. The author has exhausted the dramatic possibilities of the submerged Freudian conflict and, except for *Le Jardinier d'Ispahan*, he does not again attempt the sustained study of the evolution of a conscious unspoken passion. *La Louise* and *Les Sœurs Guédonec*, the only two perfect examples of the later " silent " play, are short, their subject matter leaving little room for dramatic development, and it becomes increasingly difficult to situate some of Bernard's " borderline cases ".

In *La Louise* and *Les Sœurs Guédonec* Bernard shows us the silent transformation of apparently second-rate characters, or rather he reveals a hidden person, the real and essentially good person. There is no suggestion of Freudian repression. In these plays Bernard is nearer to Maeterlinck, who believes in the essential purity of souls, once the veneer of worldly materialism has been removed. The fundamental goodness is brought to the surface by the presence of pure beings.

La Louise [1] has as its scene a village in the fighting zone in 1917. A friend of Pierre Garbin plans as a joke to billet him on Louise, an attractive young woman who has only half a bed to offer. Louise, whose manners have always been free and easy with soldiers, is touched by the respect that Pierre shows her, by his sincere love for his wife and by the moving confidences he makes. In the end she gives him her room, declaring that she

[1] First performed 6th May 1931.

has another for herself. When he has retired, she opens the other door of the room—it is the door of a cupboard—takes out a blanket and lies on the floor.

When Louise enters the room she sees Pierre sobbing over his wife's photograph. She stands watching him for a while. During her silence we see the dawn of new sentiments in her soul, or perhaps the memory of former purity relived. The transformation is completed by Pierre's moving words. Intelligent and sensitive like the poet Arvers, he refuses to make " literature " of his feelings. " Oui, tous les hommes que vous avez vus, et qui vous ont parlé d'amour tout de suite, ne savaient pas ce que c'était. . . . Moi . . . moi, je n'en parle pas. . . . C'est trop grand, c'est trop précieux. . . . En parler, ça me gênerait." So far Jean-Jacques Bernard's silences have proceeded mainly from his desire for realism. People do not express their deepest emotions ; it is not in their nature to do so. In this passage there is a suggestion of the Maeterlinckian idea that the quality of the emotion deteriorates at the coarse impact of the spoken word.

Louise seizes Pierre's truth immediately. " Oui, vous, une femme, vous pouvez comprendre ", says Pierre. " Eux, ils ne peuvent pas. Ils sont trop bruyants pour entendre ces choses mystérieuses. Vous, vous les sentez directement. Pas besoin d'explication." We have a recurrence here of the themes of feminine intuition and " communication directe " which appear so often in the dramas of Maeterlinck.

In *Les Sœurs Guédonec*,[1] a short play of two acts, we witness the bringing to the surface of maternal instincts in two miserly, dried-up old maids. The mayor of a small Breton town has asked them to board some little orphans from Paris as part of a holiday scheme. They consent in the end when they hear that they will be paid for it, but they soon regret their decision, for the noisy children create confusion in their home. With a sigh of relief they see them at last depart, and, left alone, they begin to count the bank-notes which they have just received from the mayor. But

[1] First performed 20th Nov. 1931.

they cannot get used to the silence. Each furtively wipes away a tear. In silence is reborn the tender love almost extinguished by years of avarice and selfishness. In silence is found the essential self. Here the author dispenses completely with analysis ; the principal characters are two simple souls—there is no contrasting lucid character—and the transformation is represented by external realism ; little gestures, commonplace words, attitude, reveal the old maids to us. A cinematic device is used to bring out the pathos of Albert, the smallest and timidest of the three boys. He cries, he is afraid at first to join in the noisy games of the other two, and stands forlornly in front of the door with his bundle, outlined against the bright background. He makes a special appeal to the crusty old maids. " Même Albert ", they say when a neighbour comes in to tell them how the children went off to the station singing at the tops of their voices.

Deux Hommes [1] is hardly a typical example of the *Théâtre de l'Inexprimé*, but it is concerned with an important aspect of the Unexpressed : that spiritual communication which may be established between sensitive beings, even when they are enemies in war ; and it contains much of Bernard's philosophy of life. Although the play is for the most part explicit, it is the silent look at the beginning which draws together the German prisoner and the French soldier and culminates in their expression of common thoughts. Both see in Jeanne d'Arc a messenger of love. Nations have distorted her thought and made her a messenger of hatred. . . .

> HERMANN. Une figure comme elle, c'est l'amour des hommes qui la modèle. Comment veux-tu retrouver la vraie Jeanne, d'ailleurs ? Ou le vrai saint François ? Ou le Christ vrai ? La vérité, c'est leur légende . . . (. . .) La seule que nous puissions saisir, c'est la vérité du cœur.
>
> ROBERT (. . .). Il faut bien, en effet, que le cœur nous aide à franchir certaines murailles où se heurte la raison.
>
> HERMANN. C'est là que peuvent nous aider les légendes,

[1] " Pièce inédite ", included in vol. v of *Théâtre* with *Nationale 6* and two short sketches.

car au moins elles répondent à des interprétations, à des besoins collectifs, qui renferment leur part de vérité, d'humanité.

Bernard's whole conception of the drama, especially as shown in his " silent " plays, springs from this idea that the heart seizes truths which are beyond the range of reason, that the heart alone can break down barriers and that salvation comes only from within. That is the substance of his plays *A la recherche des cœurs, Jeanne de Pantin* and *Le Roy de Malousie.*

In *A la recherche des cœurs,*[1] a play which treats of the relations between an employer and his workmen, the main crisis, the decisive change of heart, is expressed in silence. This work, which deals not only with individuals but with a group, begins to betray striking inadequacies in the technique of the Unexpressed.

In his preface to the play the author denies having attempted to write a social drama . . . " le problème envisagé reste toujours le mystère du cœur humain. Mais, alors que mes autres pièces montraient le cœur humain dans ses aspirations amoureuses, celle-ci vise à le placer dans son existence sociale." Having become through force of circumstances the manager of a large factory, Charles Durban has had to give up the communist ideas to which he had once inclined as a consequence of the 1914 war. His sincere affection for his workmen does not prevent him from showing himself uncompromisingly firm when threatened with a strike. He has refused to receive Dariel, the communist delegate who wanted to ask him to take back the workmen he had dismissed for sabotaging a machine. Claire, his wife, learning that Dariel is a former war comrade who, sharing the horrors of the trenches, had once been very close to Charles' heart, realizes that her husband has never ceased to be tormented by an inner conflict. She desires his spiritual salvation. " C'est Dariel qui a connu le vrai Charles. Voilà ton mal, ton déséquilibre ! Voilà le drame de ta vie. . . . Tu es un étranger qui vit chez toi. . . ."[2] He receives Dariel.

[1] First performed 30th Oct. 1931.   [2] Act II.

Les deux hommes se regardent et c'est un regard profond
qui va loin dans le passé, mais dont rien, ni dans les gestes, ni
dans la voix, ne saurait trahir l'émotion. Figés dans une
immobilité glacée, les deux hommes sont l'un devant l'autre,
comme des adversaires. Enfin, Dariel parle, mais ce sont des
paroles banales, dites sur un ton indifférent.[1]

Charles makes up his mind. To become what he was, to
become free once more, he would logically have to hand over
the factory to the workmen and sacrifice the future of his children.
Claire supports him. The result is complete isolation. The
workmen are suspicious of this unexpected change. The other
capitalists withdraw their patronage. The very existence of the
factory is threatened and Charles appeals to the workers. They
must choose between a grim struggle for two years to obtain
new clients and shameful security, which will involve Charles'
leaving them so that other capitalists may buy the firm. The
workmen suspect that the whole situation has been contrived by
Charles in order to reduce them to subjection. He is fired upon.
Mortally wounded, he hears at last what he had longed for so
ardently, proof of the sincere affection of his workmen and, before
he dies, he expresses his faith in the future. The men of our times
are not yet ripe for liberty, but we must do all in our power to
prepare for a new age, though we may never see it ourselves.
The workmen, who now begin to believe that Charles is the
victim of a plot of capitalists who have paid someone to fire on
him, swear to avenge him and sing the " Internationale ".

The author disclaims having written a partisan or a problem
play. " De pareils ouvrages n'ont de vie que s'ils restent encore
et toujours dans le domaine du cœur, seul domaine où l'on puisse
réellement faire œuvre d'art, et par conséquent, œuvre utile." [2]
It is, he maintains, a sentimental play, in which the partners are
not a man and a woman, but a man and a crowd. Is it possible
to deal adequately with such a theme by the methods of the
Théâtre de l'Inexprimé? According to Bernard, betterment in

---

[1] Act II.   [2] Preface to *A la recherche des cœurs*.

any sphere of life can come about only through a change of heart. In the Theatre of the Unexpressed a change of heart is something deep and secret which takes place in silence, when some chord has been struck in the hidden soul by an external incident, or when a kindred spirit, by its mere presence, almost telepathically awakens a response. By its nature such action seems to be confined to the individual. " Crowd psychology " exists, but it results from simple, elemental emotions. In the domain of subtler feelings the crowd remains a collection of individuals. Bernard has been forced to reduce the components of the group to a kind of uniformity in order that the crowd should respond in a uniform manner to Charles' approaches, with the result, no doubt unintentional, that they are a second-rate lot, timid, cowardly, suspicious, masochistic and, it seems, distinctly un-French. The gift of the factory on a First of May meeting only succeeds in creating hostility. From the moment Charles mounts the steps (which he had symbolically descended in order to reach the hearts of his men) and speaks to them as a master, lashing them with words of anger and scorn, the crowd, eager to be governed, testifies its approval. Surely this grovelling to an industrial Führer gives a most unrealistic picture of French workmen ? Also, the workers are unconvincingly inconsistent. If they were willing to accept the hardships of a strike, why will they not accept a struggle for the well-being of the factory in which they now have a common share ?

Such as Bernard has been forced to create them, they do not as a crowd respond to Charles' efforts to reach out to them. But " communication directe " does take place between Charles and Dariel and it is conveyed by means of the significant look. This look is not so charged with dramatic force as those we saw in *Martine* and *Le Printemps des autres*. There the characters were dominated by a simple passion, whether conscious or unconscious, which had swelled into a crisis of silence. Here the look contains mixed emotions, remembrance of the past, a consciousness of the present change in relationship between the two men and is intended to indicate an approaching change of heart in Charles. The silence is overweighted and we are dangerously near Lord Burleigh's famous shake of the head. The effect of Dariel's presence is emphasized by his departing silhouette on which the eyes of Claire and Charles are fixed—another cinematic touch—and Charles' dreamy recollections of their war-time friendship. "Pendant deux mois, chaque soir, dans le même abri, où nous risquions de mourir, lui et moi n'avons fait qu'un homme (. . .) Et aujourd'hui tu as vu. . . . Cette muraille entre nous. . . ."[1] Claire encourages him to put his true free self before family interests and—yet another cinema "shot"— he remains motionless at the open door of the factory which has meant so much inner turmoil.

Between Charles and Dariel "communication directe" is a possibility. Although Dariel is a representative of the workers, he is an intellectual, even a leader type like Charles. Between Charles and the crowd there can be no rapprochement. Loving them on account of their weakness and their inarticulate simplicity, he never succeeds in making himself understood by them. The idea which seems to emanate from the play would be that the working classes will be saved only when they succeed in establishing "communication directe" with the employers, that is to say, when by inward regeneration they become men like the best type of employer—Charles, and when employers become like the best type of working-class man—Dariel, and the two sides can freely communicate. It is not impossible for a kind of spiritual communication to be established among members of a group. Certain types of religious gatherings give evidence of this, and in Maeterlinck's *L'Intruse* and *Les Aveugles* we have also examples of a kind of telepathic communication in groups. But to seek a solution of social questions by such means without taking into account social, economic and political, as well as psychological and moral factors, is an excess of simplification. For a social play—and in spite of the author's

[1] Act II.

P

disclaimers this must in a sense be a social play—the methods of the Unexpressed are inadequate.

Nationale 6[1] is, in my opinion, one of Bernard's weaker efforts. It represents the *Théâtre de l'Inexprimé* in a state of decadence, with escapism, romantic imagination and silences running riot. The hero of the play is the road Nationale 6. For Francine and her father it is the symbol of adventure, of the great outer world, from which their little isolated house separates them. They spend most of their time—Michel, the father, is retired and Francine has apparently nothing else to do—in gazing through the window which looks out on to the road, and imagining the beautiful countries to which it leads and the destinations of the passing motor-cars. Francine is even convinced that this road is going to bring her one day the Prince Charming of her dreams. And indeed, one day, two strangers knock at the door to ask for assistance on account of a motor smash. Antoine Vanier, the famous author, and his son, Robert, were on their way to Nice to sail three weeks later for India. As the car is completely destroyed, they accept Michel's invitation to stay with them.

In the third act Robert, while painting Francine's portrait, chatters gaily. Francine interprets his words as a declaration of love. Antoine, who has meantime fallen in love with Francine, approaches her, and she, thinking he is speaking for his son, betrays her feelings for him, to Antoine's dismay. During dinner, without the situation being put into precise words, the truth is made known to Francine. It has become necessary to depart sooner than had been intended. They will always remember with pleasure this charming stay. Francine " baisse les yeux vers son assiette et demeure immobile. Il semble que les autres n'aient rien voulu remarquer. . . . Michel laisse tomber la bouteille de champagne, elle se brise." The road has betrayed Francine and her father. The dangerous bend which has caused the accident will be eliminated and the southward-bound cars

[1] First performed 18th Oct. 1935.

will no longer pass their door. In the end, Francine and her father make up their minds to love the house for its own sake. " Ainsi," says Michel, " nous n'avons plus besoin de la route ? " " Mais non, papa," replies Francine, " puisqu'elle nous a conduits chez nous."

" Cet excès de gentillesse, je l'avoue, dépasse mes forces ", says P. Brisson.[1] Most of the contemporary critics, however— even the redoubtable Dubech—acknowledge the freshness and charm of the work. Émile Mas is reminded of the author of *L'Épreuve*.[2] But Angélique's apparent misunderstanding and her quiet grief are so much more moving because Marivaux has made her a real person, and her thwarted love is real love. In this fantasy, reminiscent of J. M. Barrie's less fortunate attempts, Francine and her father are utterly remote from everyday life, two charming eccentrics obsessed and even slightly crazed by the fascination of Nationale 6. The symbolism of the road plays a disproportionate rôle in the play and the characters suffer accordingly. In contrast to Marie-Louise of *L'Invitation au voyage*, the form of escapism from which they suffer is permanent and ineradicable ; they wallow in it, and a state of normality has apparently never existed for them, and never will. " Où est la fantaisie, papa ? " says Francine. " Qu'est-ce que c'est que ça ? Où est la vie ? Où est le rêve ? Pourquoi les séparer ? " [3] Even after her disappointment in love she starts to imagine what a beautiful story could be made out of her " grief ".

It is consequently impossible to be really moved by the silences in this saccharine play. The dramatic silence can be effective only if it expresses, or is bound up with, genuinely felt human emotion, even if, as in *L'Invitation au voyage*, that emotion is the result of self-delusion. Vague romantic yearnings are not in themselves dramatic material. When Robert mentions that he and his father were eventually bound for India—the very place Michel and Francine had been nostalgically discussing—the

---

[1] *Figaro*, 20th Oct. 1935, R.
[2] Quoted in the *La Petite Illustration*, 23rd Nov. 1935.   [3] Act I.

two latter start and exchange a silent look full of inexpressible emotion. Such emotion can mean little to the normal spectator. When Antoine and Robert by tactful suggestion make her realize that her love is not returned, Francine's silence is pathetic in a small way ; how much less pathetic is her situation than the similar one between Saulnier and Madeleine in Vildrac's *Madame Béliard*! Some of the silences strike one as being forced. Antoine who has come in gazes at Francine " qu'il semble apercevoir pour la première fois " and continues to do so while she gazes after the departing Robert. And at the end of Act II Francine, after proposing the health of Antoine, with a slight tremble in her voice proposes that of Robert ; Robert looks at her rather surprised, again " comme s'il la voyait pour la première fois, et ne la quitte plus des yeux ". This last silent look seems gratuitous, since it does not lead to any emotion on the part of Robert. The whole point of the play is that he is not in love with Francine and does not realize that she is in love with him. The silence might, of course, indicate that he has for the first time become conscious of her beauty as a possible subject for painting, in which case the weakness is apparent ; the same kind of silence has to serve to indicate a deep emotion or a fact of lesser interest. And the ambiguity itself is a further point for criticism.

In *Nationale 6* the author develops a tendency similar to that of Maeterlinck in *Aglavaine et Sélysette*. The characters are excessively self-conscious and talk too much about everything, including silence ; thus they are in practice a contradiction of the author's theories. " Maman ne sait pas se taire," says eighteen-year-old Francine to her father, " toi, tu sais." Then we have this sort of false and irritating dialogue reminiscent of some of Barrie's excesses in whimsy :

> Élisa [Francine's mother].   Quelle pluie !
> Francine. Il pleut ?
> Michel. Il pleut ?
> Élisa. Vous ne vous en étiez pas aperçus ?   Vous ne regardez donc jamais par la fenêtre ? . . .

FRANCINE. Il pleut par la fenêtre de maman, mais pas par la nôtre, papa !

and again, after the events of the first act : " Je savais bien que ce n'était pas une pluie comme les autres ".

Characteristic of Bernard's " silent " heroines, Francine has a highly developed intuition ; it functions in respect of motor-cars ! She *knows* that such-and-such a car is bound eventually for India. Why ? She just knows. You have to know how to look at them.

There is an effective enough contrast between the normal, practical Élisa and her fantastic husband and offspring. Realistic-ally enough, it is she who starts dreaming when told of Francine's supposed engagement, while Michel and Francine treat the fabric of their imagination as solid reality.

The inadequacy of *Nationale 6* arises mainly from the fact that the author once more abandons realism, without attempting, as he did in *L'Ame en peine*, to put something strong and moving in its place. Both are plays of symbolism, but whereas *L'Ame en peine* deals with one of the most fundamental aspects of humanity, the yearning for complete and perfect love, which shall be a crowning fulfilment of life, *Nationale 6* is concerned with the vague whimsies of two silly people, wholly wrapped up in them-selves and unequal to the smallest demands of life.

Le Jardinier d'Ispahan [1] is based on Bernard's novel *Madeleine Landier*.[2] It is an interesting study of a conflict within a young society woman between the sensuality she has inherited from her mother and the finer instincts which the memory of her father represents. The struggle is complicated by the tormenting doubt that the man she remembers with so much respect and devotion may not, after all, be her father. Attracted by the muscular strength of Daniel, an ex-sailor and the brother of the " gardienne ", she tries to fight her growing infatuation by marrying a less athletic specimen whom she does not love. The infatuation only increases, and she finds herself breaking up

---

[1] First performed 12th Apr. 1939, but begun in 1935.   [2] 1933.

Daniel's marriage with Germaine, her mother's godchild, who drowns herself in despair. There is some similarity here with Clarisse's behaviour in *Le Printemps des autres*, but the conflicting emotions and the train of actions set going by the illicit passion are on a conscious level. The strange duality of Madeleine's nature, the mixture of sincere affection for Germaine and heartless cruelty—she recalls significantly how she sometimes beat Germaine when they were both little—is subtly rendered. At the moments when the unlawful passion takes the upper hand, there seems to be a temporary suspension of normal standards and a pushing aside of natural affection. Yet even while Madeleine is " inhabited " by that passion, normal standards and natural affection remain still within the range of consciousness. Germaine pleads with her to dismiss Lucie, the common, good-looking maid whom she has engaged for the secret purpose of enticing Daniel away from his young wife, and repeats words which Lucie reported that Madeleine said to her, when she complained of being sent to prepare the country house for the family's visit : " Et de quoi vous plaignez-vous ? Je vous envoie avec un beau garçon." Madeleine is sincerely distressed. " Moi ! J'ai dit ça ! Moi ! Moi ! Ce n'est pas possible. . . ." If the incident has been forgotten it is not for long. Left alone she repeats mechanically : " Est-ce possible ? . . . Moi . . . moi. . . . Est-ce possible ? " and it is clear that she means : " I have been capable of this. Can I really be such a person ? "

At various stages Madeleine's emotional turmoil, though not its essential cause, is put into words. She begs her husband to save her, to take her away. She is determined to honour her father's memory. " Je veux être une femme fidèle ! Je veux être une femme propre ! Je le veux ! Je le veux ! Je le veux ! " In the end she wildly confesses to Daniel how she has been responsible for Germaine's death.

Some use of the Unexpressed is made in this play. In the first act, without direct expression, a fairly complicated psychological action is indicated by extreme compression of incident and

juxtaposition of contrasting situations. Madeleine has described
to an old family friend the type of man she would like to marry :
" Le visage ouvert. . . . Les yeux décidés. . . . Les bras puis-
sants. . . . Il respire la santé . . . la force. . . ." We witness
the impression made on her by her first sight of Daniel, so like
her ideal, vigorously performing a dangerous work of repair in
the courtyard. The visit of the far from brawny Robert almost
immediately afterwards increases her initial distaste for this
pathetic suitor. She subjects him to a test—to mend a fuse from
the top of a ladder. His lamentable failure, quickly followed by
the successful performance of the efficient and dexterous Daniel,
causes her to gravitate even more strongly towards the latter, as
we see from the long hypnotic stare which almost unnerves the
handsome young man. Then comes her violent revulsion from
an impossible situation, expressing itself in her sudden desperate
resolve to marry Robert. In the following acts, in addition to
her significant actions and unnaturally abrupt attitude to Daniel,
long silent looks reveal the intensification of the forbidden passion, and the final surrender takes place in silence. After Madeleine's wild confession, Daniel's look of stupor, fear and finally
desire shows that he has understood. Although Madeleine's
doubts about her father are ultimately removed, the knowledge
that his influence is there is unavailing. She has seized a metal
paper-knife and clutches it like a dagger. But instead of
striking, she succumbs to Daniel's embrace. In the last cinematic
tableau our attention is concentrated on the detail of her raised
hand clenching the knife ; gradually her hold is relaxed, the
hand opens, and in the silence of her surrender is heard the
metallic sound of the weapon dropping to the floor.

A vague impression of intangible, half-realized influences is
sometimes given. Robert, unable to fathom the true cause of
his wife's malaise, stands absorbed at the window, gazing at
Madame Landier in the garden, hypnotized by her resemblance
to Madeleine. Just before the news of Germaine's drowning,
Madeleine is in an unnatural state of tension and anxiety. In the

last act, when Daniel announces to Madame Landier, Robert and Lorin, the family friend, his intention of leaving the house with its tragic associations, there is a long silence. " Quelque chose d'indéfinissable semble avoir changé l'allure, le visage, l'humeur des trois personnages. On dirait qu'un apaisement est tombé sur eux. . . ."

Generally speaking, however, because of Madeleine's sustained consciousness of the situation, and a certain deliberate effort of will which she makes, though in vain, to overcome the unlawful passion, the Unexpressed never attains the positive dramatic force it does in *Le Printemps des autres* or other more characteristic " silent " plays.

The other known works of Bernard are more or less in the traditional style ; some of them are interspersed among the " silent " plays. The third act of *Denise Marette*,[1] which the author describes as " l'envers, la trame, l'explication secrète " of the other two, reveals, through the scenic representation of the heroine's dream, the selfishness, cynicism and small-mindedness of the father for whom she has sacrificed talent, happiness, love and her very identity. The hidden truth is " exteriorized ", and the recognition is conveyed through words instead of silence.

Le Roy de Malousie[2] is an amusing satire of the year 2004, directed mainly against the adherence to meaningless forms and traditions which blinds people to essential truths. *Jeanne de Pantin*[3] preaches once more Bernard's gospel that regeneration is possible only by a change of heart in the individual, and that a pure-hearted human being may, unknown to himself, sow seeds of courage in another. " Jeanne de Pantin " tries, like a new Jeanne d'Arc, to fight materialism. She fails ; ". . . si notre époque ne mérite pas encore sa Jeanne d'Arc, c'est faute d'une conscience morale assez pure, faute, peut-être, d'une grande foi collective qui emporterait d'un même coup d'aile toutes les

[1] First performed 20th Nov. 1925.   [2] First performed 27th May 1928.
[3] First performed 26th Nov. 1933.

âmes ".[1] In his preface to these two plays, Bernard refers to their deeper significance and maintains that the fact that they are written " sur deux plans, le plan visible et le plan profond ", relates them closely to the rest of his theatre. But we find no trace of the technique of the " silent " school. In *Jeanne de Pantin* the dream is again used, this time to reveal Jeanne's heroic ideals and inner longings. This device, expressionistic in character, is, as I have indicated with Maeterlinck, contrary to the spirit of the *Théâtre de l'Inexprimé*.

Bernard has given us two historical plays in episodic form. The heroine of *Louise de la Vallière* [2] is his favourite type of reserved woman. *Marie Stuart, reine d'Écosse* [3] contains some picturesque scenes of pantomime. In neither play, however, do we find silences charged with the positive dramatic force of the earlier works. The elaborate stage directions in the second tableau of *Marie Stuart, reine d'Écosse*, describing the content of an exchange of looks between Mary and Darnley, once more call to mind Lord Burleigh's shake of the head. Again the author appears to admit the inadequacy of the " silent " technique by resorting to the device of " exteriorization ". The fact is that in the typical plays of the *Théâtre de l'Inexprimé* the silent effects are dependent on simplicity of action as well as on passion ; the term " un classicisme nouveau " was used by some contemporary critics. In plays like *Le Printemps des autres* and *L'Invitation au voyage* we have an Aristotelian development in the psychological action. In *Martine* the author concentrates on one passion, Martine's hopeless love. But with historical plays of episodic form, spanning a long period and heavy with events, a concentrated dialogue, charged with indications of hidden emotion and culminating in silence, is impossible. Hence the Unexpressed, if used, can occupy only a minor place in such a work.

The obviously experimental nature of Bernard's *Théâtre de*

---

[1] Author's Preface to vol. iv of *Théâtre*, p. xi.
[2] First performed 30th Dec. 1943 in Geneva, but begun in 1936.
[3] Also performed in Geneva in 1943. Author's Preface dated August 1941.

l'Inexprimé and the author's emergence as a *chef d'école* were bound to rouse strong reactions, and it is necessary to deal with some of the points raised by contemporary critics. The main accusation, that of " system ", I have already discussed.

The question of medium is raised by André Beaunier.[1] The dramatist, he says, is one who works with words. If one desires to listen to silences, one does not go to the theatre. Literary art forms should be considered as tools, each best fitted for certain purposes. Bernard's material is best suited to music or poetry, and music or poetry should have been chosen to convey his message.

Bernard has, of course, consistently protested that he does not make plays out of silence, but that, using dialogue, he has made various attempts to exploit the possibilities of its complement, the Unexpressed. " Si un architecte exprimait ainsi l'importance des portes et des fenêtres : ' Les trous ont une grande valeur dans une maison ', que dirait-on des gens qui lui reprocheraient de construire des maisons en trous ? " [2] Bernard is not really abusing the medium of the drama, but using it in a special way. In order to avoid ambiguity and bring out clearly the significance of the Unexpressed, it is necessary to manipulate the dialogue with great skill. And it is undeniable that the material is dramatic. In an article entitled *Autour du théâtre du ' silence ' et de l'inexprimé*,[3] Silvio d' Amico goes as far as to say that in a play such as *L'Invitation au voyage* Bernard keeps to the tradition of the " pièce bien faite " — " en s'exprimant en sourdine " ; the structure emerges clearly through the Unexpressed, and the author practises in effect " la clarté française ".

" Toute une littérature de points de suspension . . ." says Pierre-Aimé Touchard of the *Théâtre de l'Inexprimé*.[4] Yet the skill and delicacy required to make the Unexpressed eloquent produces a commendable sobriety of language and even elegance

[1] Cutting dated 17th Feb. 1924, dossier of *L'Invitation au voyage*, R.
[2] " Quelques Précisions après deux récentes expériences ", *Comœdia*, 7th Apr. 1924, R.
[3] *Comœdia*, 12th Dec. 1925, a translation from the Italian original appearing in *L' Idea Nazionale* some months before.   [4] *Dionysos* (1938), p. 170.

of style. Bernard's fastidiousness is evident from the fact that he excluded from his complete works *La Maison épargnée*, which is nevertheless a work of quality. Paul Blanchart [1] mentions that the majority of his plays were remade or rewritten several times, and that he has destroyed a considerable quantity of literary efforts and researches. In his article *Quelques Précisions après deux récentes expériences* Bernard gives us a glimpse of his methods of work. Speaking of the problem of " le langage indirect " he says : " La première difficulté d'un tel travail est l'absence absolue d'une méthode précise. J'ai toujours pensé qu'à chaque sujet de pièce il fallait sa méthode et presque à chaque scène, pour ne pas dire à chaque réplique. On n'a pas toujours la chance de tomber au premier essai sur la seule phrase ou sur le seul mot par quoi se puisse révéler une vérité cachée. Il faut se résoudre à beaucoup de travail inutile, tel le cinégraphiste qui, pour cent mètres de pellicule, n'hésitera pas à en gaspiller mille." These successive siftings and purifications produce a language in which realism is often blended with sad poetry.

But we still have to consider whether Bernard's special use of the spoken word is, so to speak, dramatically healthy. Is not the element of the Unexpressed unduly stressed so as to impair the very nature of the art form he has chosen for his message ? If we revert to his analogy of the house, it is evident that in his *Théâtre de l'Inexprimé* the dramatic architect has not merely been emphasizing the importance of doors and windows, but constructing his edifice in such a manner as to focus all attention on these apertures. Some graceful pieces of architecture could no doubt be produced in this manner, but it is questionable if the method is the right one for a dwelling which is to be sound and habitable as well as beautiful. We have a right to expect that plays, even quietistic in nature, should have that strength and solidity inherent in the dramatic form. " Des chants révélateurs du chœur grec, des confessions classiques aux confidents et des déclarations faites au public dans des soliloques, nous sommes arrivés comme

[1] *Op. cit.* p. 29.

suprême moyen d'expression au silence. Résultat d'une décadence raffinée, mais d'une décadence.   Ici, la flamme de l'art, réduite à un filet de lumière, peut menacer de s'éteindre. . . ." Such is the conclusion of Silvio d' Amico,[1] who adds that imitators should beware of lowering the flame still further, lest only darkness remain.

Bernard's purpose in employing the Unexpressed is to convey that inner tragedy which Racine, Shakespeare and the Greeks communicate directly through the spoken word.   According to Bernard, men do not as a rule express their deepest feelings, either from natural reserve or because they are not always conscious of them.   Therefore these feelings should not be expressed on the stage.   The necessity for psychological realism in the theatre is implied, and the Unexpressed is chosen as an instrument which is to combine realism with depth of character.

Whether realism is a *sine qua non* of the modern drama is a matter which will be discussed in the final chapter.   At the moment we should note the handicaps which Bernard imposes on himself by confining his work to realism, and, within those limits, using the methods of the Unexpressed.   Although he is desirous of indicating hidden motive and feeling, he is bound to draw his characters, as it were, from the outside.   They must appear on the stage as they might appear to the spectator in everyday life.   Their speech and behaviour must not deviate from probability, and it is with a language consisting for the most part of everyday banalities that the author must work in order to make his silences eloquent.   Since there are limits to what the Unexpressed can express, and since the scope of a banal and realistic dialogue is very restricted, he is forced to confine himself to elementary passions.   And, as I previously indicated, he may not attempt to analyse these passions through the Unexpressed, for this would require an element of intellectuality which silence cannot contain.   Instead, he splits the personality into two layers, the conscious and the subconscious.   That

[1] *Loc. cit.*

which exists on each plane is in itself simple enough, and it is the interaction of conflict of the two which provides the dramatic interest. Where the subconscious does not enter, we have an uncomplicated, silent drama of situation. It is evident that the material of Bernard's drama of normal people is somewhat tenuous. The " three dimensional " psychology of his psychopathic case histories is penetrating, but lacking in richness, and it may even be questioned whether this type of deep probing is the proper business of the dramatist. The artist suggests bone and muscle in the body he represents, but he does not paint in the skeleton.

In an article on *L'Invitation au voyage* [1] Pierre Brisson makes some penetrating remarks on the art of Bernard, and condemns by implication the realism of " silence ". This art is, he says, at the same time difficult, easy and perilous : difficult because of the delicacy of touch and choice required in the dialogue ; easy because the author gets over the difficulty of how to make a person say in the theatre what he would not say in everyday life ; it is a schematic art and, " contrairement à ce qu'on peut croire, un art de surface qui se contente d'effleurer des âmes ", lacking the complexity and richness of a work of psychological analysis such as Porto-Riche's *Amoureuse*. It is perilous because it results in plays which are always the same, in a slowing down of the pace of life with characters who have only " des velléités de désirs, des embryons de passion ". Bernard's plays must, he maintains, occupy a secondary rank. For all great drama is made from accelerated movement, exceptional heroes, and features accentuated and even deformed. " La puissance créatrice s'accommode mal avec l'exactitude méticuleuse et l'expression déguisée."

Without at this stage discussing Brisson's ideas on the nature of great drama, we must in the main accept his criticisms. Bernard's *Théâtre de l'Inexprimé* is a miniature art, a theatre of intimacy, sometimes perfect of its kind, but restricted and mono-

---

[1] Cutting dated 25th Feb. 1924, dossier of *L'Invitation au voyage*, R.

tonous. When he attempts a larger canvas, when he preaches his gospel of the regeneration of mankind by an individual change of heart, he is forced to resort to more traditional methods. I have endeavoured to show that within the limits he imposes upon himself, Bernard in his " silent " plays achieves some variety. But the general impression is one of monotony. The more ambitious plays deal with conflicts between worlds of imagination and reality, resulting in psychic abnormalities ; or else we have thwarted and concealed love, a kind of " cendrillonisme ", to use a word coined by Pierre Brisson in another connection ; or, finally, the welling up of a secret spring of goodness in a second-rate character, interesting and moving, but slight material for drama.

We have, moreover, the impression that the realism which cramps the author's style is incomplete. He confines himself to psychopathic cases or to the type of person who prefers to conceal his feelings. But it can scarcely be denied that the lyrical type exists. J. M. Synge's genial Irish peasants, beggars and tinkers are drawn from life and grief finds tragic verbal expression in the keening of Gaelic country folk. Even if the dramatist limits himself to the urbane character, there are cases when, with deeply felt emotion, silence is not always realistic and its use at certain junctures in Bernard's plays actually produces the suggestion of arbitrariness and unreality. People have things out. It is almost inconceivable that two former companions in arms such as Durban and Dariel should meet again, even in awkward circumstances, and have nothing to say to each other,[1] or that a sensible old woman like Madame Mervan should not do some plain speaking to her ingenuous grandson.[2] And, despite what Yeats says, even with urbane characters, there are times when the force of the emotion and the tension of the moment create the lyrical outburst as surely as certain atmospheric conditions produce thunder and lightning. The commonest emotional phenomenon, love, which Bernard treats by " silent " methods, usually brings

---

[1] *A la recherche des cœurs.*   [2] *Martine.*

about, even in the inarticulate and unimaginative, a degree of
lyricism and poetry, and this is a rich source which the author
deliberately ignores.

Apart from considerations of realism, however, Bernard is
also concerned with the quality of the emotion represented.
" Le mot précise et cette vertu est toute sa faiblesse." [1] And we
think of Maeterlinck : " Dès que nous exprimons quelque chose
nous le diminuons étrangement ".[2] By their rigidity words
deform and alter the emotion in its essential purity. The Unexpressed enables the quality of the emotion, reflected in the
action, to emerge and appeal directly to the audience. We have
an immediate communication between two sensibilities : that of
the character and that of the spectator.

We may doubt if the simple representation of emotion is
sufficient in the drama. Man is not all emotion, and intelligence
need not be left out of the theatre because it has so often been
abused there. Human nature in all its richness and variety is the
dramatist's province. It is characteristic of man that he not only
acts and suffers, but reflects with wonder on his doings and
sufferings and with his mind endeavours to co-ordinate them into
a scheme, to make out of that bewildering material a philosophy
of life. This can only be done inwardly with words, and Maeterlinck, for all his insistence on the instrument of intuition and the
medium of silence, uses a great many words to make his philosophy clear to others. In restricting himself to emotion pure
and simple, Bernard is in another way, like those he condemns,
confining himself to a part of the realities of human experience.
He chooses to depict inarticulate beings who feel deeply but
either do not or cannot reflect upon their emotions and if they
do reach the stage of being conscious of them, fail to express
them by the spoken word. Racine, Shakespeare and the Greeks
choose men and women who live intensely with mind and word
as well as heart, and theirs is the richer reality.

<hr>

[1] *De la valeur du silence dans les arts du spectacle, loc. cit.*
[2] *Le Trésor des humbles*, p. 61.

Moreover, it is not true to say that words always have the rigidity and the deadening effect claimed by exponents of the *Théâtre de l'Inexprimé*. Bernard reacted against the sterile rhetoric of the *fin de siècle* dramatists, but it is hardly fair to condemn a form of art by the products of its inferior practitioners. Handled by genius, the variety and flexibility of words are infinite. Ambition, jealousy, love and hatred are not diminished but a thousandfold enhanced by Shakespeare's verbal imagery. Bernard's Unexpressed presents only the outward appearance of the emotion : the reflexes of a human being under its influence. Shakespeare, by grappling verbally with it, gives us its real substance and quality. But the task requires a Shakespeare.

Bernard's concentration on pure emotion at the expense of the intellectual and reflective element in man indicates an impoverishment of the human material of the drama and a consequent lack of vitality in his work. As Silvio d' Amico says, there is a suggestion of decadence, " une décadence raffinée ". The Unexpressed with Bernard is closely associated with an incompleteness of character, of which Marceline and Antoine of *L'Ame en peine* are extreme examples. There is a lack of equilibrium ; the people are, as it were, overweighted emotionally, they have no serenity and are unequal to the demands of life. Bernard's characters tend to run away from life rather than struggle with it. His is an elegiac theatre of rêverie and escape. And it becomes clear that the essential factor missing in this " silent " drama is the human will as a positive force.

A philosophy of determinism is implicit in *L'Ame en peine*, where the two principal characters move like puppets manipulated by some external agency. At one point Philippe and Marceline discuss the human will ; is it just a compromise with reality, or even an illusion ? In two later plays, *Le Jardinier d'Ispahan* and *Louise de la Vallière*, the author deals specifically with the problem of destiny. *Louise de la Vallière*, however, cannot be regarded as typical of Jean-Jacques Bernard's *Théâtre de l'Inexprimé*, and I have already indicated that a certain conscious struggle on the part of the main character in *Le Jardinier d'Ispahan* diminishes the force of the Unexpressed. In the more characteristic silent plays, except for *L'Ame en peine*, the question of determinism is not brought to the foreground, and we have to consider the place of the human will in such a drama.

I have already indicated a connection between determinism and the *Théâtre de l'Inexprimé*. The question scarcely arises in the superficial dramas of Amiel, where the Unexpressed is generally a "tour de force". Determinism is implicit in *Le Paquebot Tenacity* of Vildrac, but the fact that in the main his characters tend to show a certain energy explains why his plays are mostly on the borderline between the Expressed and the Unexpressed. Maeterlinck entirely eliminates the element of will, giving free play to the emotion of fear, through which, without the intermediary of words, the idea of the relentless advance of Fate is conveyed. His is a complete and utter fatalism. The destinies of his characters are predetermined by non-material, external forces. It is these forces which are his main concern. He is preoccupied with mystic influences rather than human beings. With Bernard psychological realism in depth is the foremost consideration. We are therefore bound to examine the question of determinism as related to individual characters, and assess the extent to which it is connected with the Unexpressed as used by Bernard.

Psychologists warn us to beware of considering the will as a separate faculty. Not the "will", but the whole self goes through the process of willing and it would be more accurate to speak of freedom of self rather than freedom of will. This we must bear in mind when using the term "free will". It is generally agreed, even by the opponents of a deterministic philosophy, that a measure of determinism exists both from external natural sources and within the individual. Canute's will is unavailing against the tide, and even the decisions of Corneille's strong characters are in part determined by their previous actions and their psychological make-up. In a sense, therefore, free will is a matter of the degree to which a character is determined.

The question of self-determinism does not arise in the theatre of Maeterlinck, since his shadowy creatures have little " character ", in the moral sense, to speak of and are " inhabited " by a superior force. In *L'Ame en peine*, the play of Bernard nearest in spirit to those of Maeterlinck, we have a similar suggestion of determinism through some arbitrary external agency which decrees that the twin souls shall never meet. Immediate reasons are of course suggested—difference in social background, class and upbringing, and, since the play is symbolic and the physical proximity of the characters is therefore to be discounted, geographical accident, blind chance. In the majority of Bernard's plays, however, as with great dramatists, the fatality is in the character. Clarisse and Marie-Louise are powerfully swayed by subconscious motives and desires which are part of their constitution, innate and inherited, and over which they have little control. Self-determinism exists with Bernard to a greater degree than in the traditional theatre. His is a drama of suffering rather than doing. As we have seen, a choice is eventually made, a course of action decided upon, but how far does this choice constitute what is normally regarded as an act of conscious will ?

An act of will as distinct from an unreflecting gratification of impulse or desire has an element of consciousness and intelligence. The volition is the outcome of a sizing up of the situation, a weighing of issues, for which clarity of vision is necessary, and this clarity can be achieved only if the problem is formulated in words, either spoken or thought—an intellectual process. The weak-willed character takes the line of least resistance and follows his emotions without question. The strong-willed man deliberates and analyses. Not that the intellectual element need be excluded from the acts of the weak-willed character. He may vacillate long before deciding upon a course of action, considering intellectually the pros and cons of the situation ; also he may rationalize an action after first yielding to impulse. But the rational element is not a *sine qua non* with the weak-willed person ; it is with the man of strong will. An act of choice, as we normally think of it, does imply deliberation before volition ; if the person really *chooses* to be ruled by passion, it is that, the other course having duly been considered, he has calculated the superior advantage or pleasure it will afford him. The process of making a choice involves a lengthy or rapid inner debate. Volition takes place with lightning speed between this inner debate and the resultant word or act. It is almost impossible to convey the whole process dramatically except by clear expressive dialogue. An author might attempt a realistic representation of an inner verbal debate taking place in silence, but the content of such a silence would be over complicated. The various issues would have to be made the subject of previous discussion and in such a case the pause, being, so to speak, a silent repetition of these arguments, would have little dramatic value. It might create a certain suspense, but, if unduly prolonged, would slow down the action unbearably.

Although some of the less important silences of Bernard, and, indeed, of any intelligent dramatist, may be a kind of echo of the dialogue, affording the listener an opportunity of musing on and appreciating the value of the words which have just been spoken, that is not their main dramatic function. Those silences which have a real significance in the play are not a reflection but a product of the preceding dialogue, in conjunction with situation and character. They are different in meaning and quality from the words that have gone before them. Something new has been created in them, something hitherto unknown has been reached deep down in the character. They have depth but no intricacy. By nature they must relate not to the intellect but to the emotions. Either they convey a positive feeling too deep to be expressed or they indicate a state of abstraction during which subconscious emotion is allowed to rise to the surface. The " silent " type feels deeply and tends to withdraw into herself—the feminine pronoun is to be noted. She is invaded by emotion proceeding from a mysterious and often unrealized source and, bewildered as she is by its strangeness, her reactions are slowed down and her state of mind is habitually vague. Vagueness of mind is, as a rule, a pleasurable, passive condition, incompatible with what we generally term strength of will. Seeing things clearly, comparing, contrasting and weighing them up involve a degree of verbal precision, to attain which requires a certain effort, already an act of will. Consequently, instead of making a real decision, entailing the possibility of governing the feelings to achieve an end thought to be desirable, the " silent " type merely inclines towards a course of action through the weight of a prevailing emotion. Clarisse's decision to go to Spain after realizing the true state of her heart is not so much an intellectual recognition of the rightness of the moral law as a revulsion from an impossible situation which has suddenly presented itself ; a new feeling, shame, overwhelms her, outweighing love for the time being. Marie-Louise sees Philippe as he really is, a mediocre type, and gravitates back to her husband with as much will-power as a stone cast in the air returns to earth. Martine does not actively exercise her will ; she suffers at the realization of the hopelessness of her love. Louise, the Guédonec sisters, do not act ; they react.

The dramatic use of the Unexpressed, deriving as it does from emotion, either conscious or unconscious, involves a discounting of the human will. As with Racine, the fatality lies in the constitution of the personality. With Racine, however, the human will, though destined to be defeated, is a force to be reckoned with, and therefore dramatic. This is not the case with Bernard and the virtual elimination of so important an aspect of human experience must necessarily devitalize his theatre.

Intellect and will are traditionally regarded as " masculine " elements in the human personality, and tragedy, Allardyce Nicoll tells us, is " masculine ".[1] Bernard's drama is " feminine " ; it is subtle, delicate, subdued and very restricted. Yet his work has much beauty and has exerted a purifying influence on a theatre tainted with commercialism and swamped with the efforts of the " Boulevard ". His special intimate poetry of

[1] Allardyce Nicoll, *The Theory of Drama* (1931), pp. 156-8.

quiet, timid souls has given us glimpses of new truths. Though we cannot exult, as in high tragedy, we muse on the mysteries of human personality and our sympathy and understanding of suffering is deepened. Like Chekhov, but with a totally different technique, he excels in rendering the pathos of humble everyday existence and bewildered souls.

Edmond Haraucourt [1] says that between the drama of Bernard and the ordinary drama there exists " la même différence qu'entre une serre d'horticulteur et une prairie au printemps; là des fleurs exubérantes et parfois magnifiques, mais facticement obtenues ; ici, des fleurettes timorées et menues, sorties de terre, semble-t-il, sans qu'on s'en occupe et qu'il faut regarder de tout près pour discerner la subtile délicatesse de leurs tons ". The comparison is not altogether exact, since it is obvious that as much art is required to produce the special effects of Bernard's *Théâtre de l'Inexprimé* as those of the traditional drama. But the general impression conveyed by Haraucourt is true. And in the rich field of the drama, beside the strong plants that shoot up proudly, there is room for the small flowers of quiet intimate pieces.

[1] Article on *L'Invitation au voyage, Information*, 22nd Mar. 1924, R.

CHAPTER X

CONCLUSION

THE *Théâtre de l'Inexprimé* represents a reaction against the abuse of the medium of the spoken word. It turns away from sterile rhetoric, violent action and intricacy of intrigue, and looks towards the mysteries of the universe and of human personality. Silence is secret, rich and fraught with potentialities. The spoken word is subordinated to it and manipulated in such a way as to reveal dramatically some of these potentialities to the spectator. In my examination of the work of the characteristic " silent " dramatists I have endeavoured to show what their use of silence can achieve. In general, the Unexpressed stimulates the imagination of the spectator to complete the idea or emotion suggested, and this participation enables the author's message to be powerfully impressed upon him. The Unexpressed gives him more time to dream ; his attention is drawn to the beauty and significance of the dialogue, and he is allowed to meditate on what has been said. In such circumstances the dialogue must have intrinsic value, economy and discretion in language are promoted, and " literature " is discouraged. The Unexpressed can give atmosphere ; as with Maeterlinck, it may act as an invisible Chorus and hint at the strangeness of unseen influences at work in the universe. Or, as with Bernard, and to a lesser extent with Vildrac, replacing soliloquy in the individual character, it may suggest depth in personality. It can reveal the subconscious at work and thus be an important element in psychological realism. Its use, springing from the desire for greater truth, must to some extent contribute to the rehabilitation of the drama, debased by " Boulevard " subjects, and reorientate it towards good and right dramatic material.

But the limitations of the *Théâtre de l'Inexprimé* are also apparent. I have tried to show that it is impossible to convey dramatically through the Unexpressed the intellectual in man. Ideas and emotions communicated through this medium must of necessity be uncomplicated and, because of the element of reason involved in an act of conscious choice, the human will as a positive force is discounted. The author is obliged to concentrate on emotion, and on a pure reproduction of emotion, instead of analysis of its substance and speculation as to its nature. Hence, instead of an active drama of analysis and reflection, we have a passive drama of reproduction. There is truth in what Benjamin Crémieux says of the " intimate " drama, in which he includes the work of Bernard, Vildrac and Amiel. " L'intimisme français c'est la ' tranche de vie ' du Théâtre Libre prolongée et renouvelée par des dramaturges ennemis du naturalisme." [1]   What philosophy there is in the Symbolist drama of Maeterlinck is bound, because of the limitations of the medium, to be of a rudimentary nature, and in the psychological realism of the later *Théâtre de l'Inexprimé* we have not philosophy but history.

The dramatic exploitation of the Unexpressed was inspired by the desire for greater truth ; its misapplication is due, I think, to a confusion between truth and realism.[2]   I have shown how the *Théâtre de l'Inexprimé* is effective in so far as it is realistic. The idea of dramatic realism is implicit in Maeterlinck's conception of the " tragique quotidien ". For him the truly tragic lies not in exceptional acts of violence but in everyday life as lived by the common people, and the Unexpressed is the fittest material for drama because in everyday life mystic silence contains what is most worth while. Vildrac is chiefly preoccupied with the bonds of love which silently unite men, and the quiet influence which one human being may exert on another. Amiel attempts

---

[1] Article on *Madame Béliard, La Nouvelle Revue Française,* 1st Dec. 1925, R.

[2] The term naturalism is used by some contemporary critics in connection with Bernard's " silent " theatre. I prefer the word realism, as we understand by naturalism that consciously scientific and pessimistic attitude in literature, which inspires, for example, the novels of Zola.

to convey the passions of the ancestral beast, which, he is convinced, lurk beneath the drawing-room conversations of inter-war drones. Bernard uses the Unexpressed mainly because he feels that motive and feeling of greatest significance in the individual are not expressed in real life.

I have attempted to make it clear that the dramatists of the Unexpressed, by neglecting the lyrical and expressive type of character and by disregarding the situation and moment of crisis where verbal expression is the natural reaction of the character, do in effect confine themselves to as small a part of reality as those they condemn. But the important question is not whether the realism of the " silent " school is an inadequate realism, but whether—even under modern conditions—realism is actually desirable in the theatre. In the previous chapter I mentioned the views of Pierre Brisson, who declares that all great theatre is made of accelerated movement, exceptional heroes, and features accentuated and even deformed, and implies that the stage is the place where the hero says what is not said in everyday life. If we accept these views, the *Théâtre de l'Inexprimé* is already judged.

In all art realism must be relative. Even in the documentary film and the naturalistic " tranche de vie " on the stage, a degree of selection and concentration has to be employed. And in the acting, even if the special unrealistic rhythm of Copeau is not adopted, yet gesture and movement must undergo certain modifications if they are to make sense on the stage. All this is highly artificial, but necessary, and it is accepted by a benevolent audience, prepared from the start to adjust its vision to the " optique du théâtre ". It is not unreasonable to expect that this " suspension of the act of comparison ", to use a phrase of Coleridge, might extend also to the matter verbally expressed on the stage. When we examine the work of dramatists whose greatness is unquestioned we see that, in different ways, the dialogue of Aeschylus, of Shakespeare, of Racine, of Chekhov, is unrealistic, that is to say, the characters speak aloud much of what is normally left unsaid in everyday life. Even today the audience accepts that convention as it accepts other theatrical conventions. It is disposed in mind for the special type of enjoyment which the drama can give, and it agrees in advance to the rules of the dramatic game. With these very great dramatists, however, it is, more than anything, the urgent truth of the work which compels acceptance of the conventions. In art truth transcends realism.

Unrealistic conventions deriving from the physical limitations of the theatre are, so to speak, of a negative quality. There are, however, positive reasons for accepting a modification of Pierre Brisson's views. In connection with Aristotle's theory of imitation Pierre-Aimé Touchard says that Aristotle " n'avait nullement en vue une imitation servile de la réalité, mais au contraire l'expression totale de la nature humaine, aussi bien dans ses virtualités que dans ses actes réels ".[1] In tragedy, says Touchard, with the constraints of everyday life removed, man lives his passions to their very limit. The theatre is the mirror of a psychological fact, " le besoin propre à l'homme d'éprouver sans cesse les limites extrêmes de sa puissance (ou de sa faiblesse, c'est-à-dire de sa puissance encore, mais dans le mal) ".[2] I accept in the main this dionysian idea of the theatre. I take the view that tragedy is an ideal of human experience ; in it man lives completely, and suffers consciously to the very utmost. It is the quintessence of living and suffering, diluted in everyday life by the multitude of acts necessary for a man to keep alive. It is the pre-eminently humanistic art, where human material, in every respect, is employed to the full. Not distortion, not acceleration, as Brisson suggests, but intensity of experience is a positive requirement of the drama. The characters, highly charged with it, are not deformed, not exceptional, but, one might say, more alive than living people. There need be no speeding up of movement—witness the pace of the Chekhovian drama—but a concentration of doing or suffering must be conveyed, and we

[1] *Dionysos* (1938), p. 33.   [2] *Ibid.* p. 15.

must feel that the human beings we see before us, even the un-heroic failures, even the lives wasted in futility, are there, elected to do and suffer for all humanity's sake.

That non-realism is a virtue of the dramatic form, may also be inferred from the quality of the aesthetic response to the greatest dramatic works. "La mission du théâtre", says Bernard, "est d'éveiller des échos dans l'âme du spectateur. Et il parviendra d'autant mieux qu'il laissera plus de place à ce besoin de rêve qui existe à l'état clair ou à l'état latent en chaque être humain. . . . Bien mieux, ce besoin de rêve, appelons-le aussi besoin d'évasion, besoin d'au-delà et la richesse en prolongements nous apparaîtra comme la qualité principale de tout ce qui fait appel à l'âme collective." [1] This is a somewhat anaemic view of the theatre, when we think of our response to *Macbeth* or to the *Agamemnon*. Although Bernard's aesthetics allow movement to the imagination, the general emotional attitude would be negative and passive. But in great tragedy the spectator participates with his whole being. The aesthetic effect is a positive feeling of exaltation and wonder. Through the actors on the stage we live a more intense life ; human experience is concentrated and heightened. Far from escaping from life, with the dramatist we plunge into it, and boldly grapple with its passion and pain ; with our vicarious suffering comes joy in the dignity of man, the sense that, in spite of all, he is in some way greater than the gods who have brought about his destruction.

It might be objected that, whatever we say of Maeterlinck, it is hardly fair to judge Bernard and the Vildrac of *Le Paquebot Tenacity* and *Le Pèlerin* by the standards of a tremendous art to which they may not intend to aspire, that serious drama is not so exacting in its requirements as tragedy, and that the restricted realism of the Unexpressed finds its proper place in this genre. Without exploring the question of genres, which is outside the scope of this study, I would say that the subject matter of the *Théâtre de l'Inexprimé* with Bernard and Vildrac is tragic. They

---

[1] *De la valeur du silence dans les arts du spectacle, loc. cit.*

desire not to present man as a social being or an interesting psychological specimen, but to hint at the beauty and strangeness of life, the pity of humanity, and yet its " worth-while-ness ". The limitations of their chosen " silent " technique prevent their works from being the tragedies they were meant to be.

Tragedy is the quintessence of human experience, comprising, as well as emotion, thought and speculation. These can be adequately conveyed by the spoken word alone, and the spoken word, the chief element of the human material of the drama, must be positively and exultantly used. This does not mean " literature " on the stage, but good, rich, highly-charged dialogue. Such dialogue is a possibility, even in the modern drama. We have only to think of the savoury Irish speech of Synge, the verbal exaltation of Shaw, the iridescent language of Giraudoux, the liturgical music of Claudel. Richness of language must of course be right in its context. The drama must have its roots in reality, though this does not necessarily imply strict realism. Once more we are confronted with the problem of conveying the tragedy of the modern urbane character, who, when deeply moved, looks into the fireplace. A lyrical outburst from a chartered accountant in his office would be as grotesque as the German monument to a noble lady whose impressive *fin-de-siècle* hat as well as her stately person is carved in stone for all eternity. The answer is that tragedy, and serious drama too, deals with men and women, not with ladies and gentlemen, and one does not select a chartered accountant *qua* chartered accountant as a subject for high dramatic art any more than one perpetuates late Victorian headgear in stone. Attempts to do so only prove the folly of the experiment. In his famous preface to *The Playboy of the Western World* J. M. Synge tells us that rich language comes readily to those who live rich lives :

> Anyone who has lived in real intimacy with the Irish peasantry will know that the wildest sayings and ideas in this play are tame indeed, compared with the fancies one may hear in any little hillside cabin in Geesala, or Carraroe, or Dingle

Bay. All art is collaboration ; and there is little doubt that in the happier ages of literature, striking and beautiful phrases were as ready to the story teller's or the playwright's hand, as the rich cloaks and dresses of his time. It is probable that when the Elizabethan dramatist took his inkhorn and sat down to his work he used many phrases that he had just heard, as he sat at dinner, from his mother or his children. In Ireland those of us who know the people have the same privilege. When I was writing *The Shadow of the Glen*, some years ago, I got more aid than any learning could have given from a chink in the floor of the old Wicklow house where I was staying, that let me hear what was being said by the servant girls in the kitchen. This matter, I think, is of importance, for in countries where the imagination of the people, and the language they use, is rich and living, it is possible for a writer to be rich and copious in his words, and at the same time to give the reality, which is the root of all poetry, in a comprehensive and natural form. . . . In a good play every speech should be as fully flavoured as a nut or apple, and such speeches cannot be written by anyone who works among people who have shut their lips on poetry.

The relative poverty of subject matter and of aesthetic response leads us to conclude that the *Théâtre de l'Inexprimé* is drama not true to the laws of its nature, and inclining to decadence, sterility and anaemia. The indispensable medium, the spoken word, is used in a negative way. In spite of its beauty, the dialogue, the very fabric of the drama, tends to become more and more tenuous and elusive. The essence of the word, spoken on the stage, lies in its ability to express meaning to listening persons in the mass, and in the vast setting of the theatre, the subtler attributes, so exquisitely turned to account in Symbolist poetry, have to be sacrificed. In large sculptured figures we expect a certain boldness of style, emphasizing the essential nature of the stone. So in the drama a certain roughness of finish stresses the essential nature of the spoken word, its capacity for meaning. The dialogue in the *Théâtre de l'Inexprimé* might be compared to the material of fretwork. Our attention is drawn to the shape of the spaces surrounded by the wood. Yet while we admire the pattern, most of us cannot but feel that wood is used to best advantage in a more massive way, when its bulk, texture, grain and colour acquire positive significance.

The healthiest type of dramatic silence is that which points to the spoken word—the silences of Aeschylus, and even those characteristic of the Romantic theatre, which are a function of the pace of the dialogue. From the deep shadows of a Rembrandt painting emerges in spiritual light the human face, and on that we gaze, not on the darkness, mysterious and suggestive though it be.

We are forced to conclude, platitudinously, that in life words are more important than silence. When the philosopher praises silence it is, or should be, because silence is the ideal medium for inner verbal activity, without which he achieves not truth but exquisite sensations. Dramatically, silence seldom does more than convey states of feeling, and even then, as with the silent anagnorisis, it is by virtue of the preceding dialogue. Speech is the glory and wealth of mankind. If the coinage is so often debased, it is the dramatist's task to mint new money which shall ring true and honour its face value. However man arrives at his truths, whether by reason or intuition, it is for the dramatist, working with words, to put those truths into words. And if they are the right words, the audience will experience not only the truths, but emotion, and something of the artist's joy in creation. The business of the artist is not to reproduce sensations or even to suggest experience, but to interpret life. Art is philosophic, not historical. Silence cannot interpret. It can only reproduce or suggest.

Accordingly, these experiments with the Unexpressed which we have been studying must be of a limited value. But their value is real. They exploit a new source of dramatic material which, if subordinated to the proper medium, can enhance it. The exploitation of the Unexpressed promotes skill in the use of the Expressed, and the medium is re-examined and assessed.

Language is purged of rhetoric, and serious dramatists are impelled to have a care with their dialogue and see to its economy and significance.

Above all, we are impressed by the mystery of silence and its potentialities. What the poet Mallarmé divined in that enigmatic blank appears wraithlike to tantalize the dramatist. If he is a great dramatist, he will not be content to reproduce silence and hint at its virtualities. He will respond to the challenge of silence and his chosen, intractable medium. He will make it his joyous task boldly to grasp its secrets, transmute them into the strong but flexible material of the drama and, in this form, share his clear vision with the people.

BIBLIOGRAPHY

PAGE

I. The Dramatists of the Théatre de l'Inexprimé   248
    (i) Dramatic Works
    (ii) Other Works discussed or mentioned

II. Specific Plays in the French Language discussed
    in Relation to the Théatre de l'Inexprimé   251

III. Works of Literary Criticism, etc.   252

IV. Articles and Interviews in Reviews, News-
    papers, etc.   256
    a. General
    b. On Specific Plays

I. THE DRAMATISTS OF THE THÉÂTRE DE L'INEXPRIMÉ

DENYS AMIEL

(i) *Dramatic Works:*

Le Clair-Obscur, typescript in the Bibliothèque de l'Arsenal, 1911.
Près de lui, calligraphic copy in the Bibliothèque de l'Arsenal, 1911.
Théâtre, Paris, Albin Michel :—

Tome I, 1925 :	*Le Voyageur.*
	Le Couple.
	Café-Tabac.
Tome II, 1928 :	*L'Engrenage.*
	Monsieur et Madame Un Tel.
Tome III, 1930 :	*L'Image.*
	L'Homme d'un soir { en collaboration avec Charles Lafaurie.
Tome IV, 1933 :	*L'Age du fer.*
	Décalage.
Tome V, 1935 :	*Trois et une.*
	L'Homme.
Tome VI, 1938 :	*La Femme en fleur.*
	Ma Liberté.
Tome VII, 1945 :	*La Maison Monestier.*
	Mon Ami.
1926 :	*La Souriante Madame Beudet* { en collaboration avec André Obey.
	La Carcasse.

Famille (avec Monique Amiel-Pétry), *Petite Illustration*, 1–1–38.

(ii) *Other Works discussed or mentioned:*

Introduction to *Henry Bataille : Le Règne intérieur*, Paris, Sansot, undated.

JEAN-JACQUES BERNARD

(i) *Dramatic Works:*

Le Voyage à deux, Paris, Librairie Théâtrale, 1910.
La Joie du sacrifice, Paris, L'Illustration théâtrale, No. 217, 1912.

La Maison épargnée, Paris, Librairie Théâtrale, 1920.

Théâtre, Paris, Albin Michel :—

Tome I, 1925 : *Le Feu qui reprend mal.*
  Martine.
  Le Printemps des autres.
  L'Invitation au voyage.

Tome II, 1927 : *Le Secret d'Arvers.*
  Denise Marette.
  L'Ame en peine.

Tome III, 1932 : *A la recherche des cœurs.*
  Les Sœurs Guédonec.
  La Louise.

Tome IV, 1934 : *Jeanne de Pantin.*
  Le Roy de Malousie.

Tome V, 1936 : *Nationale 6.*
  Les Conseils d'Agathe (dialogue à 1 voix).
  8 Chevaux, 4 cylindres, et pas de truites (sketch radiophonique).
  Deux Hommes.

Tome VI, 1946 : *Louise de la Vallière.*
  Le Jardinier d'Ispahan.

Marie Stuart, reine d'Écosse, Paris, Les Éditions Théâtrales, 1941.

La Grande B.A., un acte pour Éclaireurs, Paris, Albin Michel, 1930.

(ii) *Other Works discussed or mentioned :*

L'Épicier, nouvelles, Paris, Ollendorff, 1914.

Les Enfants jouent . . . , récits de guerre, Paris, Grasset, 1919.

Les Tendresses menacées, Paris, Albin Michel, 1924.

Madeleine Landier, roman, Paris, Albin Michel, 1933.

Témoignages, essais sur le théâtre, Paris, Coutan-Lambert, 1933.

Le Camp de la mort lente (*Compiègne, 1941–2*), Paris, Albin Michel, 1944.

Le Pain rouge, Paris, Albin Michel, 1947.

MAURICE MAETERLINCK

(i) *Dramatic Works :*

Théâtre, Brussels, Lacomblez :—

Tome I, 1911 : *La Princesse Maleine.*
  L'Intruse.
  Les Aveugles.

Tome II, 1912 :   *Pelléas et Mélisande.*
Alladine et Palomides   ⎰ Trois petits
Intérieur   ⎱ drames pour
La Mort de Tintagiles   ⎰ marionnettes.
Tome III, 1912 :   *Aglavaine et Sélysette.*
Ariane et Barbe-Bleue.
Sœur Béatrice.
Les Sept Princesses, Brussels, Lacomblez, 1891.
Monna Vanna, Paris, Fasquelle, 1902.
Joyzelle, Paris, Fasquelle, 1903.
L'Oiseau bleu, Paris, Charpentier et Fasquelle, 1909.
Marie-Magdaleine, Paris, Fasquelle, 1913.
Le Miracle de saint Antoine, Paris, Édouard Joseph, 1919.
Le Bourgmestre de Stilmonde, Paris, Édouard Joseph, 1919.
Les Fiançailles, Paris, Fasquelle, 1921.
Le Malheur passe, in *Les Œuvres Libres*, No. 54, Paris, Fayard, 1925.
Marie-Victoire, in *Les Œuvres Libres*, No. 74, Paris, Fayard, 1927.
La Puissance des morts, in *Les Œuvres Libres*, No. 64, Paris, Fayard, 1927.
Berniquel, Toulouse, Éd. des Cahiers Libres, 1929.

(ii) *Other Works discussed or mentioned :*
Le Massacre des innocents, in *La Pléiade*, 1886.
Serres chaudes, suivies de *Quinze Chansons*, Brussels, Lacomblez, 1900.
Translation from Ruysbroeck l'Admirable : *L'Ornement des noces spirituelles*, with introduction, Brussels, Lacomblez, 1891.
Translation : *Les Disciples à Saïs et les Fragments de Novalis*, with introduction, Brussels, Lacomblez, 1895.
Le Trésor des humbles, Paris, société du Mercure de France, 1896.
La Sagesse et la destinée, Paris, Fasquelle, 1898.
La Vie des abeilles, Paris, Fasquelle, 1901.
Le Temple enseveli, Paris, Fasquelle, 1902.
Le Double Jardin, Paris, Fasquelle, 1904.
L'Intelligence des fleurs, Paris, Fasquelle, 1907.
La Mort, Paris, Fasquelle, 1913.
L'Hôte inconnu, Paris, Fasquelle, 1917.

CHARLES VILDRAC

(i) *Dramatic Works :*
L'Indigent, contained in *Découvertes*, prose essays, Paris, Nouvelle Revue Française, 1912.
Michel Auclair, Paris, Nouvelle Revue Française, 1923.

Le Pèlerin, Petite Illustration of 31–7–26.
Madame Béliard, Paris, Émile-Paul, frères, 1928.
La Brouille, Paris, Émile-Paul, frères, 1931.
Le Jardinier de Samos, d'après un conte de Pierre-Édouard Lemontey, 1762–1829, Paris, Les Cahiers de " Bravo ", No. 33, 1932.
L'Air du temps, Petite Illustration of 16–4–38.
Théâtre, Paris, Gallimard, 9ᵉ édition, 1946 :—
    Le Paquebot Tenacity.
    Poucette.
    Trois Mois de prison.

(ii) *Other Works discussed or mentioned :*
Poèmes, Paris, Éditions du Beffroi, 1905.
Images et mirages, collection of poems including *l'Abbaye*, printed on the Abbaye's own press, 1907, republished under the title of *Poèmes de l'Abbaye*, Paris, Sablier, 1925.
Découvertes, Paris, Nouvelle Revue Française, 1912.
Livre d'amour, Paris, Eugène Figuière, 1910.
Livre d'amour (augmented), Paris, Nouvelle Revue Française, 1914.
Chants du désespéré, Paris, Nouvelle Revue Française, 1920.

II. SPECIFIC PLAYS IN THE FRENCH LANGUAGE DISCUSSED IN RELATION TO THE THÉATRE DE L'INEXPRIMÉ

DUJARDIN (ÉDOUARD), *Antonia*, Paris, Mercure de France, 1899.
GÉRALDY (PAUL), *Les Grands Garçons*, Paris, Delamain et Boutelleau, 1923.
GANTILLON (SIMON), *Cyclone*, Paris, Stock, 1923.
LENORMAND (HENRI-RENÉ), Théâtre Complet, Paris, Crès, 1921–6 :
    Vol. I : *Les Ratés.*
            Le Temps est un songe.
    Vol. II : *Le Simoun.*
            Le Mangeur de rêves.
LERBERGHE (CHARLES VAN), *Les Flaireurs*, Brussels, Lacomblez, 1890.
PELLERIN (JEAN-VICTOR), *Têtes de rechange*, Paris, Coutan-Lambert, 1929.
    Intimité, ibid.
RENARD (JULES), *Poil de carotte*, Paris, Flammarion, 1894.
ROMAINS (JULES), *L'Armée dans la ville*, Paris, Mercure de France, 1911.
    Théâtre, Paris, Gallimard, 1924–35 :—
    Vol. III : *Cromedeyre-le-Vieil.*
    Vol. VII : *Donogoo.*
SARMENT (JEAN), *Le Pêcheur d'ombres*, Paris, Librairie de France, 1926.

SCHLUMBERGER (JEAN), *Césaire*, Paris, Gallimard, 1943.
SCHURÉ (ÉDOUARD), *La Roussalka*, Paris, Perrin, 1902.
VILLIERS DE L'ISLE-ADAM, Œuvres complètes, Paris, Mercure de France,
    1914–29 :—
    Vol. IV :   *Axël.*
    Vol. VII : *La Révolte.*
                Le Nouveau Monde.
    Vol. VIII : *Morgane.*
                Elën.

III. WORKS OF LITERARY CRITICISM, ETC.

BAILLY (AUGUSTE), *Maeterlinck*, Paris, Firmin-Didot et Cie, 1931.
BARRE (ANDRÉ), *Le Symbolisme*, Paris, Jouve, 1912.
BATAILLE (HENRY), *A propos d'art dramatique*, preface to *La Marche nuptiale*,
    included in *Écrits sur le théâtre*, Paris, Crès, 1917.
BENDA (JULIEN), *Belphégor*, Paris, Émile-Paul, 1924.
BESANÇON (J.-B.), *Essai sur le théâtre d'Henry Bataille*, The Hague, J.-B.
    Wolters, 1928.
BIDAL (M.-L.), *Les Écrivains de l'Abbaye*, Paris, Boivin et Cie, 1938.
BISSELL (CLIFFORD H.), Introduction to *Michel Auclair*, by Charles Vildrac,
    New York, D. Appleton Century Co., 1941.
BISSON (LAURENCE), *A Short History of French Literature from the Middle
    Ages to the Present Day*, Harmondsworth, Middlesex, Penguin Books,
    1943.
BITHELL (JETHRO), *Life and Writings of Maurice Maeterlinck*, London,
    Walter Scott Publishing Co., 1913.
BLANCHART (PAUL), *Gaston Baty*, Collection " Choses et gens de Théâtre ",
    Paris, Éditions de la Nouvelle Revue Critique, 1939.
BLANCHART (PAUL), *Jean-Jacques Bernard*, " Masques ", IIᵉ cahier, Paris,
    Coutan-Lambert, 1928.
BLOCH (JEAN-RICHARD), *Destin du théâtre*, Paris, Gallimard, 1930.
BOLL (ANDRÉ), *La Mise en scène contemporaine, son évolution*, collection
    " Choses et gens de Théâtre ", Paris, Nouvelle Revue Critique, 1944.
BOURGET (PAUL), *Essais de psychologie contemporaine*, Paris, Plon, 1899.
BRAUNSCHVIG (M.), *La Littérature française contemporaine étudiée dans les
    textes (de 1850 à nos jours)*, Paris, A. Colin, 1931.
BRISSON (PIERRE), *Le Théâtre des années folles*, Collection " Bilans ",
    Geneva, Éditions du Milieu du Monde, 1943.
CHANDLER (FRANK W.), *Modern Continental Playwrights*, New York,
    Harper and Brothers, 1931.
CHARQUES (R. D.) (ed.), *Footnotes to the Theatre*, London, Peter Davies,
    Ltd., 1938.

CLARK (BARRETT H.), *A Study of the Modern Drama*, New York, D. Appleton & Co., 1925.

CLARK (BARRETT H.), *European Theories of the Drama*, Cincinnati, Stewart & Kidd Company, 1918.

CLARK (M. E. MACDONALD), *Maurice Maeterlinck, Poet and Philosopher*, London, G. Allen & Unwin, 1915.

COINDREAU (MAURICE), *La Farce est jouée. Vingt-cinq ans de théâtre français*, New York, Éditions de la Maison Française, 1942.

CRÉMIEUX (BENJAMIN), *Inquiétude et reconstruction, essai sur la littérature d'après-guerre* (" Inventaires "), Paris, R.-A. Corrêa, 1931.

CRÉMIEUX (BENJAMIN), " Les Tendances actuelles du théâtre ", Article in *L'Encyclopédie Française*, tome xvii, Section A, Ch. 2, *Les Arts du temps*, 17.30-1, Dec. 1935.

DAICHES (DAVID), *The Place of Meaning in Poetry*, Edinburgh, Oliver & Boyd, 1935.

DELPIT (LOUISE), *Paris—Théâtre contemporain* (Smith College studies in modern languages, VI, 1 and 2), Paris, Champion, 1925.

DICKINSÓN (THOMAS H.) (ed.), *The Theatre in a Changing Europe*, London, Putnam, 1938.

DUBECH (LUCIEN), *La Crise du théâtre*, Paris, Librairie de France, 1928.

DUBECH (LUCIEN), *Le Théâtre, 1918–1923*, Paris, Plon, 1925.

DUBECH (LUCIEN), *Le Théâtre français contemporain*, Les Cahiers de la République des Lettres, des Sciences et des Arts, Paris, Les Beaux-Arts, No. 3, *Où va le théâtre?*, 15–7–26.

ELLIS-FERMOR (UNA), *The Frontiers of Drama*, London, Methuen & Co., Ltd., 1945.

FLANAGAN (HALLIE), *Shifting Scenes of the Modern European Theatre*, London, George G. Harrap & Co. Ltd., 1929.

FRITH (J. LESLIE), Introduction to his English translation of the plays of Jean-Jacques Bernard, *The Sulky Fire*, London, Jonathan Cape, 1939.

GOURMONT (REMY DE), *Promenades littéraires*, 5 vols., Paris, Mercure de France, 1904–13.

HARRY (GÉRARD), *Maurice Maeterlinck*, translated by Alfred Allinson, London, George Allen & Sons, 1910.

HUNEKER (JAMES), *Iconoclasts*, London, T. Werner Laurie, 1905.

HURET (JULES), *Enquête sur l'évolution littéraire*, Paris, Charpentier, 1891.

JASPER (GERTRUDE R.), *Adventure in the Theatre. Lugné-Poe and the Théâtre de l'Œuvre to 1899*, New Brunswick, Rutgers University Press, 1947.

KNOWLES (DOROTHY), *La Réaction idéaliste au théâtre depuis 1890*, Paris, Droz, 1934.

LALOU (RENÉ), *Histoire de la littérature française contemporaine (1870 à nos jours)*, édition revue et augmentée, Paris, G. Crès et Cie, 1925.

LANSON (GUSTAVE), *Histoire de la littérature française*, 19th edition, Paris, Hachette, undated.

LECAT (MAURICE), *Le Maeterlinckianisme*, 2 vols., Brussels, Castaigne, 1937–9.

LEMAÎTRE (JULES), *Impressions de théâtre*, 11 vols., Paris, Lecène & Oudin & Boivin, 1888–1920.

LUCAS (F. L.), *Tragedy in Relation to Aristotle's Poetics*, London, Hogarth Press, 1927.

LUGNÉ-POE (AURÉLIEN-FRANÇOIS), *Le Sot du tremplin* (*La Parade*, vol. I), Paris, Gallimard, 1930.

MACKAIL (J. W.), Introduction to Maeterlinck's *Aglavaine et Sélysette*, translated by Alfred Sutro, London, Grant Richards, 1897.

MALLARMÉ (STÉPHANE), *Divagations*, Paris, Fasquelle, 1897.

MALLARMÉ (STÉPHANE), " La Musique et les lettres " (Taylorian Lecture, 1893), in *Studies in European Literature*, Oxford Clarendon Press, 1900.

MARTINO (PIERRE), *Parnasse et symbolisme*, Paris, A. Colin, 1925.

MAUCLAIR (CAMILLE), *Princes de l'esprit*, Paris, Albin Michel, undated.

MAULNIER (THIERRY), *Racine*, Paris, Redier, 1935.

MICHAUD (GUY), *La Doctrine symboliste* (Documents), Paris, Nizet, 1947.

MICHAUD (GUY), *Message poétique du symbolisme*, 3 vols., Paris, Nizet, 1947.

MODERWELL (H. K.), *The Theatre Today*, London, The Bodley Head, 1927.

MORNET (DANIEL), *Histoire de la littérature et de la pensée françaises contemporaines, 1870–1927*, 2ᵉ tirage, revu et augmenté, Paris, Larousse, 1927.

MORTIER (ALFRED), *Quinze Ans de théâtre, 1917–1932*, Paris, Messein, 1933.

NEWMAN (ERNEST), *Wagner as Man and Artist*, London, The Bodley Head, 1925.

NICOLL (ALLARDYCE), *The Theory of Drama*, London, George G. Harrap & Co., Ltd., 1931.

PALGEN (R.), *Villiers de l'Isle-Adam, auteur dramatique*, Paris, Champion, 1925.

PALMER (JOHN), *Studies in the Contemporary Theatre*, London, Martin Secker, 1927.

PEACOCK (RONALD), *The Poet in the Theatre*, London, Routledge, 1946.

PIGNARRE (ROBERT), *Histoire du théâtre*, Collection " Que sais-je ? ", Paris, Presses Universitaires de France, 1945.

PILLEMENT (GEORGES), *Anthologie du théâtre français contemporain — Le théâtre d'avant-garde*, Paris, Éditions du Bélier, 1945.

POIZAT (ALFRED), *Le Symbolisme*, Paris, Renaissance du Livre, 1919.

POULAILLE (HENRY), *Nouvel Age littéraire*, Paris, Valois, 1930.

RADINE (SERGE), *Essais sur le théâtre (1919–1939)*, Geneva, Éditions du Mont Blanc, S.A., 1944.

RAVENNES (JEAN), *Essais sur le théâtre (1923-4)*, Paris, Éditions de La Douce France, 1925.

RAYMOND (MARCEL), *Le Jeu retrouvé*, Montréal, Éditions de l'Arbre, 1943.

ROSE (HENRY), *Maeterlinck's Symbolism, The Blue Bird, and other Essays*, London, A. C. Fifield, 1910.

ROUCHÉ (JACQUES), *L'Art théâtral moderne*, nouvelle édition, Paris, Bloud et Gay, 1924.

SARTRE (JEAN-PAUL), *Situations*, i, Paris, Gallimard, 1937.

SCHURÉ (ÉDOUARD), *La Genèse de la tragédie*, Paris, Perrin, 1926.

SCHURÉ (ÉDOUARD), *Précurseurs et révoltés*, Paris, Perrin, 1904.

SÉE (EDMOND), *Le Mouvement dramatique (1929-1930)*, Paris, Les Éditions de France, 1930.

SÉE (EDMOND), *Le Théâtre français contemporain*, Paris, A. Colin, 1941.

SÉNÉCHAL (CHRISTIAN), *L'Abbaye de Créteil*, Paris, André Delpeuch, 1930.

SÉNÉCHAL (CHRISTIAN), *Les Grands Courants de la littérature française contemporaine*, Paris, Edgar Malfère, 1934.

SION (GEORGES), *Le Théâtre français d'entre-deux-guerres*, Collection " Clartés sur . . .", Tournai-Paris, Casterman, 1943.

THIBAUDET (ALBERT), *La Poésie de Stéphane Mallarmé*, Paris, Gallimard, 1913.

THOMAS (EDWARD), *Maurice Maeterlinck*, Methuen, 1911.

THOMPSON (ALAN R.), *The Anatomy of Drama*, 2nd edition, Berkeley (Cal.), University of California Press, 1946.

THOMSON (GEORGE), Introduction and Commentary, Aeschylus : *Prometheus Bound*, Cambridge University Press, 1932.

TOUCHARD (PIERRE-AIMÉ), *Dionysos, apologie pour le théâtre*, Paris, Aubier, éditions Montaigne, 1938.

WALKLEY (A. B.), *Still More Prejudice*, London, William Heinemann, Ltd., 1925.

WOOLLEY (GRANGE), *Richard Wagner et le symbolisme français*, Paris, Presses Universitaires de France, 1931.

WRIGHT (C. H. C.), *The Background of Modern French Literature*, Boston, (Mass.), Ginn & Co., The Athenaeum Press, 1926.

YEATS (W. B.), *Essays*, London, Macmillan & Co., Ltd., 1924.

IV. ARTICLES AND INTERVIEWS IN REVIEWS, NEWSPAPERS, ETC. [1]

a. *General Articles, Interviews, etc.* :

D' AMICO (SILVIO), "Le Théâtre français à l'étranger : autour du théâtre du 'silence' et de l'inexprimé", traduit en français de *l' Idea Nazionale, Comœdia*, 12–12–25, R.

AMIEL (DENYS), reply to "Enquête sur la jeune littérature : V. Les auteurs dramatiques", *Revue Hebdomadaire*, 16–12–22, R.

AMIEL (DENYS), reply to interview by Simonne Ratel, "Les Grands courants de la pensée contemporaine", *Comœdia*, 25–8–28, R.

BERNARD (JEAN-JACQUES), "De la valeur du silence dans les arts du spectacle", *Les Nouvelles Littéraires*, 25–4–31 and 9–5–31.

BERNARD (JEAN-JACQUES), reply to "Enquête sur la jeune littérature : V. Les auteurs dramatiques", *Revue Hebdomadaire*, 16–12–22, R.

BERNARD (JEAN-JACQUES), "Le Silence au théâtre", *Bulletin de la Chimère*, no. V, May 1922, R.

BERNARD (JEAN-JACQUES), "Quelques Précisions après deux récentes expériences", *Comœdia*, 7–4–24, R.

BLANCHART (PAUL), "Jean-Jacques Bernard ou l'intelligence de la sensibilité", *Chantecler*, 28–4–28, R.

DUBECH (LUCIEN), "L'École du silence", *Revue Universelle*, 1–5–24.

DUBECH (LUCIEN), "Le Théâtre de M. Jean Sarment", *Revue Universelle*, 15–4–24.

FLAT (PAUL), "Le Théâtre idéaliste. (II) M. Maurice Maeterlinck", *Revue Bleue*, 10–10–03.

HENDERSON (ARCHIBALD), "Maurice Maeterlinck as a Dramatic Artist", *Sewanee Review*, vol. xii, p. 207, 1904.

JONES (HENRY ARTHUR), "Literary Critics and the Drama", *Nineteenth Century Review*, vol. ii, p. 662, 1903.

LEMONNIER (LÉON), "Le Théâtre de Jean-Jacques Bernard", *Revue Mondiale*, date illegible, R.

LENORMAND (HENRI-RENÉ), "L'Inconscient dans la littérature dramatique", *Bulletin de la Chimère*, no. V, May 1922, R.

MAETERLINCK (MAURICE), "Menus propos — Le Théâtre", *La Jeune Belgique*, tome ix, 1890.

[1] Only those quoted or found useful have been listed. The main source is the collection of cuttings containing criticisms of plays and articles on dramatists, housed in the Bibliothèque de l'Arsenal, Paris (Collection Théâtrale Rondel), and this is indicated by the letter R. In some cases the date or the publication from which the article was extracted is not given, and occasionally the inscription giving these details is illegible. The *Bulletins de la Chimère*, also in the Collection Rondel, are complete.

Soissons (S. C. de), "Maeterlinck as a Reformer of the Drama", *Contemporary Review*, Nov. 1904.

Thomas (Louis), "Charles Vildrac", *Les Nouvelles Littéraires*, 4–8–28, R.

Turquet-Milnes (Gladys), "Bergson and Tragedy", *Contemporary Review*, Aug. 1929.

Visan (Tancrède de), "L'Idéal symboliste", *Mercure de France*, 16–7–07.

b. *Articles, etc., on Specific Plays:*

Denys Amiel : Café-Tabac :
    Lindauer (Madeleine), *Avenir*, 10–11–32, R.

Denys Amiel : La Femme en fleur :
    Bauer (G.), *Larousse Mensuel*, May 1936, R.
    Dubech (Lucien), *Candide*, 2–1–36, R.

Denys Amiel : Le Voyageur :
    Amiel (Denys), interview, *Figaro*, 3–5–23, R.
    Amiel (Denys), interview, *La Rampe*, 15–10–32, R.
    Beaunier (André), cutting dated 5–5–23, R.
    Bidou (Henry), feuilleton du *Journal des Débats*, undated, R.
    Brisson (Pierre), cutting dated 7–5–23, R.
    Gignoux (Régis), cutting dated 4–5–23, R.
    Méré (Charles), cutting dated 5–5–23, R.
    Nozière, cutting dated 6–5–23, R.

Jean-Jacques Bernard : L'Ame en peine :
    Boulenger (Jacques), *Nouveau Siècle*, 19–3–26, R.
    Brisson (Pierre), *Le Temps*, 29–3–26, R.
    Descaves (Lucien), *L'Intransigeant*, 20–3–26, R.
    Dubech (Lucien), *Action Française*, 23–3–26, R.
    Schneider (Louis), *Gaulois*, 21–3–26, R.

Jean-Jacques Bernard : Le Feu qui reprend mal :
    Bidou (Henry), feuilleton du *Journal des Débats*, 21–10–29, R.

Jean-Jacques Bernard : L'Invitation au voyage :
    Beaunier (André), cutting dated 17–2–24, R.
    Bernard (Jean-Jacques), *Le Journal*, 23–2–24, R.
    Brisson (Pierre), cutting dated 25–2–24, R.
    Haraucourt (Edmond), *Information*, 22–3–24, R.

Jean-Jacques Bernard : Martine :
    "Alceste", *Comœdia*, 14–11–34, R.
    Bidou (Henry), *Figaro*, 26–11–34, R.
    Mas (Émile), *Petit Bleu*, 14–11–34, R.

Jean-Jacques Bernard : Nationale 6 :
    BRISSON (PIERRE), *Figaro*, 20–10–35, R.
    CRÉMIEUX (BENJAMIN), *Je suis partout*, 26–10–35, R.

Jean-Jacques Bernard : Le Printemps des autres :
    BEAUNIER (ANDRÉ), cutting dated 20–3–24, R.
    BRISSON (PIERRE), *Les Annales*, 30–3–24, R.
    REY (ÉTIENNE), *Opinion*, 28–3–24, R.

Jean-Jacques Bernard : Le Secret d'Arvers :
    DUBECH (LUCIEN), *Action Française*, 20–6–26, R.
    LENORMAND (HENRI-RENÉ), *Chantecler*, 12–6–26, R.
    WISNER (RENÉ), *Carnet*, 13–6–26, R.

Paul Géraldy : Les Grands Garçons :
    BEX (MAURICE), cutting dated 12–11–22, R.
    FISCHER (MAX et ALEX), cutting dated 21–11–22, R.
    GIGNOUX (RÉGIS), cutting without source or date, R.
    SOUDAY (PAUL), cutting dated 19–11–22, R.

Charles van Lerberghe : Les Flaireurs :
    LEMAÎTRE (JULES), feuilleton du *Journal des Débats*, 13–1–96.

Jean-Victor Pellerin : Intimité :
    PELLERIN (JEAN-VICTOR), *Bulletin de la Chimère*, no. V, May
      1922, R.

Charles Vildrac : La Brouille :
    BOISSY (GABRIEL), *Comœdia*, 2–12–30, R.

Charles Vildrac : Le Paquebot Tenacity :
    FONTRAILLES (PIERRE), cutting dated 7–3–20, R.
    LUGNÉ-POE, cutting dated 9–3–20, R.
    RAGEOT (GASTON), cutting dated 27–3–20, R.

Charles Vildrac : Madame Béliard :
    BERTON (CLAUDE), *Nouvelles Littéraires*, 17–10–25, R.
    BRISSON (PIERRE), feuilleton du *Temps*, 12–10–25, R.
    CARDONNERET (G. LE), *Journal*, 12–10–25, R.
    CRÉMIEUX (BENJAMIN), *Nouvelle Revue Française*, 1–12–25, R.
    FLERS (ROBERT DE), *Figaro*, 19–10–25, R.
    GIGNOUX (RÉGIS), *Comœdia*, 10–10–25, R.

INDEX

Principal references are in italic type

Abbaye, L', 126
Abbaye de Créteil, *121-3*, 126, 134, 140, 141, 142, 143
Aeschylus, 8, 10 and n., 28, 50, 70, 103, 187, 240, 245
Agamemnon, 8, 10 n., 242
Age du fer, L', 168
Aglavaine et Sélysette, 79, 88, *89-92*, 95, 220
Aiglon, L', 135
Aimer, 116
Air du temps, L', 134, *139-40*
A la recherche des cœurs, *214-18*
Alladine et Palomides, *78-83*, 90
Ame en peine, L', 81, *205-10*, 211, 221, 232, 233, 234
Amico, Silvio d', 226, 228, 232
Amiel, Denys, 51, 106, 107, 111, 116, 120, 139, 141, 143, *144-71*, 233, 239
Amoureuse, 229
Annunzio, Gabriele d', 145
Antigone, 9
Antoine, André, 18, 21, 44, 102, 103
Antonia, *32-3*
Appia, Adolphe, 103
" A propos d'art dramatique " (Preface to *La Marche nuptiale*), 12, 144
Aquinas, Thomas, 40
Arcos, René, 121, 122
Ariane et Barbe-Bleue, 92
Aristophanes, 9
Aristotle, 1, 199, 241
Armée dans la ville, L', 123, *124-5*, 133
Art théâtral moderne, L', 103 n.
Aubes, Les, 124
Autour du théâtre du " silence " et de l'inex-primé, 226
Aveugles, Les, 44, 53, *67-70*, 73, 80, 94, 185, 217
Axël, 34, 35, 36, *37-9*

Bailly, Auguste, 78 n.
Balzac, 13 n.
Barrie, J. M., 219, 220

Bataille, Henry, *12-14*, 20, 144 and n., 145, 150, 158
Baty, Gaston, 32, 102, *103-12*, 152, 153
Baudelaire, 19, 21, 22, 46, 200
Bazalgette, 123 n.
Beaubourg, Maurice, 43 n.
Beaunier, André, 226
Becque, Henry, 18, 20
Bérénice, 14, 136
Bergson, 20, 102, 105, 123
Bernard, Jean-Jacques, 5, 7, 9, 15, 24, 36, 41, 51, 52, 61, 77, 81, 82, 92, 96, 106, 107, 108, 111, 112, 113 and n., 114, 116, 118, 119, 120, 125, 127, 129, 132, 133, 134, 135, 137, 139, 141, 142, 143, 144, 149, 151, 153, 163, 166, 167, 168, 170, 171, *172-237*, 238, 239 and n., 240, 242
Bernard, Tristan, 177
Bernstein, Henry, 12, 20, 158
Bidal, M.-L., 122, 123 and n.
Bidou, Henry, 181
Bithell, Jethro, 55 n., 56
Bjoernson, 21, 44
Blanchart, Paul, 105, 153, 173, 177, 191, 200, 206, 227
Bloch, Jean-Richard, 101
Boehme, Jakob, 46
Boulenger, Jacques, 206
Bourget, Paul, 19, 20
Bourgmestre de Stilemonde, Le, 93
Brieux, Eugène, 12, 20
Brisson, Pierre, 151, 219, 229, 230, 240, 241
Brouille, La, *140-1*
Brunetière, Ferdinand, 21
Burne-Jones, 46, 72

Café-Tabac, *153-6*
Camp de la mort lente, Le, 178
Carcasse, La, 168
Carlyle, 46, 47 and n., 48, 88
Césaire, 110
Chants du désespéré, 126
Chat maigre, Le, 206

Chekhov, 129, 155, 210, 237, 240
Chevillard, 31
Chimère, La, 105, 106, 107, 175
Choephoroe, 50
Christine, 116
Clair-Obscur, Le, 145
Clarke, Barrett H., 93
Claudel, Paul, 31 n., 33, 44, 243
Clerget, Paul, 45
Coindreau, Maurice, 180
Coleridge, 240
Comte, Auguste, 17
Conquérants, Les, 126
Copeau, Jacques, 102, 103, 240
Corbeaux, Les, 18
Corneille, 233
Couple, Le, 159, *161-3*, 169
Courtès, 45
Cousine Bette, La, 13 n.
Craig, Gordon, 103
Crémieux, Benjamin, 101, 116, 120, 123,
    170, 199, 239
Crime and Punishment, 112
Critic, The, 7
Cromedeyre-le-Vieil, 123, 125, 130, 133
Cromwell, Preface to, 62
Curel, François de, 12, 20
Cyclone, 109

Darzens, 46
Daudet, 17
Debussy, 59
Décalage, 168
Découvertes, 123, 127, 128
Denise Marette, 224
Descaves, Lucien, 206
Deux Hommes, *213-14*
Diderot, *5-7*, 14, 45
Disciple, Le, 20
Divagations, 26
Donnay, Maurice, 20
Donogoo, 132
Dostoievski, 21
Double Jardin, Le, 88, 93
Dubech, Lucien, 153, 192, 193, 206, 208,
    219
Duhamel, Georges, 121, 123 n.
Dujardin, Édouard, *32-3*
Dullin, Charles, 101 n., 102
Dumas *fils*, 12

Écrivains de l'Abbaye, Les, 122
Elën, 35, 36
Eliot, George, 21
Ellis-Fermor, Una, 3 n.

Emerson, 46, 88
Enfants jouent, Les, 178
Engrenage, L', 159
Enquête sur l'évolution littéraire, 21
En revenant, 127
Épicier, L', 177, 178
Épreuve, L', 184, 219
Escholiers, Les, 44
*Essai sur les données immédiates de la
    conscience*, 20
Évolution créatrice, L', 20

Faguet, Émile, 6, 45
Famille, 168
Fausses Confidences, Les, 15, 184
Femme en fleur, La, 159, *164-8*, 171
Fernández, Ramón, 102
Feu qui reprend mal, Le, 176, *180-1*, 189,
    190, 195, 202
Fiançailles, Les, 88, 93
First Principles, 21
Flaireurs, Les, 63
Flers, Robert de, 142
Foire sur la place, La, 121
Fort, Paul, 44
France, Anatole, 206
Freud, 101, 105, 108, 175, 177, 206
Frith, J. Leslie, 206
Frogs, The (Ranae), 9, 10 n.
Frontiers of Drama, The, 3 n.
Fuchs, Georg, 103

Gantillon, Simon, 62, *109-10*
Géraldy, Paul, 100, *116-19*, 120
Gignoux, Régis, 185
Giraudoux, Jean, 243
Gleizes, Albert, 121, 122
Gourmont, Remy de, 31 n., 40
Grands Garçons, Les, 117

Hamlet, 42, 49, 55, 56, 60, 111
Haraucourt, Edmond, 237
Hauptmann, G., 21, 44
Hegel, 34
῝Εκτορος λύτρα, 10 n.
Hernani, 1
Homer, 10 n.
Homme, L', 159, 168
Homme d'un soir, L', 168
Hôte inconnu, L', 88
Hugo, Victor, 30, 36, 62, 64
Hulsman, G., 72
Huneker, James, 59
Huret, Jules, 21, 46, 53

Ibsen, 3, 21, 30, 31 n., 42, 43, 44, 64
Iliad, 10 n.
Image, L', 168
Images et mirages, 126
Inconscient dans la littérature dramatique L', 175
Indigent, L', 128, 129
Intelligence des fleurs, L', 88
Intérieur, 44, 53, 73, 78, *83-5*, 87
Intimité, 107, 153
Intouchable, L', 178
Intruse, L', 44, 53, *62-7*, 68, 69, 70, 73, 86, 87, 94, 217
Invitation au voyage, L', 106, 115, 152, 176, 181, 189, 196, *199-205*, 210, 219, 225, 226, 229

James, William, 123
Jardinier de Samos, Le, 140
Jardinier d'Ispahan, Le, 36, 190, 211, *221-4*, 232, 233
Jeanne de Pantin, 214, *224-5*
Jeu de l'amour et du hasard, Le, 15
John Gabriel Borkman, 42
Joie du sacrifice, La, *176-7*
Jones, P. Mansell, 123
Jouvet, Louis, 102
Joyzelle, 79, 92

Kahn, G., 35
Kant, 34, 46
King Lear, 49, 55, 111
Knowles, Dorothy, 30 n., 71, 75, 173

Laforgue, Jules, 31 n., 46
Leblanc, Georgette, 54, 88, 89
Lecat, Maurice, 54, 55
Leclerq, Jules, 67
Lectures on Dramatic Literature, 4 *and* n.
Lemaître, Jules, 63, 72, 87, 98
Lemonnier, Léon, 180
Lenormand, Henri-René, 62, 101, *108-9*, 175, 189, 193
Lerberghe, Charles van, 31 n., 63
Linard, 121
Lindauer, Madeleine, 155
Livre d'amour, 123, 126, 127
Lodovici, Cesare, 210
Louise, La, 92, *211-12*
Louise de la Vallière, 225, 232
Lucrèce Borgia, 8
Lugné-Poe, Aurélien-François, 44, 45, 102

Macbeth, 49, 55, 111, 242
Madame Béliard, 116, *136-8*, 142, 220

Madame Bovary, 112
Madeleine Landier, 221
Maeterlinck, Maurice, 1, 6, 16, 24, 30, 31 n., 34, 35, 40, 43, 44, 45, *46-99*, 105, 107, 110, 111, 120, 122, 125, 130, 132, 133, 135, 139, 141, 143, 145, 152, 153, 163, 168, 170, 171, 173, 174, 175, 176, 180, 184, 185, 190, 191, 203, 207, 209, 211, 212, 217, 220, 225, 231, 233, 234, 238, 239, 242
Maeterlinckianisme, Le, 54
Maison épargnée, La, 176, *179-80*, 184, 189, 190, 195, 202, 227
Maison Monestier, La, 168
Ma Liberté, 159, 168
Mallarmé, 23, *24-30*, 33, 42, 46, 74, 246
Mallet, Félicia, 45
Mangeur de rêves, Le, 108, 189
Manifeste des Cinq, 21
Marie-Magdaleine, 93
Marie Stuart, reine d'Écosse, 225
Marivaux, *14-15*, 117, 176, 183, 184, 219
Martin, Henri, 121
Martine, 9, 92, 106, 113 n., 119, 139, 173, 176, 177, *182-91*, 192, 195, 196, 197, 202, 216, 225
Martino, Pierre, 41 n.
Mas, Émile, 219
Masque, Le, 13, 144 n.
Massacre des innocents, Le, 55
Master Builder, The, 42
Matière et mémoire, 20
Mauclair, Camille, 23, 71
Maulnier, Thierry, 11
Mendès, Catulle, 46
Meuble, Le, 177
Meyerhold, 103
Michel Auclair, 134
Mikhael, 46
Mirbeau, Octave, 20, 56
Molière et Copeau, 102
Mon Ami, 159, 161, *163-4*, 169, 170
Monna Vanna, 93
Monsieur et Madame Un Tel, *159-61*
Morgane, 35, 36
Mornet, Daniel, 22
Morris, William, 46
Mort, La, 88
Mort de Tintagiles, La, 78, *86-8*, 93, 135
Musset, Alfred de, 1, 11, 183

Nationale 6, 92, 137, *218-21*
Newman, Ernest, 29
Nicoll, Allardyce, 236

Nietzsche, 123
Noces d'argent, Les, 100, 117
Nouveau Monde, Le, 35, 36
Novalis, 46, 88
Nozière, 150

Obey, André, 156
Ode on Intimations of Immortality, 66
Oiseau bleu, L', 88, 93, 209
On ne badine pas avec l'amour, 183

Pain rouge, Le, 178
Palmer, John, 116
Paquebot Tenacity, Le, 103, 129-34, 137, 233, 242
Parisienne, La, 18, 20
Parnasse et symbolisme, 41 n.
Pêcheur d'ombres, Le, 113-15
Péladan, 31 n.
Pèlerin, Le, 127, 132, 134-6, 137, 242
Pelléas et Mélisande, 44, 59, 69, 73-8, 79, 85, 153, 181, 204
Pellerin, Jean-Victor, 107-8, 153
Persae, 8, 10 n.
Phèdre, 14, 61
Pirandello, 101, 199
Pitoëff, G., 102, 109
Pitoëff, L., 102
Playboy of the Western World (The) (Preface to), 243-4
Poe, Edgar Allan, 46
Poèmes (Vildrac), 126
Poèmes de l'Abbaye, 126
Poètes et la poésie, Les, 123 n.
Poil de carotte, 19
Poizat, Alfred, 89
Porto-Riche, Georges de, 20, 116, 117, 145, 158, 229
Poucette, 138-9, 149
Près de lui, 145
Princesse Maleine, La, 55-62, 68, 71, 80, 93
Printemps des autres, Le, 61, 166-7, 175, 176, 189, 190, 193-9, 200, 202, 204, 210, 216, 222, 224, 225
Prometheus Bound, 8, 10 n., 50
Puissance des morts, La, 93, 152
Puvis de Chavannes, 46

Quelques Précisions après deux récentes expériences, 227
Quillard, 31 n., 46

Rabelais, 121, 133
Rachilde, 44

Racine, 11, 14, 15, 176, 189, 194, 228, 231, 236, 240
Ranson, 70
Ratel, Simonne, 144
Ratés, Les, 108
Raymond, Marcel, 103
Récréation, La, 127
Règne intérieur, Le, 144 n.
Régnier, Henri de, 44
Renan, Ernest, 19
Renard, Jules, 19, 145
Révolte, La, 34, 35, 36
Revue Wagnérienne, La, 31, 32
Robert et Marianne, 116
Rolland, Romain, 121
Romains, Jules, 105, 122, 123-6, 127, 132
Roman naturaliste, Le, 21
Rossetti, 46
Rostand, Edmond, 135
Rouché, Jacques, 103 n.
Roussalka, La, 31
Roy de Malousie, Le, 214, 224
Ruy Blas, 8
Ruysbroeck, 46, 88

Sagesse et la destinée, La, 88, 89
Saint-Pol-Roux, 31 n., 46
Sarcey, Francisque, 17
Sardou, 12, 17
Sarment, Jean, 113-15, 120
Sartre, Jean-Paul, 19
Schlegel, August Wilhelm von, 4 and n.
Schlumberger, Jean, 110
Schneider, Louis, 206
Schopenhauer, 34, 46, 71
Schuré, Édouard, 31 and n., 32
Scribe, 12, 17
Secret d'Arvers, Le, 9, 149, 182, 191-3
Sée, Edmond, 43 n., 196
Sept Princesses, Les, 70-2, 83, 85
Serments indiscrets, Les, 184
Serres chaudes, 55 and n.
Shakespeare, 15, 28, 42, 46, 56, 60, 61, 62, 76, 111, 228, 231, 232, 240
Shaw, George Bernard, 243
Sheridan, 7
Silence au théâtre, Le, 191
Simoun, 108-9
Sœur Béatrice, 92
Sœurs Guédonec, Les, 211, 212-13
Sophocles, 9
Souriante Madame Beudet, La, 116, 156-158, 169, 170
Spectacle dans un fauteuil, Un, 1

Spencer, Herbert, 21
Stanislavski, 103
Strindberg, 44
Strowski, Fortunat, 136
Studies in the Contemporary Theatre, 116
Sudermann, 21
Suppliants, The (Supplices), 10 n., 50
Surprise de l'amour, La, 15, 184
Swedenborg, 46
Swinburne, 46
Synge, J. M., 230, *243-4*

Taine, 17, 19
"Talks with French Poets in 1913–14",
  123 n.
Tancrède, 6
Tempest, The, 111
Temple enseveli, Le, 88
Temps est un songe, Le, 109
Tendresses menacées, Les, 178
Terre, La, 21
Têtes de rechange, *107-8*
Théâtre d'Art, 44
Théâtre de l'Œuvre, 44, 102
Théâtre des Arts, 103 n.
Théâtre du Vieux Colombier, *102-3*
Théâtre Funambulesque, 45
Théâtre Libre, 1, 18, 21, 44, 239
Théâtre Montparnasse, 105
Théâtre sera sauvé, Le, 105
Thomson, George, 10 n.
Toi et moi, 116
Tolstoi, 21
Touchard, Pierre-Aimé, 226, 241
Tragique quotidien, Le, 49, 55

Trésor des humbles, Le, 47, 54, 56, 66, 73,
  83, 88, 90, 122, 173
Tristan and Isolde, 34
Trois et une, 168
Trois Mois de prison, 140, 141
Turgeniev, 44

*Valeur du silence dans les arts du spectacle,
  De la*, 172, 173
Valkyrie, The, 30
Veber, Pierre, 102
Verhaeren, Émile, 31 n., 44, 124 n.
Verlaine, 21, 112
Vie des abeilles, La, 88
Vieil Homme, Le, 145
Vie muette, La, 43 n.
Vie unanime, La, 122, 123 n.
Vildrac, Charles, 103, 116, 120, *121-43*,
  171, 220, 233, 238, 239, 242
Villiers de l'Isle-Adam, 31 n., *33-40*, 46
Visite, 128, 129
Voltaire, 6
Volupté de l'honneur, La, 101 n.
Voyage à deux, Le, *176-7*
Voyageur, Le, 106, 107, 139, 145, *146-53*,
  157, 162, 170, 171

Wagner, 23, 26, *29-31*, 32, 33, 202
Whitman, 55 n., 123 *and* n.
Wild Duck, The, 42
Wisner, René, 193
Woolley, Grange, 31 n.
Wordsworth, 66

Yeats, W. B., 4, 230

Zola, 17, 18, 239 n.